A Bombshell in the Baptistery

A Bombshell in the Baptistery

An Examination of the Influence of George Beasley-Murray on the Baptismal Writings of Select Southern Baptist and Baptist Union of Great Britain Scholars

JUSTIN NALLS

☙PICKWICK *Publications* • Eugene, Oregon

A BOMBSHELL IN THE BAPTISTERY
An Examination of the Influence of George Beasley-Murray on the Baptismal Writings of Select Southern Baptist and Baptist Union of Great Britain Scholars

Copyright © 2019 Justin Nalls. All rights reserved. Except for brief quotations in critical publications or reviews, no part of this book may be reproduced in any manner without prior written permission from the publisher. Write: Permissions, Wipf and Stock Publishers, 199 W. 8th Ave., Suite 3, Eugene, OR 97401.

Pickwick Publications
An Imprint of Wipf and Stock Publishers
199 W. 8th Ave., Suite 3
Eugene, OR 97401

www.wipfandstock.com

PAPERBACK ISBN: 978-1-5326-5308-7
HARDCOVER ISBN: 978-1-5326-5309-4
EBOOK ISBN: 978-1-5326-5310-0

Cataloguing-in-Publication data:

Names: Nalls, Justin, author

Title: A bombshell in the baptistery : an examination of the influence of George Beasley-Murray on the baptismal writings of select Southern Baptist and Baptist Union of Great Britain scholars / by Justin Nalls.

Description: Eugene, OR : Pickwick Publications, 2019 | Includes bibliographical references.

Identifiers: ISBN 978-1-5326-5308-7 (paperback) | ISBN 978-1-5326-5309-4 (hardcover) | ISBN 978-1-5326-5310-0 (ebook)

Subjects: LCSH: Baptism. | Southern Baptist Convention. | Baptists—England. | Beasley-Murray, George Raymond, 1916–2000.

Classification: LCC BX6331.3 N15 2019 (print) | LCC BX6331.3 (ebook)

Manufactured in the U.S.A.   MARCH 7, 2019

"Scripture quotations are from the ESV® Bible (The Holy Bible, English Standard Version®), copyright © 2001 by Crossway, a publishing ministry of Good News Publishers. Used by permission. All rights reserved."

To Cassie, who values God's glory, the church's good, and my faithfulness enough to make countless sacrifices that made this project possible. *Sine qua non.*

Table of Contents

Acknowledgments xi

Introduction 1
    A Brief Biography of George-Beasley-Murray 2
    Claims About the Significance of Beasley-Murray's Work on Baptism 3
    The Contribution of This Project 5
    Scope of This Project 6
    Definition of Terms 7
    Structure of the Argument 8
    The Author's View 9

PART I: GEORGE BEASLEY-MURRAY AND BAPTISM

1: Antecedents of George Beasley-Murray's Baptismal Theology 13
    The Sacramental Resurgence 14
    Beasley-Murray's Training as a Biblical Scholar 24
    Major Influences 27
    Conclusion 38

2: George Beasley-Murray's Baptismal Theology 39
    Beasley-Murray's Understanding of the Meaning of Baptism 39
    Possible Misunderstandings Acknowledged and Addressed 52
    Beasley-Murray and the Baptist Tradition 57
    Beasley-Murray and the Paedobaptist Tradition 61
    Initial Resistance to the Sacramental Resurgence 67
    Conclusion 69

PART II: GEORGE BEASLEY-MURRAY AND SOUTHERN BAPTISTS

3: Southern Baptist Contextual Factors 73
    Three Factors 73
    The Campbellite Controversy 74
    The Lack of Sacramentalism in Southern Baptist History 77
    The Inerrancy Controversy 83
    Conclusion 88

4: Thomas Nettles 89
    A Biographical Sketch of Thomas Nettles 89
    Thomas Nettles' View of Baptism 90
    Nettles' Appropriation of the Work of Beasley-Murray 101
    Conclusion 107

5: Timothy George 108
    A Biographical Sketch of Timothy George 108
    Timothy George's View of Baptism 110
    George and Ecumenism 118
    George and the Reformers 119
    George's Appropriation of the Work of Beasley-Murray 122
    Conclusion 126

6: Thomas Schreiner 127
    A Biographical Sketch of Thomas Schreiner 127
    Thomas Schreiner's View of Baptism 128
    Schreiner's Appropriation of the Work of Beasley-Murray 139
    Conclusion 145

PART III: GEORGE BEASLEY-MURRAY AND BUGB BAPTISTS

7: Baptist Union of Great Britain Contextual Factors 149
    Three Factors 149
    The Oxford Movement 150
    The Ecumenical Movement 156
    The Charismatic Movement 165
    Conclusion 169

8: Nigel Wright 171
    A Biographical Sketch of Nigel Wright 171
    Nigel Wright's View of Baptism 174
    Wright's Appropriation of the Work of Beasley-Murray 182
    Conclusion 185

9: John Colwell 186
    A Biographical Sketch of John Colwell 186
    John Colwell's View of Baptism 187
    Influences on Colwell's Baptismal Theology 202
    Baptism, Manic Depression, and the Charismatic Movement 204
    Colwell's Appropriation of the Work of Beasley-Murray 207
    Conclusion 210

10: Anthony Cross 212
    A Biographical Sketch of Anthony Cross 213
    Anthony Cross and George Beasley-Murray 215
    Anthony Cross's View of Baptism and His Appropriation
        of George Beasley-Murray 216
    Concluding Observations 238

Conclusion 241
    Major Conclusions 241
    Further Research 245

Bibliography 247

Acknowledgments

SO MANY PEOPLE HAVE had a hand in helping me complete this project In them, I have seen the body of Christ at work, and for that I am filled with joy and gratitude. I would like to thank my parents, Jim and Linda, and my siblings, David and Amanda, whose support has been significant at every stage of my academic pursuits. Thanks to my grandmother, Thelma, who has been a constant source of encouragement. I would also like to thank my in-laws, Charles and Tempie, who have helped our family throughout this entire process.

I am very grateful for my church family, Ingleside Baptist Church. They have consistently asked about my research, prayed for me, encouraged me, celebrated with me, and helped with yard work so that I could spend time reading and writing. Special thanks to my Lead Pastor, Tim McCoy, and my Executive Pastor, Andy Johnson, who have encouraged me in my pursuit of a PhD and publication of the thesis.

My doctoral supervisors, Graham Watts and Peter Morden, provided much guidance, feedback, and thought-provoking conversation along the way. At many points, they kept me convinced that there was indeed a light at the end of the tunnel.

I appreciate Timothy George, Thomas Schreiner, Tom Nettles, Nigel Wright, John Colwell, and Anthony Cross, all subjects of chapters in this book who have been willing to correspond with me on numerous occasions. Thanks also to Fisher Humphreys, who has had many conversations with me about this work, and over the years has kept me mindful that theology can be a great service to the church.

Diana Kim, Triston Smith, and Autumn Vineyard have all helped me acquire sources. I am thankful for their friendship and their help.

To those friends who read parts of the book and suggested needed edits—including Aaron Adams, Laurie Ennis, Mark Hudgins, and Tara Fox: Excellence honors God and inspires people. Thanks for your help in maintaining high standards.

Introduction

THE FOCUS OF THIS book is situated at the intersection of my academic interests and pastoral concerns. My academic interests have long been related to the doctrine of the church. During my time in divinity school, I was introduced to the concept of open-membership, which is the practice of allowing into membership of baptist churches those who have not experienced believer baptism.[1] Researching and writing on that topic consistently led me back to the meaning of baptism. As a Southern Baptist pastor, issues related to baptism are also pastorally practical. People often have questions about when they should be baptized or whether they should be (re)baptized. Again, the primary issue in these questions is the meaning of baptism. In order to reflect on these issues theologically, I began this project. The initial scope was much broader than the final product. I began by investigating the connection between people's understanding of the meaning of baptism and their approach to open-membership throughout Baptist history. That developed into a focus on the meaning of baptism, and particularly the work of George Beasley-Murray.

I first read Beasley-Murray in divinity school while researching and writing about Baptist approaches to open-membership. Early in this current project I read more of his work. I came to respect Beasley-Murray as a scholar primarily because of his methodology. His theological conclusions related to baptism result from thorough exegesis of biblical texts. As someone who affirms the absolute authority of the Bible, I believed I had to take his work seriously. The more I read his work and reflected on it, I

---

1. First through a lecture by John Piper at Beeson Divinity School, and then in the work of Paul Fiddes, *Tracks and Traces,* 141–48. This led to exploration of Augustine's approach to (re)baptism during the Donatists controversy; see Augustine, "Faith and Creed;" Augustine, "On Baptism, Against the Donatists."

wondered to what extent, if any, it had shaped Baptist thinking about the meaning of baptism.

A BRIEF BIOGRAPHY OF GEORGE BEASLEY-MURRAY

George Beasley-Murray was born in London in 1916.[2] He was baptized in an Anglican church as a baby[3] and at the age of four was baptized again in a Roman Catholic Church.[4] In 1932 he was converted during a weeklong "mission" at the Free Church he was attending. He heard a sermon by a student of Spurgeon's College[5] on the meaning of Christ's death, and for the first time "learned that the cross was for my sake."[6] He was then baptized as a believer.[7]

Beasley-Murray studied at Spurgeon's College and earned an external BD from the University of London (1941).[8] From 1941 to 1948 he served as pastor of Ashurst Drive Baptist Church in the suburbs of London and earned an MTh from King's College, London (1948).[9] From 1948 to 1950 he served as pastor of Zion Church in Cambridge while earning a BA and MA from Cambridge University (1950). He then began teaching New Testament at Spurgeon's College and also completed a PhD at the University of London, which was published as *Jesus and the Future*.[10] From 1956 to 1958 he taught New Testament at The Baptist Theological Seminary in Ruschlikon, Switzerland. The next 15 years were spent as the Principal of Spurgeon's College. During that time he received a DD from the University of London. In 1973, he went to The Southern Baptist Theological Seminary in Kentucky, where he taught New Testament until

---

2. Biographical information found in Gloer, *Eschatology and the New Testament*, viii; Garrett, *Baptist Theology*, 387–95; and Beasley-Murray, *Fearless for Truth*.

3. Beasley-Murray, *Fearless for Truth*, 5.

4. Beasley-Murray, *Fearless for Truth*, 7.

5. Spurgeon's College is referenced throughout the book, as several of the scholars who are discussed, including Beasley-Murray, have connections to it. The origins of the college, founded by Charles Spurgeon, go back to 1855. For a history of Spurgeon's College, see Randall, *School of the Prophets*.

6. Beasley-Murray, *Fearless for Truth*, 13.

7. Beasley-Murray, *Fearless for Truth*, 14.

8. Garrett, *Baptist Theology*, 388.

9. Garrett, *Baptist Theology*, 388.

10. Garrett, *Baptist Theology*, 388.

1980. His final twenty years were spent in England, where he continued to write.[11]

During the course of his career, Beasley-Murray wrote commentaries on Ezekiel,[12] Matthew,[13] Mark,[14] John,[15] 2 Corinthians,[16] Philippians,[17] James, 1 Peter, Jude, 2 Peter,[18] and Revelation.[19] Beyond his commentaries, Beasley-Murray focused much of his writing on three topics—baptism, Jesus and the future, and the kingdom of God. R. Alan Culpepper has asserted that Beasley-Murray wrote "the definitive monograph for this generation" on all three topics.[20]

CLAIMS ABOUT THE SIGNIFICANCE OF BEASLEY-MURRAY'S WORK ON BAPTISM

In 1963 George Beasley-Murray published *Baptism in the New Testament*.[21] The book, in which he argues that baptism in the New Testament period was a means of divine grace, was neither his first nor his last on the subject. However, it was quickly recognized as a significant contribution in the area of baptismal theology. In a review of the book in 1963, Dale Moody wrote,

> There is little doubt that the publication of Baptism in the New Testament by G. R. Beasley-Murray, Principal of Spurgeon's College in London, will mark a new stage in discussions that relate to baptism. This will be especially true among Baptists, who for the most part came late to the debate, but world Christianity is not likely to ignore a work so genuinely ecumenical and so scholarly composed. Southern Baptists, among whom much of

---

11. Garrett, *Baptist Theology*, 388.
12. Beasley-Murray, "Ezekiel," *The New Bible Commentary*, 645–47.
13. Beasley-Murray, *Matthew*.
14. Beasley-Murray, *Commentary on Mark Thirteen*.
15. Beasley-Murray, *Gospel of John*.
16. Beasley-Murray, "2 Corinthians."
17. Beasley-Murray, "Philippians."
18. Beasley-Murray, *General Epistles*.
19. Beasley-Murray, *Book of Revelation*.
20. Culpepper, "George Beasley-Murray," 576.
21. Beasley-Murray, *Baptism in the New Testament*.

this material was presented, are sure to profit as much as they may be amazed by a book of this type.[22]

Five years later, Moody referred to *Baptism in the New Testament* as "the best one volume on New Testament baptism."[23] That same year, William Hull referred to it as a "bombshell in the baptistery."[24]

In 1983 Michael Walker claimed that *Baptism in the New Testament* had revolutionized Baptist understanding of baptism.[25] In 1990, Alan Culpepper said it would be "the definitive work on the subject for years to come."[26] In 2000 Anthony Cross considered the publishing of *Baptism in the New Testament* to mark the point at which there was a generally accepted approach among Baptists to thinking about baptism.[27] Cross claims, "There is no doubt that *Baptism in the New Testament* is the single most important and lasting contribution made by any Baptist this century to the baptismal debate, and more than adequately fulfilled the hopes of the many who had for so long called for a major Baptist work to be published."[28] In a 2000 review, J. Mark Beach writes, "G. R. Beasley-Murray's book *Baptism in the New Testament*, written almost forty years ago, remains the definitive statement and defense of the believers' baptism position. This study has stood the test of time and is probably the most widely quoted book in contemporary discussions on baptism in the English language."[29] At about the same time, Douglas Sparkes claimed that "it is still the standard reference work to those who explore this theme."[30] James Leo Garrett contends that it has "probably been the most frequently quoted or cited monograph on Christian baptism during the twentieth century."[31] Stanley Fowler has referred to it as "the crowning achievement of the Baptist contribution to the discussion of baptismal theology."[32] Writing in 2005, David Wright argued that *Baptism in the*

---

22. Moody, "Baptism in the New Testament," 232.
23. Moody, "Baptism in Recent Research," 21.
24. Hull, "Baptism in the New Testament," 3.
25. Walker, "Baptists at Worship in the Twentieth Century," 24.
26. Culpepper, "George Beasley-Murray," 576.
27. Cross, *Baptism and the Baptists*, 243.
28. Cross, *Baptism and the Baptists*, 202.
29. Beach, "Baptism in the New Testament," 203.
30. Sparkes, "Revd Dr. George Raymond Beasley-Murray," 14.
31. Garrett, "Baptists Concerning Baptism," 58.
32. Fowler, *More Than a Symbol*, 133.

New Testament "now stands as a landmark in the modern scholarly *retractatio* of early Christian Baptism."[33]

Although *Baptism in the New Testament* has received much attention, Anthony Cross has noted that Beasley-Murray's contribution has not been limited to that one work, and this book will therefore take into account other works as well. Referring to his larger corpus, Cross claims that Beasley-Murray wrote "what are undoubtedly the most eloquent, theologically balanced and important contributions any Baptist has made to the baptismal debate."[34]

THE CONTRIBUTION OF THIS PROJECT

Since the time that Beasley-Murray wrote about baptism, there has been much agreement that his works have had a lasting impact. This book goes beyond those claims in several ways. First, while a number of people have claimed that his work has been influential, I am not aware of any work that examines the arguments of more recent scholars in order to demonstrate that Beasley-Murray has influenced the debate about the meaning of baptism. Doing so is the primary aim of this book. This will serve the specific purpose of helping us better understand the current baptismal debate and will provide some insights that may prove helpful to those wanting to contribute to the debate moving forward. It will serve the more general purpose of helping us see the impact a single scholar can have on a debate and why certain scholars may have more influence than others.

Second, this book adds needed nuance to the claims about Beasley-Murray's significance by demonstrating how Beasley-Murray's work has shaped the debate. Some of the statements made about his work may be taken to imply that Beasley-Murray has won the debate. However, as will be seen in the following chapters, what Christopher Ellis wrote in 1996 remains true: Baptists still have "a wide range of views about baptism."[35] I have not, therefore, argued that Beasley-Murray has won the debate or even that all of the scholars in this book have been led in a sacramental direction by him. I have argued, rather, that he has influenced the debate to a significant extent and has done so in a variety of ways.

33. Wright, *What Has Infant Baptism Done to Baptism?*, 5.
34. Cross, *Baptism and the Baptists*, 227.
35. Ellis, "Baptism and the Sacramental Freedom of God," 23.

Third, the consideration of both Southern Baptist and BUGB Baptist[36] scholars is also a distinct contribution of this project. I am interested in the effect of Beasley-Murray on BUGB Baptists because that is his own tradition. As a Lecturer and Principal of Spurgeon's College and a pastor of two churches, he had the potential to influence the thinking of many BUGB Baptists. I am also interested in the effect of Beasley-Murray on Southern Baptists, and for two reasons. First, that is my own tradition and I want to better understand it. Second, Beasley-Murray taught at The Southern Baptist Seminary from 1973 to 1980. That position provided him the opportunity to influence the thinking of many Southern Baptists.

Evaluating Beasley-Murray's influence within these two traditions will provide necessary focus for this study. It will also allow for some comparison of Southern Baptist and BUGB Baptist thinking about baptism. Although it will not be possible to survey all the baptism-related literature, by considering the writings of scholars from both traditions, as well as contextual factors that are particularly relevant to the two groups, we can get a sense of the how the debate has developed, and what Beasley-Murray's role has been, within each tradition.

SCOPE OF THE PROJECT

Even within these two traditions additional focus is needed. I have chosen, therefore, to examine the work of three scholars within each tradition. In choosing which scholars to include two factors were taken into account. The primary factor is the amount of work each person has published on the issue of baptism. The second criterion is a personal connection to Beasley-Murray.

It should be noted that there are other BUGB Baptists and Southern Baptists who have written on baptism yet are not included in this book for a variety of reasons, including not having a clear connection to Beasley-Murray, not having published as much on baptism as the scholars who were selected, or in one case having published one of his most significant works before Beasley-Murray published *Baptism in the New Testament*. Among Southern Baptists, these include Dale Moody,[37] Oscar

---

36. The term "BUGB Baptist" is used throughout the book to refer to scholars who are affiliated with the Baptist Union of Great Britain.

37. Moody, *Baptism;* Moody, *Word of Truth;* Moody, "Shaping of Southern Baptist Polity"; Moody, "Nature of the Church."

Brooks,[38] James Leo Garrett,[39] Fisher Humphreys,[40] as well as the numerous contributors to *Believer's Baptism*.[41] Among BUGB Baptists are Paul Fiddes,[42] Brian Haymes,[43] Christopher Ellis,[44] and Paul Beasley-Murray.[45]

DEFINITION OF TERMS

"Sacrament"

Several terms will be used throughout this book that require some explanation. The first is the term "sacrament," with its related term "sacramental." Anthony Cross is correct in his assertion that "there is no agreed definition of the term 'sacrament.' 'Sacrament' is a term that has to be defined by the writer using it, not read into by the reader."[46] Writing in 1948, L. A. Read argued that "sacrament" lacks a clear definition.[47] Beasley-Murray acknowledged that the term "sacrament" is ambiguous and can be used by different people to mean different things.[48] He also indicated that he was not greatly concerned to defend the term "sacrament," though he did not believe that the ambiguous use of the term by some writers is sufficient reason to discard it.[49]

The primary element that various understandings of "sacrament" have in common is the conviction that God is active in baptism. There is disagreement concerning precisely what it is that he is doing, making the

---

38. Brooks, *Drama of Decision*.
39. Garrett, "Baptists Concerning Baptism," 52–67; Garrett, *Systematic Theology*.
40. Humphreys, *Thinking About God*.
41. Schreiner and Wright, *Believer's Baptism*.
42. Fiddes, "Baptism and Creation"; Fiddes, *Participating in God*; Fiddes, "Ex Opere Operato."
43. Haymes, "Baptism as a Political Act"; Haymes, *A Question of Identity*.
44. Ellis, "Baptism and the Sacramental Freedom of God."
45. Beasley-Murray, *Radical Believers*; Beasley-Murray, "Believers' Baptism."
46. Cross, "Faith-Baptism," 25. For various definitions of "sacrament," see Augustine, *On the Catechizing of the Uninstructed*, 26.50; "Sacrament" in Livingstone, *Oxford Concise Dictionary*, 508; and Cross, *Recovering the Evangelical Sacrament*, 188; Fahey, "Sacraments," 271; Clark, *Approach to the Theology*, 32; Guzie, *Book of Sacramental Basics*, 53; Cross, "Evangelical Sacrament," 199.
47. Read, "Ordinances," 8.
48. Beasley-Murray, *Baptism Today*, 13
49. Beasley-Murray, "Sacraments," 3.

term "sacrament" somewhat elastic and allowing for a range of nuances. Nevertheless, the dividing line between a sacramental view and a non-sacramental view is the belief that God is active in the baptismal event. Throughout this book, I will use the terms "sacrament" and "sacramental" to refer to this basic conviction about baptism.

"ex opere operato"

In discussions of a sacramental view of baptism another term that is often used is *ex opere operato*, a term that appears frequently in this book. The phrase translates into English "by the very fact of the action's being performed,"[50] and in relation to baptism suggests that the act of baptism has an effect upon the person baptized even if the person baptized has no faith of his own.[51] As Baptists, the scholars under consideration in this book affirm the necessity of faith in biblical baptism and therefore reject an *ex opere operato* view of baptism. Even when they suggest that infant baptism may be a valid practice, they continue to affirm that at some point the person baptized must exercise faith in the gospel in order to experience all the benefits associated with baptism.

At times, the term "mechanical" is used as a synonym for *ex opere operato*. Additionally, opponents of a sacramental view sometimes use the term "magical," which appears to be a pejorative way of referring to an *ex opere operato* view. "Magical" appears in quotations of scholars throughout this book, but because of the pejorative nature of the term, I have avoided using it as much as possible.

STRUCTURE OF THE ARGUMENT

The first section of the book will focus on George Beasley-Murray. Chapter 1 explores three factors that affected Beasley-Murray's thinking about baptism. Chapter 2 will examine Beasley-Murray's baptismal theology.

The second section of the book will focus on Beasley-Murray's impact on the arguments of three Southern Baptists. Chapter 3 will consider three contextual factors that have shaped Southern Baptist thinking about baptism. Chapter 4 will consider Beasley-Murray's impact on the argument of Thomas Nettles. Chapter 5 will consider Beasley-Murray's

---

50. *Catechism of the Catholic Church*, 319.
51. Livingstone, *Oxford Concise Dictionary*, 206.

influence on the argument of Timothy George. Chapter 6 will consider the role of Beasley-Murray's work in the argument of Thomas Schreiner.

The third section of the book mirrors the second section and will focus on Beasley-Murray's influence on the arguments of three BUGB Baptists. Chapter 7 will present three contextual factors that have shaped BUGB Baptist thinking about baptism. Chapter 8 will focus on Beasley-Murray's influence on Nigel Wright's argument related to the meaning of baptism. Chapter 9 will focus on Beasley-Murray's impact on the argument of John Colwell. Chapter 10 will examine the role of Beasley-Murray's work in Anthony Cross's argument.

It is appropriate at this point to acknowledge the overlap between much of Cross's work and this book. Cross has published work on the baptismal theology and practice of British Baptists in the twentieth century. While there are some points of contact between his work and this book, there are also differences. Perhaps the most significant is that, as noted above, this book examines baptismal theology beyond Britain by considering scholars within the Southern Baptist Convention. The second major difference is that this book, while taking into account a range of factors, focuses on one factor in the baptismal debate, namely the work of George Beasley-Murray. Cross acknowledges Beasley-Murray's role in the theological developments of the twentieth century, but does not demonstrate the extent of Beasley-Murray's impact on the baptismal theology of specific scholars.

The Conclusion will summarize the major findings and suggest some directions in which additional research is needed.

THE AUTHOR'S VIEW

The fundamental questions of this project are historical in nature: Has Beasley-Murray affected the debate about the meaning of baptism? And if so, in what ways? Nevertheless, the project necessarily deals with the theology of baptism. It may be helpful at this point, then, to make clear my own position, which is summed up in the New Hampshire Confession of Faith,

> Christian baptism is the immersion in water of a believer in Christ, into the name of the Father, and Son, and Holy Ghost; to show forth in a solemn and beautiful emblem his faith in the

crucified, buried, and risen Savior, with its effect in our death to sin and resurrection to a new life.[52]

In others words, baptism is an expression of a person's faith in response to the gospel of Jesus Christ.

In the New Testament, when a person repents of his sin and believes in Jesus, his repentance and belief are expressed through the act of baptism, which occurs immediately, or at least very near the time that repentance and belief take place. In the New Testament, therefore, baptism is very closely associated with conversion. It is never portrayed as the cause of salvation. Indeed, salvation is always by grace through faith. Baptism, then, expresses faith in the God who saves by grace.

---

52 New Hampshire Confession of Faith.

PART 1

George Beasley-Murray and Baptism

1

Antecedents of George Beasley-Murray's Baptismal Theology

THE FOCUS OF THIS book is the impact of George Beasley-Murray on the baptismal debate among Southern Baptist and BUGB Baptist scholars in the years following his publications on baptism. The debate, however, did not start with Beasley-Murray. This chapter will show how he fits into the ongoing debate and will show that Beasley-Murray's understanding of baptism was shaped, in part, by other scholars. It will therefore make clear that not all of Beasley-Murray's arguments were original, even among Baptists. Yet it is the contention of this book that, because he made them forcefully and prolifically, he is largely responsible for their influence.

This chapter comprises three main sections. The first provides an overview of the sacramental resurgence, a movement beginning in the 1920s in which a series of British Baptist scholars argued for a sacramental understanding of baptism. The second section argues that Beasley-Murray's training as a New Testament scholar affected his methodology, which in turn affected his theology of baptism. The third section analyzes some of the scholars whose work on baptism Beasley-Murray has appropriated into his own.

THE SACRAMENTAL RESURGENCE

The sacramental resurgence began in the 1920s. For the next four decades, a number of influential British Baptist scholars published works arguing for a sacramental understanding of baptism. Some critics believed that a sacramental view of baptism was foreign to Baptist life and that those pushing for it were doing something that had never been done among Baptists. For example, Baptist historian Robert Baker preached a sermon at Southwestern Baptist Theological Seminary in the mid-1960s, claiming that the sacramental thought developing among British Baptists was an innovation.[1] The truth is that sacramentalism has been part of Baptist life from the beginning. This is the thesis of Stanley Fowler's book, *More Than a Symbol*, a thesis he successfully defends.[2] He traces a line of sacramental thought from the seventeenth century that runs through the works of numerous Baptist leaders and confessions. Indeed, William Kiffin,[3] Benjamin Keach,[4] Andrew Fuller,[5] Daniel Turner,[6] and Robert Hall, Jr.[7] all believed that the New Testament presents a sacramental understanding of baptism.

The sacramental thought in the twentieth century, then, was not an innovation. It was, however, a shift. Though a sacramental understanding of baptism had been present in Baptist thought for three hundred years, it had been a minority view. Fowler points out that prior to the twentieth century there was an anti-sacramental consensus.[8] It is that consensus that Wheeler Robinson had in mind when he called for a "recovery of a lost sacramental emphasis."[9] Alec Gilmore also acknowledged that by

---

1. Baker, "Baptist Sacramentalism," 406–20.
2. Fowler, *More Than a Symbol*.
3. Kiffin, *Sober Discourse*, 11.
4. Keach, "Keach's Catechisms," 253.
5. Fuller's view of baptism is not entirely clear, but Fowler believes him to lean in a sacramental direction. See Fowler, *More Than a Symbol*, 50.
6. Fiddes, "Daniel Turner," 126; Covenant of 1780 of a Group of Christians.
7. Hall believed that baptism in the New Testament was sacramental. However, he did not believe that baptism as it was practiced in his own day was sacramental. Hall, *Works of Robert Hall*, 218; Walker, *Baptists at the Table*, 63.
8. Fowler, *More Than a Symbol*, 89.
9. Robinson, "Five Points of a Baptist's Faith" 9. According to Fowler, it is unclear whether Robinson is referring to the early Baptist tradition or the apostolic teaching, though the latter is more likely in light of the absence of any reference to early Baptists (Fowler, *More Than a Symbol*, 97).

holding to a sacramental view of baptism he was going against the majority of Baptists. He writes,

> Since the authority of the scriptures and the New Testament in particular has always been one of the foundation stones of Baptist principles, and since in the providence of God new light and truth are continually breaking forth from His word, Baptists of all people must beware of ignoring the findings of modern biblical scholarship because those findings happen to conflict with present practices or with positions adopted by some of their earliest advocates.[10]

Gilmore goes on to claim, "Baptism is clearly more than Baptists have traditionally understood by it."[11] So even though some Baptists had held to a sacramental view in the past, their position had been the minority view among Baptists. Those involved in the resurgence were hoping to change that.

Wheeler Robinson

According to Fowler, H. Wheeler Robinson was at the forefront of the sacramental resurgence.[12] Robinson, an Old Testament scholar who was Principal of Regent's Park College[13] and began publishing on the issue in the 1920s, affirmed in no uncertain terms a sacramental view of baptism. He believed that God was at work in the act of baptism to give grace to the person baptized. The reason more Baptists did not agree, he claimed, was because they had reacted to a wrong understanding of the relationship between baptism and grace implied in infant baptism, and had therefore become suspicious of any relationship between baptism and grace.[14] That position left many Baptists claiming that baptism is important solely because Jesus had commanded it, and failed to provide any actual meaning of baptism.[15]

---

10. Gilmore, *Baptism and Christian Unity*, 59–60.
11. Gilmore, *Baptism and Christian Unity*, 76.
12. Fowler, *More Than a Symbol*, 89.
13. For a brief biography of Robinson, see Garrett, *Baptist Theology*, 350–55.
14. Robinson, *Life and Faith of the Baptists*, 146.
15. Robinson, "Place of Baptism," 214.

Robinson, however, was more concerned with articulating the meaning of baptism than simply affirming that Jesus commanded it.[16] He claimed that there are four truths about the sacraments that are generally agreed upon: 1) the inward reality is a divine act; 2) God is not bound by the sacraments; 3) faith is necessary to receive God's gifts; 4) a person can receive more in the sacraments than he realizes.[17] In other places, he offers more detail concerning what is actually received in baptism. At its core, baptism is a means of putting on Christ, which is to be united with Christ in his death and resurrection.[18] Even more specifically, he argues that baptism in the New Testament implies three things: cleansing from sin, the gift of the Spirit, and a deep, experiential union with Christ in his redeeming acts.[19]

In his book, *Baptist Principles*, Robinson deals with the relationship between the outward expression of baptism and the inward realities experienced in baptism. He writes, "The baptism of the New Testament is the immersion of intelligent persons as the expressive accompaniment of their entrance into a new life of moral and spiritual relationship to God in Christ."[20] He goes on to point out that baptism in the New Testament is so closely identified with the experience it initiates, that it is virtually impossible to talk about baptism without talking about the experience.[21]

Robert Walton

Robert Walton was part of a group of young Baptist ministers that met in 1941 for prayer and theological study. They gave special attention to the doctrine of the church. Walton was asked to prepare a draft of a book containing their thoughts, which was published in 1946 as *The Gathered Community*. While he took responsibility for the final form, he states that the book is "a piece of group thinking."[22]

In the book, Walton puts forth a sacramental view of baptism. As did Robinson, Walton conceded that a sacramental view was not in his

16. Robinson, *Life and Faith*, 81.
17. Robinson, *Christian Experience*, 187.
18. Robinson, *Life and Faith*, 145.
19. Robinson, *Life and Faith*, 145.
20. Robinson, *Baptist Principles*, 12.
21. Robinson, *Baptist Principles*, 13.
22. Walton, *Gathered Community*, 8.

time common among Baptists, nor was it the majority view among the early Baptists.[23] Though it was contrary to much of his own tradition, one of his guiding principles was the conviction that the spiritual operates through the material. The clearest example of this principle is the incarnation.[24] That is not the only example, though. Creation and the church are other material means through which God works.[25] In that sense, many things can be sacramental. Yet baptism and the Lord's Supper are unique in that they point to the incarnation, death, and resurrection of Jesus in a way that other material things do not.[26]

For Walton, the water of baptism is an instrument through which God acts.[27] In particular, it is the "effective sign" of our union with Christ.[28] He emphasized two results of God's activity in baptism. The first is that the person baptized is brought into the church. The second result of baptism is the gift of the Holy Spirit. He recognized some tension between the claim that the Spirit is given in baptism and his belief that baptism follows conversion.[29] Walton asks, "Do men receive no guidance and persistent direction from the Holy Spirit, no encouragement to inquire and no illumination of a puzzled or darkened mind before they come to the waters of baptism? Are they not standing there making their confession because the Spirit has brought them?"[30] His solution is to make a distinction between the work of the Spirit which brings a person to faith, and the gift of the Spirit that a person receives when he enters into the Christian community through baptism. That distinction allows him to conclude that while there remains an intimate connection between baptism and the Spirit, the Spirit is nevertheless at work before and after baptism as well.[31]

---

23. Walton, *Gathered Community*, 156.
24. Walton, *Gathered Community*, 155.
25. Walton, *Gathered Community*, 156.
26. Walton, *Gathered Community*, 159.
27. Walton, *Gathered Community*, 158.
28. Walton, *Gathered Community*, 159.
29. Walton, *Gathered Community*, 27.
30. Walton, *Gathered Community*, 30.
31. Walton, *Gathered Community*, 30.

Neville Clark

Neville Clark, at that time a Baptist pastor in Rochester,[32] understood baptism as an act "behind which stands a depth of meaning related to divine action."[33] He agreed with those who hold a symbolic view that baptism is "an outward manifestation" of a response to the gospel.[34] His emphasis, however, is consistently on what God does in baptism, not what man does.[35]

The belief that God is active in baptism results from Clark's interpretation of Rom 6:3, which he understands as a reference to water-baptism which provides insight into the meaning of the rite.[36] In his view, since baptism marks a person's union with Christ in his death and resurrection, baptism is also connected to forgiveness and the giving of the Holy Spirit.[37] In fact, Clark argues that being in Christ, being in the Church, and being in the Spirit all refer to the same reality.[38] Convinced that all these things take place in baptism, Clark asserts that baptism marks the beginning of salvation.[39] He acknowledges that in Acts there are different patterns—sometimes Spirit then water, sometimes water then Spirit. That is because Luke is primarily concerned about the expansion of the church, not a precise history of events related to baptism.[40] For Clark, the biblical witness is clear and consistent—it is in baptism that a person is united to Christ and receives all the benefits that go with that union.

Christian Baptism

In 1959, Alec Gilmore, at that time a pastor in Northampton,[41] edited a book, *Christian Baptism*, which comprised a collection of essays on

---

32. Gilmore, *Christian Baptism*, 9.
33. Clark, "Christian Initiation," 156.
34. Clark, *An Approach to the Theology of the Sacraments*, 21.
35. Clark, "Christian Initiation," 161.
36. Clark, *Approach to the Theology*, 24.
37. Clark, *Approach to the Theology*, 21.
38. Clark, *Approach to the Theology*, 25.
39. Clark, *Approach to the Theology*, 25.
40. Clark, *Approach to the Theology*, 20.
41. Garrett, *Baptist Theology*, 542.

baptism written by British Baptists.[42] Collectively, the contributors spent over 100 pages of the book exegeting specific passages on baptism. They also argued for a sacramental view on theological grounds. It is understandable why Anthony Cross considers *Christian Baptism* to be "the most important book" on the meaning of baptism during the resurgence.[43]

The first essay to deal with the meaning of baptism is Alec Gilmore's "Jewish Antecedents." For the purpose of this study, the most significant part of Gilmore's essay is the section titled, "Whereas the old covenant had a 'sign,' the new covenant had an 'effective sign.'" In that section Gilmore writes,

> Paul acknowledges a link between faith and the way it is awakened or sustained, and the Christian church has followed him in this approach. The Anglican, for instance, believes that in Scripture baptism signifies the public acknowledgment of Jesus as Lord, and that the blessings of baptism flow from the union with Christ thus gained. The Free Churchman, similarly, would endorse the view of P.T. Forsyth that baptism is the sacrament of the new birth, not in the sense that it produces the regeneration, but in the sense that it richly conveys it by our personal experience into its home. Outside this country, Karl Barth has done as much as anyone in recent years to counteract extreme sacramentalism, but he too sees the special work of baptism to be that of sealing; it is the sealing of the letter which Jesus Christ has written in His person and with His work. Thus understood, he goes on to argue that in the words of Scripture we must say of it that it saves, sanctifies, purifies, mediates, and gives the forgiveness of sins and the grace of the Holy Spirit.[44]

As will be discussed below, one of the criticisms of *Christian Baptism* was that its authors were promoting baptismal regeneration. The authors denied the accusation. In fact, in the very next essay, R. E. O. White claims that the silence on baptism in the gospels serves as a warning against making baptism necessary for salvation.[45] Nevertheless, in light of Gilmore's above statement, along with similar statements by the other contributors, the critics' concern about baptismal regeneration is understandable.

42. Gilmore, *Christian Baptism*.
43. Cross, *Baptism and the Baptists*, 228.
44. Gilmore, *Christian Baptism*, 62.
45. Gilmore, *Christian Baptism*, 98.

In his essay, "Baptism in the Acts of the Apostles," S.I. Bruce, Lecturer in New Testament Studies at University College of North Wales,[46] contends that in Acts, human activity and divine activity are both present in baptism. In response to the suggestion of Markus Barth that baptism is solely a human act, Bruce writes,

> We have no right, however, to think of the human activity in baptism as the all-important factor. We must remember the significant fact that in Christian baptism the candidate does not baptise himself. . . . The Christian convert was baptised by someone who was acting as the representative of his Lord. Only when the two sides of baptism, the human and the divine, are seen together is Luke's picture viewed whole.[47]

George Beasley-Murray contributed an essay titled "Baptism in the Epistles of Paul." Beasley-Murray's baptismal thought will be examined in much more detail in the next chapter, but his contribution to *Christian Baptism* is noteworthy. His thesis is that in the New Testament baptism is the appropriate response to the gospel. Specifically, it is an expression of faith in Christ. He writes, "Since faith in Jesus as the risen Lord brings justification, and confession of His name deliverance from this world and the life of the age to come, the baptismal act in which both are expressed is the supreme moment in the believer's experience of salvation. . . . For Paul the inner and outer acts of the decision of faith and its expression in baptism form one indissoluble event."[48] He points out that Paul links baptism with justification and sanctification.[49] He does not suggest that baptism causes either, only that it is associated with them.

In his essay, "Baptism in the Fourth Gospel and the First Epistle of John," D. R. Griffiths, Lecturer in Biblical Studies at University College, Cardiff,[50] goes further than any other contributor in his understanding of what happens in baptism. He considers baptism to be the "definite moment" when purification takes place,[51] and when the Christian dies with Christ and is saved as a result of that union.[52] His conclusion is that

---

46. Gilmore, *Christian Baptism*, 9.
47. Gilmore, *Christian Baptism*, 127.
48. Gilmore, *Christian Baptism*, 129–30.
49. Gilmore, *Christian Baptism*, 142.
50. Gilmore, *Christian Baptism*, 9.
51. Gilmore, *Christian Baptism*, 176.
52. Gilmore, *Christian Baptism*, 179.

entrance into the kingdom of God is impossible except by means of rebirth in water-baptism and the giving of the Spirit, which are inextricably connected.[53] This conclusion left the authors of *Christian Baptism* open to the accusation that they were excluding the unbaptized from salvation and the church, an accusation that will be dealt with below.

Neville Clark contributed the essay, "The Theology of Baptism." His primary concern is the subjects of baptism, but he also deals with the meaning of baptism.[54] He claims that baptism "implies, embodies and effects forgiveness of sin, initiation into the church and the gift of the Holy Spirit" and "effects initiation into the life of the blessed Trinity."[55] When establishing the results of baptism, he makes no mention of faith. Only later in his essay does he affirm that faith is necessary, but then continues to give priority to the divine activity in baptism.[56]

R. E. O. White

According to Michael Walker, R. E. O. White's *Biblical Doctrine of Initiation* was one of two works which "revolutionised the Baptist understanding of the initiating sacrament."[57] In it, White, who held pastorates in Wales, England, and Scotland before becoming a tutor in New Testament in the Baptist Theological College of Scotland,[58] claims that throughout Scripture, what is required to enter the covenant community is faith and repentance in response to the divine initiative. In the New Testament, that faith is expressed in baptism.[59] He argues that Paul's view of baptism was sacramental, but is careful to point out that it was not conceived by Paul as *ex opere operato*. Baptism was for those who had heard, understood, and believed the message of the *kerygma*.[60] He affirms that faith is too important to Paul to allow for a mechanical view of baptism.[61] For

---

53. Gilmore, *Christian Baptism*, 158.
54. Gilmore, *Christian Baptism*, 311.
55. Gilmore, *Christian Baptism*, 308–9.
56. Gilmore, *Christian Baptism*, 311.
57. Quoted in Porter and Cross, *Baptism, the New Testament*, 37. The other work was *Baptism in the New Testament* by Beasley-Murray.
58. For a brief biography of White, see Garrett, *Baptist Theology*, 541.
59. White, *Biblical Doctrine of Initiation*, 203.
60. White, *Biblical Doctrine of Initiation*, 218.
61. White, *Biblical Doctrine of Initiation*, 219.

Paul, then, baptism effectively unites a person to Christ only because for Paul baptism is always faith-baptism.[62]

In White's view, Peter also puts forth a sacramental view of baptism. His understanding of baptism is perhaps clearest in his statement in 1 Pet 3:21 that "baptism saves." It does so, according to White, by uniting the baptized person to Christ in his death and resurrection.[63] John, too, presents a sacramental view of baptism, evident in the fact that in John water-baptism and Spirit-baptism are portrayed as coincidental.[64]

White's conclusion is that baptism is confessional in nature.[65] It has a "spiritual endowment," meaning it is "an effective rite of actual fulfillment."[66] He continues, "The example of Jesus, the use of his name, the claim to his authority, the awareness of eschatological fulfillment, the baptised's reception of the Spirit, the reality of spiritual initiation—all underline the fact that the event of baptism is more than the act of the baptised."[67] He is careful to note, though, that the sacrament is not efficacious because of the thing done, but because of the doing of the thing. The response of faith on the part of the baptized is necessary, and actually invests the rite with meaning. At the same time, the activity of God is necessary for the rite to have sacramental meaning.[68] He concludes,

> efficacy belongs strictly neither to the element, nor to the rite, but to the action of God within the soul of the baptised who at that time, in that way, is making his response to the grace offered to him in the gospel. . . . On the one side, the faith of the person doing the appointed thing invests the rite at that moment, for himself, with sacramental meaning; on the other side, God accepting this response, in fulfillment of His promise in the gospel invests the rite at that moment, for that convert, with sacramental power.[69]

---

62. White, *Biblical Doctrine of Initiation*, 226.
63. White, *Biblical Doctrine of Initiation*, 231.
64. White, *Biblical Doctrine of Initiation*, 255.
65. White, *Biblical Doctrine of Initiation*, 271.
66. White, *Biblical Doctrine of Initiation*, 273.
67. White, *Biblical Doctrine of Initiation*, 274.
68. White, *Biblical Doctrine of Initiation*, 308.
69. White, *Biblical Doctrine of Initiation*, 308.

Alec Gilmore

In 1966 Alec Gilmore published *Baptism and Christian Unity*, the final major work in the sacramental resurgence. In it he argues along similar lines as the others mentioned above. He contends that in the New Testament, faith and baptism are inseparable,[70] and are considered "two sides of the same thing."[71] His insistence on the necessity of faith prevents baptism from being understood as *ex opere operato*. From a Baptist point of view, God takes the initiative in baptism, but faith is required to receive the grace He gives.[72] At times, however, Gilmore seems to go beyond associating faith and baptism by nearly identifying them. For example, he refers to Alan Richardson, who claimed that we should not speak of justification by faith, but of justification by faith and baptism.[73] Prior to baptism, a person must recognize what God has done in Christ and must desire to accept that gift.[74] According to Gilmore, though, such a recognition and desire do not constitute the kind of faith through which a person is united to Christ. Such faith can only be expressed in baptism.

He goes on to attempt to refute the distinction between the material and the symbolic, and goes quite far in this effort. He refers to a study by A. Wikenhauser, who argued that union with Christ cannot be brought about by faith alone, else baptism would be reduced to a mere symbol.[75] Gilmore appears to agree with this idea. In fact, he goes so far as to imply that the spiritual cannot exist without the material.[76]

It is clear then that Beasley-Murray did not start the debate about the meaning of baptism among Baptists. In fact, other respected scholars published substantial works on baptism both before and around the same time that he was publishing his works on the topic. Yet he seems to have influenced the debate to a greater extent than even the others who contributed to the resurgence.

---

70. Gilmore, *Baptism*, 17.
71. Gilmore, *Baptism*, 59.
72. Gilmore, *Baptism*, 18.
73. Gilmore, *Baptism*, 24.
74. Gilmore, *Baptism*, 67.
75. Gilmore, *Baptism*, 55.
76. Gilmore, *Baptism*, 55.

BEASLEY-MURRAY'S TRAINING AS A BIBLICAL SCHOLAR

Beasley-Murray acknowledged that one of the factors that led him to his conclusions about baptism was the approach he took when considering what the Bible teaches about baptism.[77] This section will elucidate what his approach was, and will show the relevance of his approach for his conclusions.

James Leo Garrett has classified Beasley-Murray as a "biblical theologian." He claims, "Baptists have characteristically sought to base their doctrinal affirmations upon specific passages within the Bible," and understands this to be the approach of Beasley-Murray.[78] Beasley-Murray arrived at his position by examining in detail passages of Scripture that are relevant to baptism. Much of his work is essentially thorough exegesis of particular texts. Beasley-Murray was deliberate in this approach and was aware of the fact that others took a different approach. He also believed that the different approaches helped explain, at least in part, different conclusions. In his first published work on the sacraments, Beasley-Murray focused primarily on the exegesis of Rom 6:4–8, Gal 3:27, and 1 Pet 3:21. From those passages he concludes that the most important thing in baptism is what God does. He then asks, "If this be valid exegesis, how can one assert that the important thing in Baptism is what we give God?"[79] He goes on to point out that objections to a sacramental view of baptism "are usually on other than exegetical grounds."[80]

One specific example he points to is John Calvin's interpretation of John 3:5. Calvin acknowledged that "the greater part of expounders" take "water" as a reference to baptism, but he disagreed.[81] He believed that such an understanding "confines salvation to the outward sign," making baptism absolutely necessary for salvation, which he found "absurd."[82] Calvin concludes, "I cannot bring myself to believe that Christ speaks of baptism; for it would be inappropriate."[83]

---

77. Beasley-Murray, "Sacraments," 4.
78. Garrett, *Baptist Theology*, 343.
79. Beasley-Murray, "Sacraments," 4.
80. Beasley-Murray, "Sacraments," 4.
81. Calvin, *Commentary on the Gospel According to John*, 110.
82. Calvin, *Commentary on the Gospel According to John*, 110.
83. Calvin, *Commentary on the Gospel According to John*, 110; In Calvin, *Commentary Upon the Acts of the Apostles*, 454, Calvin also separates the Spirit and baptism

Beasley-Murray believed that Calvin's conclusion was determined not by sound exegesis, but by prior theological assumptions. He claimed, "Calvin's exegesis was forced on him because he could not endure the idea that baptism was necessary to salvation, but that deduction from the words does not necessarily follow and they must be allowed their proper force without prejudice."[84]

Calvin himself claimed that a person should interpret specific passages in light of his theology. In his preface to *Institutes of the Christian Religion* he writes,

> Now my design in this work has been to prepare and qualify students of theology for the reading of the divine word, that they may have an easy introduction to it, and be able to proceed in it without any obstruction. For I think I have given such a comprehensive summary, and orderly arrangement of all the branches of religion, that, with proper attention, no person will find any difficulty in determining what ought to be the principal objects of his research in the scripture, and to what end he ought to refer any thing it contains.[85]

It is unclear whether Beasley-Murray would argue with Calvin's approach on principle. He did believe, however, that Calvin's theological beliefs prevented Calvin from properly interpreting at least one particular passage.

One of the reasons for Beasley-Murray's biblical approach was his own conviction concerning the way Christians should decide what to believe.[86] Another reason was his training. Beasley-Murray was by training a New Testament scholar. Though most of the people with whom he studied do not show up often in his work, they likely influenced his approach by helping him develop as an exegete.[87] While at Spurgeon's College, Beasley-Murray studied New Testament with Percy Evans, who held a sacramental view of baptism.[88] He cites Evans in *Baptism in the New Testament* in regards to a specific exegetical point concerning 2 Cor

in his commentary on Acts. He argues that Acts 10:48 indicates that "the Spirit is not included in baptism."

84. Beasley-Murray, *Baptism in the New Testament*, 228n2.

85. Calvin, *Institutes*, 4–5.

86. Beasley-Murray, "I Still Find Infant Baptism Difficult," 226; Beasley-Murray, *Baptism in the New Testament*, 263.

87. Details about Beasley-Murray's education can be found in Beasley-Murray, *Fearless for Truth*; and Garrett, *Baptist Theology*, 388.

88. Evans, *Sacraments in the New Testament*.

1:21, and disagrees with his former teacher on that point.[89] Nevertheless, it is significant that his first New Testament teacher was a sacramentalist and someone that Beasley-Murray continued to interact with in his own work.

Beasley-Murray also studied at King's College, London, where he earned both an MTh and a PhD under the supervision of New Testament scholar R. V. G. Tasker. However, Beasley-Murray does not refer to Tasker at all in *Baptism in the New Testament*, which suggests that Tasker may not have had much direct influence on Beasley-Murray's view of baptism. His lack of influence is also evident in one other way. Tasker wrote a commentary on the book of John, a book to which Beasley-Murray gave much attention. In fact, he later wrote a commentary himself on John. Throughout his writings, John 3:5 was an important passage for his understanding of baptism. Interestingly, Tasker did not mention baptism at all in his explanation of John 3:5. In Beasley-Murray's commentary on John he mentions several people who had influenced him, including some who had written commentaries on John.[90] Tasker was not among those he mentioned.

Beasley-Murray earned an MA at Cambridge under the supervision of New Testament scholar P. Gardner Smith. Smith seems to have had a more direct impact on Beasley-Murray's thought than did Tasker. Beasley-Murray referred to Smith twice in *Baptism in the New Testament*. The first time he cites Smith is in support of the possibility that John 20:21 may be an allusion to the baptizing activity of the disciples.[91] The second time he cites Smith is also approvingly, in support of the claim that John's baptism was for the revelation of the Messiah.[92] In his commentary on John, Beasley-Murray points out that he was guided in his studies by Smith, who also introduced him to the work of New Testament scholar E. C. Hoskyns, who led him to the work of New Testament scholar Adolf Schlatter, who proved to be a major influence on Beasley-Murray.[93]

Although there were others who had more influence on Beasley-Murray's baptismal thought, Evans, Tasker and Smith are noteworthy because of their training of Beasley-Murray in New Testament studies.

---

89. Beasley-Murray, *Baptism in the New Testament*, 273.
90. Beasley-Murray, *John*, x–xi.
91. Beasley-Murray, *Baptism in the New Testament*, 80.
92. Beasley-Murray, *Baptism in the New Testament*, 218.
93. Beasley-Murray, *John*, x–xi.

MAJOR INFLUENCES

In addition to his academic supervisors, there are a number of other scholars who should be considered major influences on Beasley-Murray. There were literally hundreds of scholars with whom he interacted in his works,[94] but among them some stand out as more significant than others for a number of reasons. One group which stands out are those that Beasley-Murray himself acknowledges as being major influences. In his commentary on John, for example, he refers to the "crystal-clear exegesis" of C. H. Dodd.[95] He states that he was guided in his studies by P. Gardner Smith. He also mentions the work of Hoskyns and Schlatter, and claims Raymond Brown and Rudolf Schnackenburg wrote the most influential commentaries on John.[96]

A second group which stands out as especially influential are those that Beasley-Murray cites early in his career. Since in his earliest work on baptism Beasley-Murray held a sacramental view, scholars that he interacts with only in his later writings may have confirmed his views or been helpful on particular points, but they are not responsible for his sacramental stance. To see those who may have been more helpful in arriving at a sacramental position, we must look to those to whom he refers early in his career. In his first work on baptism, an article published in 1948 titled "The Sacraments," he refers to Dodd, Barth and Brunner.[97] In a 1956 article, "The Church of Scotland and Baptism," he refers to Adolf Schlatter.[98] In his influential essay, "Baptism in the Epistles of Paul," published in 1959, he refers to a number of people, most frequently Adolf Schlatter, Rudolf Butlmann, C. H. Dodd, Rudolf Schnackenburg, W. F. Flemington, G. Bornkmann, Oscar Cullmann, and G. W. H. Lampe.[99]

A third group which stands out are those people that Beasley-Murray cites often. In his major work *Baptism in the New Testament*, there are many people he cites once or twice. There are others that he cites dozens of times. Among the most cited are Rudolf Bultmann, Oscar Cullmann, C. H. Dodd, W. F. Flemington, Joachim Jeremias, G. W. H. Lampe, Adolf Schlatter, Rudolf Schnackenburg, and H. Windisch. When considering

---

94. In *Baptism and the New Testament* alone he cites over three hundred people.
95. Beasley-Murray, *John*, x.
96. Beasley-Murray, *John*, x–xi.
97. Beasley-Murray, "Sacraments."
98. Beasley-Murray, "Church of Scotland and Baptism," 9.
99. Beasley-Murray, "Baptism in the Epistles of Paul."

Beasley-Murray's influences, special attention will be given to the major influences, especially those who fall into more than one of the above categories.

Two Brief Observations

Before examining in greater detail the major influences on Beasley-Murray, two observations should be made. First, most of the scholars with whom Beasley-Murray interacts are outside the Baptist tradition, including Dodd (Congregationalist), Flemington (Methodist), Schlatter (German Evangelical), Schnackenburg (Catholic), Barth (Reformed), Cullmann (Lutheran), Bultmann (Lutheran) and Jeremias (Lutheran). According to R. Alan Culpepper, it was R. Newton Flew, a New Testament scholar and principal of Wesley House, Cambridge, who encouraged Beasley-Murray to read scholars from other traditions.[100] This would seem to be a significant factor in Beasley-Murray's arrival at a sacramental position. As has been discussed, the majority of Baptist leaders before Beasley-Murray did not hold a sacramental view of baptism. By being willing to interact with other traditions, Beasley-Murray was exposed to much sacramental thought not always present in Baptist life. He was also guided in his exegesis by people who did not read the Bible through traditional Baptist lenses. They may have worn lenses that were colored by their own ecclesiastical traditions, but they nevertheless provided Beasley-Murray with a wider range of interpreters with whom he could interact.

The second observation is that most of Beasley-Murray's major influences were primarily biblical scholars, not theologians.[101] There were some who were theologians, such as Barth and Brunner. The majority, however, were biblical scholars. Those include Dodd, Flemington, Jeremias, Schlatter, Schnackenburg, Windisch, Bultmann, Cullmann, Evans, Hoskyns, Westcott, Tasker, Dibelius, Bornkamm, and Heitmuller. This bias towards New Testament scholars is consistent with Beasley-Murray's overall approach. His primary task was to understand the meaning of specific texts, and in that process he interacted with other biblical scholars

---

100. Culpepper, "George Beasley-Murray," 571.

101. It is sometimes difficult to make a distinction between a New Testament scholar and a theologian, as some people studied and even taught in both fields. For purposes of this study, an attempt has been made to consider the primary focus of each scholar.

who have addressed in a detailed way the exegetical issues of passages related to baptism.

An Examination of the Major Influences

Though not one of his supervisors, perhaps the most influential person with whom Beasley-Murray studied was the Cambridge New Testament scholar C. H. Dodd. As noted above, in the introduction to his commentary on John, Beasley-Murray referred to the influence of the "crystal-clear exegesis" of Dodd.[102] Culpepper claims that Dodd influenced Beasley-Murray to write on the text itself and not just quote other people's opinions.[103] That is certainly characteristic of Beasley-Murray's approach. In "The Sacraments," his first work on the topic, he mentions other scholars briefly, but most of the article is simply exegesis.

Beyond influencing his methodology, Dodd is one of the scholars with whom Beasley-Murray interacts most frequently. His view of baptism, then, is worth considering. Dodd understood baptism to be a response of faith to the gospel. He considered an appeal for repentance and the offer of forgiveness to be an essential component of the apostolic preaching, and saw such an appeal in Acts 2:37–38, which calls people to be baptized in response to the gospel.[104] Baptism, according to Dodd, was an expression of faith and repentance. Consequently, he claims that Paul would not have considered the question of whether faith without baptism would make a person a member of the Body.[105] Faith was always recognized by the administration of baptism.[106]

In Dodd's view, Paul did not give "overwhelming importance" to the rite *per se*, but did understand it to unite a person to Christ.[107] The physical act itself cannot accomplish anything unless it is a symbol of what really happens inwardly.[108] It was for Paul "the act by which [a person] entered into the Christian communion,"[109] and "the effectual sign"

---

102. Beasley-Murray, *John*, x.
103. Culpepper, "George Beasley-Murray," 571.
104. Dodd, *Apostolic Preaching*, 29.
105. Dodd, *Epistle of Paul to the Romans*, 86.
106. Dodd, *Epistle of Paul to the Romans*, 87.
107. Dodd, *Meaning of Paul*, 118.
108. Dodd, *Meaning of Paul*, 119.
109. Dodd, *Meaning of Paul*, 119.

of Spirit-baptism.[110] Since baptism was an expression of faith in Christ, "The whole sacrament is an act by which the believer enters into all that Christ did as his Representative."[111] Dodd was clear that in baptism "is something actually done."[112] Before it, a person was not a member of the Church. After it, he is.[113] "He is now in Christ."[114]

Dodd's influence on Beasley-Murray is apparent in a number of works. In "The Sacraments" he credits Dodd, along with Brunner, for helping him see that in the New Testament *keygma* precedes *didache*.[115] In "Baptism in the Epistles of Paul" he refers to Dodd's commentary on Rom 6, once approvingly and once disapprovingly.[116] In *Baptism in the New Testament*, he cites Dodd often. He agrees with a number of Dodd's statements in his Romans commentary[117] and appeals to *The Apostolic Preaching and its Developments* in support of his argument that faith and repentance expressed in baptism is the proper response to the proclamation of God's saving acts.[118] Throughout Beasley-Murray's work, then, the influence of C. H. Dodd is apparent.

Another major influence was German Evangelical Adolf Schlatter. Though he taught theology as well, Schlatter was primarily a New Testament exegete.[119] Concerning his view of baptism, Schlatter believed that in the New Testament baptism was the appropriate response of faith upon hearing and believing the message of the gospel.[120] It was "active repentance."[121] There was, therefore, no separation between baptism and

---

110. Dodd, *Meaning of Paul*, 131.
111. Dodd, *Epistle of Paul to the Romans*, 87.
112. Dodd, *Epistle of Paul to the Romans*, 87.
113. Dodd, *Epistle of Paul to the Romans*, 87.
114. Dodd, *Epistle of Paul to the Romans*, 87. Dodd claims that in baptism a person is made a member of the body of Christ, and is therefore united to Christ. Beasley-Murray believed that Dodd had reversed the order, and claimed in baptism a person was united to Christ and therefore made a member of Christ's body.
115. Beasley-Murray, "Sacraments," 5.
116. Beasley-Murray, "Baptism in the Epistles of Paul," 132, 139.
117. Beasley-Murray, *Baptism in the New Testament*, 133, 138.
118. Beasley-Murray, *Baptism in the New Testament*, 381.
119. Elwell and Weaver, *Bible Interpreters*, 60–61, 66.
120. Schlatter, *Theology of the Apostles*, 44.
121. Schlatter, *Theology of the Apostles*, 45.

the call to faith.¹²² To be baptized was to confess Jesus as Lord,¹²³ which brought a person into union with Christ.¹²⁴ As a result of that union, the baptized person was given grace, including forgiveness of sins and the gift of the Spirit.¹²⁵ Union with Christ also brought the baptized person into the church:

> But how were men to become members of the Church and partakers of her privileges? From the beginning the answer was unhesitatingly by baptism. . . . There can be no doubt that it was connected with repentance and conversion. It was an act of contrition, in which the candidate repudiated his old life, acknowledged his guilt, and sought purification.¹²⁶

Schlatter's influence shows up early and often in Beasley-Murray's work. In "The Church of Scotland and Baptism," published in 1956, Beasley-Murray quotes Schlatter, who claimed that Paul can "express the Gospel not in half measure, but completely, without mentioning the sacraments at all. But if they come into view he connects with them the entire riches of the grace of Christ, because he sees in them the will of Jesus not partially but fully stamped and effective." Beasley-Murray states, "I assent to that statement."¹²⁷

In "Baptism in the Epistles of Paul," Beasley-Murray cites Schlatter frequently when dealing with specific texts.¹²⁸ In *Baptism in the New Testament*, Schlatter is among those most frequently cited by Beasley-Murray. He is often in agreement with Schlatter. For example, he agrees that according to Rom 6:8 faith is a necessary component of baptism.¹²⁹ He agrees that in the New Testament the gospel was heard and accepted in baptism.¹³⁰ He agrees that in baptism a person is united to Christ and given all the blessings that go with that union.¹³¹ Beasley-Murray's overall thesis in *Baptism in the New Testament*, then, is consistent with Schlatter's

---

122. Schlatter, *Theology of the Apostles*, 45.
123. Schlatter, *Theology of the Apostles*, 46.
124. Schlatter, *Church in the New Testament Period*, 32.
125. Schlatter, *Church in the New Testament Period*, 27.
126. Schlatter, *Church in the New Testament Period*, 26.
127. Beasley-Murray, "Church of Scotland and Baptism," 9.
128. Beasley-Murray, "Baptism in the Epistles of Paul."
129. Beasley-Murray, *Baptism in the New Testament*, 156.
130. Beasley-Murray, *Baptism in the New Testament*, 204.
131. Beasley-Murray, *Baptism in the New Testament*, 210.

view of baptism in the New Testament. The similarity is also seen in Beasley-Murray's article, "The Holy Spirit, Baptism and the Body of Christ." He quotes with approval the statement by Schlatter,

> The blessing that is bestowed upon the baptised man does not consist in an individual gift of grace, nor on a particular religious condition, but in a union with Christ, by which the totality of God's gifts are obtained. For which reason the baptismal preaching consistently uses the whole Gospel in its entirety for the interpretation of baptism.[132]

A third major influence was Rudolf Schnackenburg, a Roman Catholic New Testament scholar. In 1946 he published a dissertation on baptism. A revised version of that work was translated by Beasley-Murray and published in 1964 as *Baptism in the Thought of St Paul*. In the translator's preface, Beasley-Murray wrote, "No treatment known to me of Paul's teaching on baptism is so profound as that contained within these pages."[133] Schnackenburg's stated goal was to investigate the relevant biblical text as a New Testament scholar and not as a defender of Catholic doctrine. In his words, "The book does not repudiate the Roman Catholic standpoint, but an endeavor is made in it to investigate the Pauline texts, according to the historical-critical method which all scholars in the New Testament field are obliged to observe."[134] Beasley-Murray took the same approach as a Baptist, arguing for what he saw in the New Testament and not necessarily for what was common among Baptists.

In his book, Schnackenburg examines specific passages which deal with baptism, including 1 Cor 6:11, Eph 5:26, Titus 3:5, 1 Cor 1:13 and Rom 6:11. These passages led him to a sacramental understanding of baptism. He claims that a person is united to Christ in baptism[135] and consequently dies and rises with Christ in baptism.[136] He therefore considers baptism to be a "means of salvation,"[137] and argues that for Paul, baptism is "for every man the regular means of becoming a Christian."[138] He also understood faith to be an essential component of baptism in the

---

132. Beasley-Murray, "Holy Spirit, Baptism and the Body of Christ,"
133. Schnackenburg, *Baptism in the Thought*, Translator's Preface.
134. Schnackenburg, *Baptism in the Thought*, Author's Preface.
135. Schnackenburg, *Baptism in the Thought*, 30.
136. Schnackenburg, *Present and Future*, 101.
137. Schnackenburg, *Baptism in the Thought*, 106.
138. Schnackenburg, *Baptism in the Thought*, 125.

New Testament. Baptism without faith is "unimaginable" for the early church.[139]

Schnackenburg's sacramental stance also appears in his commentary on the Gospel of John, which in Beasley-Murray's opinion, was one of the two most influential commentaries on John.[140] Commenting on John 3:5, which mentions water but not baptism, Schnackenburg claims, "Every Christian hearer or reader must have thought at once of baptism."[141] In his opinion, the only reason anyone would question a reference to baptism in John 3:5 is because of a prejudice that John has no interest in the sacraments.[142]

In "Baptism in the Epistles of Paul," Beasley-Murray refers to Schnackenburg frequently. He refers to Schnackenburg's argument that being "in Christ" involves being "with Christ" in his suffering, a relationship brought about by baptism. Beasley-Murray says of this argument, "Schnackenburg's discussions of this matter . . . constitute the profoundest treatment I have seen of this element in Paul's baptismal theology and are worthy of closest study."[143]

Beasley-Murray also interacts with Schnackenburg in *Baptism in the New Testament*. In his discussion of Rom 6:1–11 he agrees with Schnackenburg's view that "the parallel formulated of the resurrection in v. 4, 'as Christ . . . so also we,' applies to our entire relation to the redemptive event."[144] In his discussion of Col 2:6, he credits Schnackenburg for the insight that Paul's effort to counter a false theology moves him to explain baptism in theological terms and so make clear "the nature of the sacrament itself."[145]

Another influence was W. F. Flemington, a Methodist who taught New Testament at Cambridge. Flemington's baptismal thought is detailed in his book, *The New Testament Doctrine of Baptism*, published in 1957. The similarities between his book and Beasley-Murray's *Baptism in the New Testament* are striking. Both books begin with an examination of the antecedents of Christian baptism, including Jewish washings, proselyte

---

139. Schnackenburg, *Baptism in the Thought*, 126.
140. Beasley-Murray, *John*, xi. The other was written by Raymond Brown.
141. Schnackenburg, *Gospel According to St. John*, 369.
142. Schnackenburg, *Gospel According to St. John*, 369.
143. Beasley-Murray, "Baptism in the Epistles of Paul," 137.
144. Beasley-Murray, *Baptism in the New Testament*, 141.
145. Beasley-Murray, *Baptism in the New Testament*, 156.

baptism, the baptism of John and the baptism of Jesus. Both books go on to examine the New Testament evidence concerning baptism in Acts, the letters of Paul, the writings of John, then finally in other authors.

Flemington argues that in Acts baptism is most frequently linked with "hearing the word" and "believing," and is also associated with repentance, forgiveness and the gift of the Holy Spirit.[146] In Paul, baptism is primarily associated with faith, justification and sonship.[147] Paul, Flemington claims, saw baptism as an act by which converts were united to Christ and his body, and therefore marked for the Christian a transition from the old life to the new.[148] He concluded, "In baptism itself something happened. The symbolism was not only expressive but also effective."[149] Because Paul's understanding of baptism holds together God's gracious action in Christ and man's response of faith, his view "cannot truly be characterised as other than sacramental."[150]

Flemington's influence is seen first in "Baptism in the Epistles of Paul." In his discussion of Rom 6:1–11, Beasley-Murray refers approvingly to Flemington's argument that faith in Jesus must be seen as the background of the entire passage,[151] as well as Flemington's view that in 1 Cor 6:11 Paul links baptism with justification and sanctification.[152] Flemington's influence is also apparent in *Baptism in the New Testament*, in which Beasley-Murray refers to Flemington's understanding of baptism as "a sacrament of the Gospel"[153] and "the *kerygma* in action."[154] He agrees with Flemington that the mention of baptism in Eph 5 indicates the significance of baptism,[155] and they share the opinion that 1 Pet 3:21 presents baptism as a prayer for a good conscience.[156] The number of times that Beasley-Murray cites Flemington approvingly in arguably his two most influential works on baptism indicates the significance of Flemington's influence.

146. Flemington, *New Testament Doctrine*, 49–50.
147. Flemington, *New Testament Doctrine*, 58.
148. Flemington, *New Testament Doctrine*, 59.
149. Flemington, *New Testament Doctrine*, 82.
150. Flemington, *New Testament Doctrine*, 84.
151. Flemington, *New Testament Doctrine*, 134.
152. Flemington, *New Testament Doctrine*, 142.
153. Beasley-Murray, *Baptism in the New Testament*, 99.
154. Beasley-Murray, *Baptism in the New Testament*, 121.
155. Beasley-Murray, *Baptism in the New Testament*, 199.
156. Beasley-Murray, *Baptism in the New Testament*, 261.

The number of times Beasley-Murray cites Rudolf Bultmann, a German Lutheran New Testament scholar, suggests that Bultmann was another major influence. In addition to engaging with Bultmann in "Baptism in the Epistles of Paul,"[157] Beasley-Murray interacts with Bultmann a great deal in *Baptism in the New Testament*. He agrees with Bultmann's assertion that Paul's teaching on baptism is more "decisive" than Luke's,[158] and with Bultmann's insight that in Acts 4 there is a hint of baptism in connection with salvation.[159] They both acknowledge that in the Cornelius story baptism and the Spirit were separated, but believe that situation to be exceptional,[160] and are in agreement that 1 Pet 3:21 teaches that baptism is a prayer.[161] Beasley-Murray also translated Bultmann's commentary on John into English.[162]

There are also, however, points of disagreement between the two. Beasley-Murray did not agree that early Christian baptism had essentially the same meaning as John's baptism[163] or that the phrase "with water" in John 3:5 was added by a redactor.[164] And while Bultmann held a sacramental view of baptism, he believed that the idea of sacramentalism rested on assumptions from primitive religion. This belief led him to what was to Beasley-Murray's mind a rather mechanical view in which the right words and right actions turn a natural event into a supernatural one. Beasley-Murray rejected this understanding of the sacraments.[165]

Another German New Testament scholar to receive much attention from Beasley-Murray was G. Bornkmann. Among the many references in *Baptism in the New Testament* is Beasley-Murray's mention of Bornkmann's claim that Acts indicates that God is not bound by the sacraments,[166] a theme which was significant in Beasley-Murray's view of baptism. He agrees with Bornkmann that in baptism a person participates in the death and resurrection of Jesus, though Beasley-Murray

---

157. Beasley-Murray, "Baptism in the Epistles of Paul," 132. He is referring to Bultmann, *Theology of the New Testament*, 333.
158. Beasley-Murray, *Baptism in the New Testament*, 95.
159. Beasley-Murray, *Baptism in the New Testament*, 98.
160. Beasley-Murray, *Baptism in the New Testament*, 108.
161. Beasley-Murray, *Baptism in the New Testament*, 264.
162. Bultmann, *Gospel of John*.
163. Beasley-Murray, *Baptism in the New Testament*, 99.
164. Beasley-Murray, *Baptism in the New Testament*, 228.
165. Beasley-Murray, *Baptism in the New Testament*, 264.
166. Beasley-Murray, *Baptism in the New Testament*, 120.

thinks that the relationship between baptism and death and resurrection involves more than this.[167] He also agrees with Bornkmann's interpretation of Col 2:11–12, which is that the circumcision of Christ refers to the death of Christ, and that in baptism a person is united to Christ in his death.[168]

Though most of Beasley-Murray's influences were biblical scholars, he did interact with some theologians as well. One of the theologians he cited most often was the Lutheran Oscar Cullmann. Cullmann also wrote a book titled *Baptism in the New Testament*, originally published in 1950 and written in large part as a response to Karl Barth's challenge to infant baptism.[169] Though Beasley-Murray disagreed with Cullmann concerning the proper subjects of baptism, there was significant agreement between the two concerning the meaning of baptism. For Cullmann, the most important thing about baptism by the Christ, as opposed to John's baptism, is the giving of the Holy Spirit.[170] He refers to baptism as "the sacrament of the transmission of the Holy Spirit,"[171] and argues that an individual's participation in the death and resurrection of Jesus results from baptism.[172]

Despite the points of agreement, many of Beasley-Murray's references to Cullmann in *Baptism in the New Testament* are for the purpose of refuting Cullmann's views. For example, he rejects Cullmann's claim that the relationship between baptism and death and resurrection results from Jesus' teaching about his own baptism,[173] and rejects Cullmann's claim that death and resurrection, understanding, and faith are all separate realities from baptism.[174] He disagrees with Cullmann's argument that the circumcision of Christ in Col 2 refers to baptism,[175] as well as Cullmann's view that allusions to baptism are all throughout John.[176]

Karl Barth was another theologian with whom Beasley-Murray interacted, and with whom, like Cullmann, he had points of agreement

---

167. Beasley-Murray, *Baptism in the New Testament*, 131.
168. Beasley-Murray, *Baptism in the New Testament*, 153, 155.
169. Cullmann, *Baptism in the New Testament*, 7.
170. Cullmann, *Baptism in the New Testament*, 10.
171. Cullmann, *Baptism in the New Testament*, 10.
172. Cullmann, *Baptism in the New Testament*, 14.
173. Beasley-Murray, *Baptism in the New Testament*, 128.
174. Beasley-Murray, *Baptism in the New Testament*, 145.
175. Beasley-Murray, *Baptism in the New Testament*, 153.
176. Beasley-Murray, *Baptism in the New Testament*, 207.

and points of disagreement. Barth believed that those who are united to Christ actually died with him on the cross and were actually raised with him from the grave.[177] However, he did not believe that such a union took place in baptism. He understood the New Testament to make a distinction between water-baptism and Spirit-baptism,[178] and saw water-baptism as a "representation" of a person's union with Christ.[179] While he was comfortable with the terms "sign" or "seal," he claimed that baptism is "primarily" a symbol[180] and claimed that the "essence of baptism" is to be a picture.[181] Though they had some differences, Beasley-Murray still shows points of agreement with Barth. For example, in *Baptism in the New Testament*, he agrees with Barth's contention that both grace and faith are essential parts of man's response to the gospel.[182]

While Barth is mentioned here primarily for the purposes of showing that Beasley-Murray did interact some with theologians, perhaps the most noteworthy aspect of Beasley-Murray's interaction with Barth is how little he refers to Barth. Despite the prominence of Barth, in *Baptism in the New Testament* Beasley-Murray mentions Barth only six times.

The final theologian to be discussed here is the Catholic theologian Joseph Crehan. Crehan is significant not for the frequency with which Beasley-Murray interacts with him, but for the way in which he influenced Beasley-Murray. In *Early Christian Baptism and the Creed*, Crehan argues that the confession of Jesus as Lord was an integral part of baptism in the New Testament. He begins with the second account of the baptism of Paul. Acts 22:16 indicates that in baptism Paul called upon the name of the Lord. Crehan contends, then, that from the beginning baptism was accompanied with a confession of Jesus as Lord.[183] For him, "baptism into the Name of Christ" means that the person baptized called upon the name of the Lord in baptism.[184] He also claims that the most likely reading of the eunuch's baptism includes him calling on the name of the

---

177. Barth, *Teaching of the Church*, 11.
178. Barth, *Teaching of the Church*, 12.
179. Barth, *Teaching of the Church*, 9.
180. Barth, *Teaching of the Church*, 13.
181. Barth, *Teaching of the Church*, 15.
182. Beasley-Murray, *Baptism in the New Testament*, 271.
183. Crehan, *Early Christian Baptism*, 7.
184. Crehan, *Early Christian Baptism*, 8.

Lord.[185] This close connection between confession and baptism is evident in Beasley-Murray, who refers to Crehan in support of it.

In "Baptism in the Epistles of Paul," Beasley-Murray begins with a discussion of Rom 10:9–10, which makes no mention of baptism. Since it does mention confession, however, Beasley-Murray sees in it a reference to baptism. He writes, "The significance of this saying, in which no mention of baptism occurs, lies in the virtually unanimous conviction of modern scholars that its summary of the Christian confession as "Jesus is Lord" is a citation of the primitive baptismal confession, made by a candidate about to be baptised."[186] The one source he cites is *Early Christian Baptism and the Creed* by Crehan. With that principle in place from early on in his works on baptism, Beasley-Murray was able to see references to baptism in passages which do not explicitly mention baptism.

CONCLUSION

When Beasley-Murray began publishing works on baptism, he was joining a movement that had been arguing for a sacramental view of baptism for approximately 30 years. In his works on baptism, Beasley-Murray appropriated a range of scholars in a variety of ways. Some influenced his methodology, while others influenced his interpretation of specific passages of Scripture and his theological conclusions. Nevertheless, though their ideas and arguments have been assimilated into his work, he makes his own argument for a sacramental understanding of baptism, and it is his argument that has been a key factor in shaping the recent debate. It is to that argument that we now turn our attention.

---

185. Crehan, *Early Christian Baptism*, 8.
186. Beasley-Murray, "Baptism in the Epistles of Paul," 128.

2
George Beasley-Murray's Baptismal Theology

THIS CHAPTER WILL PRESENT Beasley-Murray's contribution to the baptismal debate. The first section will draw from his various works to provide a comprehensive examination of his understanding of the meaning of baptism. This will be followed by a section that addresses ways in which some of the people who responded to Beasley-Murray's work misunderstood parts of his argument. Next, we will consider Beasley-Murray's theological relationships to the Baptist tradition and the paedobaptist tradition, respectively. We will conclude by showing that Beasley-Murray's argument was not accepted by all, but there was, rather, some resistance to it.

BEASLEY-MURRAY'S UNDERSTANDING OF THE MEANING OF BAPTISM

Union With Christ Attributed to Both Faith and Baptism in Scripture

The first key to unlocking Beasley-Murray's baptismal thought is to understand that in his view, faith and baptism should be held together. Beasley-Murray arrived at this conclusion primarily by examining the Scriptures. A number of passages attribute a person's position in Christ, and all the resulting benefits of that position, to faith. Other passages attribute a person's position in Christ, and the exact same benefits, to baptism. This fact led Beasley-Murray to conclude that there is a more intimate and necessary relationship between faith and baptism than is often thought, either by paedobaptists or Baptists. A brief examination of some of the relevant passages will demonstrate this point.[1]

Several passages claim that people are united to Christ through their faith in him. Eph 3:17 says, "so that Christ may dwell in your hearts through faith." Col 2:12b claims that Christians "were also raised with Christ] through faith in the powerful working of God." Other passages claim that people are united to Christ through baptism. Col 2:12a reads, "having been buried with [Christ] in baptism." While Gal 3:26 states, "for in Christ Jesus you are all sons of God, through faith," verse 27 continues, "For as many of you as were baptized into Christ Jesus have put on Christ."

The same is true of the benefits that result from being in Christ. For example, some passages associate forgiveness of sins with faith. Acts 15:9 says that "God cleansed their hearts through faith." 1 John 1:9 indicates that God will forgive sins if people confess, with no mention of baptism. Acts 2:38, however, associates forgiveness with baptism: "Repent and be baptized every one of you in the name of Jesus Christ for the forgiveness of your sins." Acts 22:16 reads, "Rise and be baptized and wash away your sins, calling on his name."

Similarly, some passages associate the inheritance of the kingdom of God with faith. John 3:15, which is in the context of Jesus teaching about entering the kingdom, says that whoever believes in the Son of Man will have eternal life. Mark 10:15 records Jesus' statement, "Truly, I say to you, whoever does not receive the kingdom of God like a child shall not enter it." Considering the absence of any mention of baptism, this reception most likely refers to faith. Other passages associate the inheritance of the kingdom of God with baptism. In John 3:5 Jesus states, "Truly, truly, I say to you, unless one is born of water and the Spirit, he cannot enter the kingdom of God."[2]

Some passages attribute justification to faith. Rom 3:28 says, "For we hold that one is justified by faith apart from works of the law." Other passages associate justification with baptism. 1 Cor 6:11 claims, "But you were washed, you were sanctified, you were justified in the name of the Lord Jesus Christ and by the Spirit of our God."

---

1. Beasley-Murray considers these passages in *Baptism Today*, 27–36.

2. Beasley-Murray acknowledged that some respected theologians deny that John 3:5 refers to water-baptism. He, however, was confident that the mention of water was a reference to water-baptism.

The same pattern can be seen concerning the reception of the Holy Spirit. Some passages associate the giving of the Holy Spirit with faith. Gal 3:2 asks rhetorically, "Did you receive the Spirit by works of the law or by hearing with faith?" Gal 3:4 provides the answer to that question: " . . . so that we might receive the promised Spirit through faith." Other passages associate the reception of the Holy Spirit with baptism. Acts 2:38 says, "Repent and be baptized every one of you in the name of Jesus Christ for the forgiveness of your sins, and you will receive the gift of the Holy Spirit."

In *Baptism Today and Tomorrow* Beasley-Murray provides some background concerning this insight. He was part of the Faith and Order Commission of the World Council of Churches that produced a work called *One Lord, One Baptism*.[3] He recounts that he was

> assigned the task . . . to investigate the relation of baptism to faith (a dangerous assignment to hand a Baptist!). Apart from the obvious necessity of evaluating afresh statements in which faith and baptism were directly related in the New Testament, it occurred to me that it might be profitable to tabulate the associations of baptism in the New Testament writings and those of faith, and see to what extent there was a correlation between the two.[4]

One Lord, One Baptism summarizes Beasley-Murray's findings, stating, "Baptism and faith are inseparably joined in the New Testament. The full range of salvation is on the one hand promised to faith *sine qua non*, and on the other hand is associated with baptism."[5]

Faith and Baptism Should Not Be Separated

Beasley-Murray is well aware that one set of passages attributes union with Christ to faith, and another set of passages attributes it to baptism. He recognizes the need, therefore, to offer a credible explanation of this fact. He puts his conclusion mildly by stating, "It would seem that baptism and faith turning to the Lord are the exterior and interior of one reality."[6]

3. Beasley-Murray, "Obituary."
4. Beasley-Murray, *Baptism Today*, 27.
5. World Council of Churches Commission on Faith and Order, *One Lord One Baptism*, 61.
6. Beasley-Murray, "Authority," 66.

His position is put more directly and more clearly in his claim that faith in Jesus as Lord and baptism in the name of the Lord are viewed as one in the New Testament.[7] In other words, to be baptized is to respond to the gospel in faith. To put it the other way around, the proper response to the gospel is baptism, which is the expression of faith in Christ. The two should not be separated.

A number of passages appear to directly support this view. Acts 2:38 clearly links faith and baptism. Gal 3:26–27 uses faith and baptism almost interchangeably. Col 2:12 also seems to use faith and baptism interchangeably. Beasley-Murray sees in these passages evidence that the expression of faith and the experience of baptism are one and the same.[8]

Once this principle is in place, the meaning of other passages can be seen more clearly. 1 Cor 6:11, for example, suggests that justification, consecration by the Spirit, and baptism all occur at the same time, forming a "coincidental action."[9] Beasley-Murray acknowledges that Paul may be using those terms loosely, but contends that even if such is the case, this verse still shows that baptism and faith are more closely related than is often thought.[10] In a similar way, he argues that John 3 presents the confession of faith, the gift of Christ, the work of the Spirit, and baptism as "one complex event."[11] He even sees the same idea at work in Paul's statement, "The life I now live in the flesh, I live by faith in the Son of God" (Gal 2:20). Beasley-Murray contends that rebirth which makes this life of faith possible began in baptism.[12] Once again, faith and baptism cannot be separated. It is in this light that Beasley-Murray suggests using the term "conversion—baptism."[13] He argues that in the New Testament, "the spiritual realities of conversion and baptism are merged together, for in that context they do fall together."[14] In a lecture delivered in 1970 he stated,

---

7. Beasley-Murray, *Baptism Today*, 54.
8. Beasley-Murray, "Faith," 41.
9. Beasley-Murray, *Baptism in the New Testament*, 164.
10. Beasley-Murray, *Baptism in the New Testament*, 164.
11. Beasley-Murray, "John 3:3–5," 169.
12. Beasley-Murray, *Baptism in the New Testament*, 141.
13. Beasley-Murray, "Holy Spirit," 39. Also Beasley-Murray, "The Holy Spirit, Baptism and the Body of Christ," 180.
14. Beasley-Murray, "Second Chapter of Colossians," 476.

The descriptions of baptism in the New Testament, and the indications of the apostolic teaching on its meaning, make it plain that the early church viewed baptism as the completion of conversion to God. The baptism of John the Baptist is described by Mark as a "repentance baptism" (Mark 1:4), and scholars are agreed that in this context repentance means "turning to God"; i.e. what we mean by conversion. This way of viewing baptism became normative in the Christian church, whatever else was attached to the significance of the rite.[15]

Since in the New Testament baptism and conversion were "inseparable," the blessings of salvation are associated with both baptism and conversion.[16]

Baptism as a Confession of Faith

The precise relationship of faith to baptism is expressed in a number of ways. First, the baptismal event is said to be a confession of faith. Beasley-Murray got this idea primarily from 1 Pet 3:21: "Baptism, which corresponds to this, now saves you, not as a removal of dirt from the body but as an appeal to God for a good conscience, through the resurrection of Jesus Christ" (ESV). For Beasley-Murray, the key to a correct interpretation of this verse is the word translated "appeal" by ESV, which can mean "promise" or "appeal." Beasley-Murray comments, "Here the essential feature of baptism is represented not as the washing of the body, but as a spiritual transaction in which the baptised one makes an appeal to God in faith and prayer (*or in which he makes a declaration of faith*) and experiences the power of the risen Lord to save" (italics mine).[17]

In another place, he makes a similar comment on the same passage. "The cleansing in baptism is gained not through the application of water to flesh, but through *the pledge of faith* and obedience therein given to God, upon which the resurrection of Jesus Christ becomes a saving power to the individual concerned" (italics mine).[18] It is for this reason that Beasley-Murray can refer to baptism as "repentance-baptism."[19] In baptism, a person turns from sin toward his new Lord, Jesus.

15. Beasley-Murray, "Worship and the Sacraments."
16. Beasley-Murray, "Worship and the Sacraments."
17. Beasley-Murray, "Authority," 65.
18. Beasley-Murray, *Baptism in the New Testament*, 262.
19. Beasley-Murray, "I Still Find Infant Baptism Difficult," 232.

He understands Acts 2:38 to also indicate that baptism is an expression of faith. For the Jews in Acts 2:38, baptism involved confessing Jesus as their Messiah and Lord. "Never was the significance of Christian baptism so plain as in the day it was first administered!"[20]

Although Rom 10:10–13 makes no mention of baptism, Beasley-Murray sees this same connection in those verses. They read, "For with the heart one believes and is justified, and with the mouth one confesses and is saved. For the Scripture says, 'Everyone who believes in him will not be put to shame.' For there is no distinction between Jew and Greek; for the same Lord is Lord of all, bestowing his riches on all who call on him. For 'everyone who calls on the name of the Lord will be saved.'" Beasley-Murray contends that this passage reflects the situation in baptism, in which the baptized confesses Jesus as Lord. He refers to this as "the climax of faith."[21]

Baptism as an Appeal

The second way in which Beasley-Murray understands the relationship between faith and baptism is to see baptism as faith making an appeal to God for forgiveness and acceptance. It is not only a confession of what one believes, but is also a prayer asking God to act. Beasley-Murray raises the question, if God gives life through the preached word, what does baptism have to do with new life? His answer is that in baptism a person appeals, or prays, to God for a clear conscience and forgiveness.[22]

This understanding is also rooted primarily in 1 Pet 3:21. Once again, his commentary on that verse is insightful. "Here the essential feature of baptism is represented not as the washing of the body, but as a spiritual transaction in which *the baptised one makes an appeal to God in faith* and prayer (or in which he makes a declaration of faith) and experiences the power of the risen Lord to save" (italics mine).[23] "The crucial feature in baptism," he states, "is not its being a washing in water, but its aspect as 'an appeal to God for a clear conscience' and its relating of the believer to

---

20. Beasley-Murray, "Holy Spirit," 31.
21. Beasley-Murray, "Faith," 140.
22. Beasley-Murray, *General Epistles*, 53–54.
23. Beasley-Murray, "Authority," 65.

the resurrection of Christ."[24] Baptism itself is the appeal for forgiveness.[25] A person hears the gospel preached, believes that God will forgive him, and goes to the waters of baptism to make that request.

Baptism as Reception of the Gospel

The third way Beasley-Murray describes the relationship of faith to baptism focuses on baptism as a reception of the gospel. In baptism, the baptized not only asks for forgiveness, but in faith receives that forgiveness. Admittedly, the gospel is heard in faith prior to baptism,[26] but it is in baptism that faith receives the gift of God promised in the gospel.[27] Exactly what that gift is will be discussed below. The primary point to be grasped here is that the faith necessary to receive the gift is expressed in baptism.

This is what Beasley-Murray has in mind when he claims that in the baptismal event the proclamation of the gospel and the hearing of faith meet.[28] Baptism is an expression of the gospel in that it pictures the death and resurrection of Christ, even to the one baptized. Baptism is also the way in which a person receives the gospel that is expressed. It is understandable, then, why Beasley-Murray agrees with C. H. Dodd that the call to be baptized is a necessary part of the preaching of the gospel.[29]

A similar point is made by portraying baptism as the meeting place of Christ and the baptized person. Commenting on Col 2:12, Beasley-Murray states, "This saying appears to mean that baptism is the context in which God makes effective the redemptive action of Christ in the life of the penitent one exercising faith in him."[30] He is even more explicit in his claim that baptism is the context in which the believer and Christ meet in the Holy Spirit.[31] Not only is baptism a confession of faith and an appeal of faith, it is also the place a person goes to receive Christ as savior and

---

24. Beasley-Murray, *General Epistles*, 49.
25. Beasley-Murray, "Faith in the New Testament," 141.
26. Beasley-Murray, *Baptism Today*, 41.
27. Beasley-Murray, *Baptism in the New Testament*, 304.
28. Beasley-Murray, *Baptism in the New Testament*, 304.
29. Beasley-Murray, *Preaching the Gospel*, 15.
30. Beasley-Murray, "Authority," 65.
31. Beasley-Murray, "John 3:3–5," 170.

Lord in faith. It is the "occasion and means" of receiving blessings from the Lord.[32]

United to Christ in Baptism

The essential content of what is promised in baptism is Christ himself. Writing about Gal 3:26–27, Beasley-Murray notes, "It is faith which receives *Christ* in baptism" (italics mine).[33] By responding in faith a person is united to Christ. One way Scripture speaks about this reality is to say that a person puts on Christ. Gal 3:27, for example, uses that language and connects the putting on of Christ to baptism. Beasley-Murray insists that the flow of thought in that passage demands the conclusion that the putting on of Christ takes place in baptism.[34]

More specifically, the person is united to Christ in his death and resurrection. According to Beasley-Murray, baptism has a threefold effect. First, it relates the baptized person to the death and burial of Christ. Second, it involves a corresponding death and resurrection in the life of the baptized person. Third, it involves dying to an old way of life and rising to a new way of life.[35] It is the first of these that is foundational. The baptized person does not merely die to sin, but in some mysterious sense, the person actually dies. Being united to Christ is more than benefitting from his death. It involves somehow dying with him on a cross approximately two thousand years ago and being buried with him in his tomb.

It also involves the same kind of union with Christ in his resurrection. Beasley-Murray sees the "relating of the believer to the resurrection of Christ" as a "crucial feature" of baptism.[36] As with the union in Christ's death and burial, the baptized person does not merely benefit from the resurrection, but is actually united to Christ in the resurrection, so that the person is raised together with Christ. Baptism is "a real going down to death with Christ, a real rising to new life in him."[37] What must be remembered is that the participation and the act which signifies that participation should not be separated. Baptism not only represents the

32. Beasley-Murray, *Baptism in the New Testament*, 102.
33. Beasley-Murray, "Authority," 64.
34. Beasley-Murray, *Baptism in the New Testament*, 148.
35. Beasley-Murray, *Baptism in the New Testament*, 304.
36. Beasley-Murray, *General Epistles*, 49.
37. Beasley-Murray, *Christ Is Alive*, 122.

union, but effects it. Beasley-Murray states, "We are involved in the death and resurrection of Christ through baptism."[38]

He also understands the second chapter of Colossians to teach that a person is united to Christ in baptism. In his view, that passage indicates that Christ has undergone a "circumcision" on the cross, and Christians share in that event.[39] When Paul moves to baptism, then, he shows how closely baptism is related to the Christian's union with Christ in his death and resurrection.[40] Beasley-Murray concludes, "The primary declaration of baptism therefore is, '*I was with him there, on the cross, and in his grave.*'"[41] Nothing more important can be said about baptism. The union which takes place in baptism is the single most important feature of the act. "The primary significance of baptism," writes Beasley-Murray, "is its relating the believer to the once for all reconciliation that took place on Golgotha."[42]

A natural corollary of that view is the belief that conversion takes place in baptism. Beasley-Murray is forthright about his position on this point. He directly denies that in the New Testament conversion took place before baptism.[43] Even more directly, he claims that in the New Testament "baptism was conversion."[44] To separate baptism and conversion, then, is to change the meaning of baptism from what it was in the New Testament. In "The Church of Scotland and Baptism," he responds to the claim that in baptism the person baptized (even an infant) is united to Christ and receives all the benefits that go with that union. He states that baptism can only be spoken of in those terms so long as conversion and baptism are held together.[45] Once they are separated, as in infant baptism—and as in most Baptist churches—baptism cannot be said to unite a person to Christ.[46]

---

38. Beasley-Murray, *Christ Is Alive*, 122.
39. Beasley-Murray, "Second Chapter of Colossians," 474.
40. Beasley-Murray, "Second Chapter of Colossians," 475.
41. Beasley-Murray, "Second Chapter of Colossians," 475.
42. Beasley-Murray, *Baptism in the New Testament*, 155.
43. Beasley-Murray, *Baptism in the New Testament*, 277.
44. Beasley-Murray, *Baptism Today*, 93.
45. Beasley-Murray, "Church of Scotland and Baptism," 9.
46. Beasley-Murray, "Church of Scotland and Baptism," 9.

Other Benefits Are Received in Baptism

If it is the case that a person is united to Christ in baptism, it logically follows that it is also in baptism that a person receives all that is his in Christ. Beasley-Murray makes this point when he claims that Col 2:12 does not allow Rom 6 to be interpreted as purely symbolic. Instead, Rom 6 must be understood to mean that in baptism God unites the person to Christ and freely gives that person all things.[47]

There are, according to that view, a number of benefits that are given and received in baptism. One is membership in the church, the body of Christ. Beasley-Murray contends that when a person is united to Christ, that person is inevitably joined to the body of Christ.[48] While nearly all, if not all, theologians agree that there is a necessary connection between Christ and his body, and that a person who is united to Christ is inevitably united to his body, the emphasis in Beasley-Murray's thought is that this all takes place in baptism. He also sees the same idea at work in Col 1:13, which makes reference to redemption and the forgiveness of sins. Since redemption and the forgiveness of sins take place in Christ, Beasley-Murray concludes the verse should be understood in a baptismal context.[49] In baptism, a person in faith receives Christ and all that he offers. According to him, Acts 2:38 makes this clear. In that passage, "Proclamation of the gospel, repentance of the hearers, baptism in faith, forgiveness, the gift of the Spirit, enrollment in the Church, are all joined so as to form one unbroken whole. Without doubt those who participated in the event of that momentous day would ever after look back on it as a unified experience of the grace of God."[50]

The Relationship of the Holy Spirit to Baptism

One gift to which Beasley-Murray gives much attention is the Holy Spirit. The relationship of the Holy Spirit to baptism must be clear if either is to be properly understood. In Beasley-Murray's view, it is baptism that is most frequently misunderstood, which produces deficiencies in the

---

47. Beasley-Murray, "Holy Spirit, Baptism, and the Body of Christ," 178.
48. Beasley-Murray, "Holy Spirit and the Church," 94.
49. Beasley-Murray, *Baptism in the New Testament*, 160.
50. Beasley-Murray, "Holy Spirit," 1–32.

church's understanding of the Holy Spirit.[51] Some biblical scholars and theologians claim that the gift of the Spirit is not clearly associated with baptism in the Bible. Leon Morris, for example, argues that John 3:5, which Beasley-Murray understood to make a clear connection between the Spirit and baptism, simply indicates that the new birth is an activity of the Spirit. He does not claim that baptism is in view.[52] John Owen acknowledged a connection, but understands water-baptism to be the sign and seal of Spirit-baptism.[53] Graham Cole states, "With regard to baptism, apart from clear references to baptism with or by the Spirit, as in the case of 1 Cor 12:3, and in Acts 2:38, there is little explicit linkage between baptism and the Spirit in the Scriptures."[54] He concludes, "there are good reasons for adopting a moderate skepticism toward overinflated claims concerning the specifics of the Holy Spirit's role in the administration of the dominical ordinances."[55]

For Beasley-Murray, the key to grasping the correct relationship of baptism to the Holy Spirit is to grasp the relationship between Christ and the Holy Spirit. For Beasley-Murray, it is impossible to have one without the other. From his perspective, then, we are united to Christ in baptism and therefore are also given the Holy Spirit in baptism.[56] It is unthinkable to be in Christ and not have the Holy Spirit. It is equally unthinkable to have the Holy Spirit and not be in Christ. The two go together. That is why Beasley-Murray claims that even if the Scriptures never explicitly linked baptism and the Spirit, they would still provide sufficient evidence that the Spirit is received in baptism.[57] More recently, Moule seems to have reached a similar conclusion by considering the association of various concepts in the New Testament. He points out that nearly every religion makes symbolic use of water. However, Christianity alone involves this "nexus of ideas and events: water-Spirit-death-life-sonship."[58]

Though Beasley-Murray would be convinced that the Spirit is received in baptism even if the Scriptures did not make that point explicitly,

---

51. Beasley-Murray, *Baptism Today*, 8.
52. Morris, *Spirit of the Living God*, 12.
53. Owen, *Holy Spirit*, 120.
54. Cole, *He Who Gives Life*, 223.
55. Cole, *He Who Gives Life*, 224.
56. Beasley-Murray, "Holy Spirit, Baptism, and the Body of Christ," 179.
57. Beasley-Murray, *Baptism Today*, 55.
58. Moule, *Holy Spirit*, 33.

he nevertheless believes that the Scriptures do in fact make it explicit. It is not solely a case of connecting theological dots. Three passages in particular make it clear that the Spirit is given in baptism. The first is Acts 2:38, which records Peter saying, "Repent and be baptized every one of you in the name of Jesus Christ for the forgiveness of your sins, and you will receive the gift of the Holy Spirit." Peter explicitly connects baptism, faith, and the Holy Spirit. 1 Cor 6:11 also links the Holy Spirit to baptism: "But you were washed, you were sanctified, you were justified in the name of the Lord Jesus Christ and by the Spirit of our God." Beasley-Murray understands the phrase "you were washed" as a reference to water-baptism. Sanctification and justification both happen in baptism. They are granted in the name of Jesus and by the Holy Spirit. The Holy Spirit must be given, then, in the act of baptism.[59] A third passage in which Beasley-Murray sees the connection between baptism and the Spirit is John 3:5, which says, "unless one is born of water and the Spirit, he cannot enter the kingdom of God." Beasley-Murray states, "It is difficult to avoid seeing in this expression a reference to baptism."[60] He explicitly rejects the idea that "water" refers to ordinary birth.[61] For Nicodemus, the experiences of baptism and the reception of the Spirit were separated by time. Since Pentecost, those two experiences have been brought together.[62]

Because of this view, Beasley-Murray refuses to separate water-baptism and baptism in the Holy Spirit. He claims that "baptism in its New Testament context is always a baptism of the Spirit."[63] Baptism is the individual counterpart to the pouring out of the Holy Spirit at Pentecost.[64]

> To imagine that one could be in Christ, in the Body, in the Kingdom, participating in the life of the new age and therefore be

---

59. Beasley-Murray, *Baptism in the New Testament*, 164.

60. Beasley-Murray, "Holy Spirit," 19.

61. Beasley-Murray, "Holy Spirit," 19.

62. Beasley-Murray, "Holy Spirit," 20. This view is also expressed in *John*, 48–49. He claims that the interpretation of "of water and Spirit" as referring to natural birth and spiritual birth, respectively, does not do justice to the expression. He points out that some scholars consider "water and" to be an interpolation from a copyist, or even from John himself, but states that such claims are unprovable. Beasley-Murray concludes that the reference is to baptism in water and baptism in the Spirit, which since Pentecost have been conjoined.

63. Beasley-Murray, "Holy Spirit, Baptism, and the Body of Christ," 180.

64. Beasley-Murray, *Baptism Today*, 56.

> a new creature, born anew and renewed by the Spirit, yet not possess the Spirit of Christ, the Spirit of the Body, the Spirit of the Kingdom and the life of the new age is to be guilty of serious misunderstanding of the Apostolic teaching. Where Christ is, there is his Spirit. A man is either in Christ or not in Christ.[65]

In Beasley-Murray's view, then, Baptists can be, and often are, guilty of missing this point. Instead of believing that the Spirit is received after baptism, however, they tend to believe the Spirit is received before baptism. They make an inappropriate distinction between water-baptism and Spirit-baptism, as though they are two independent realities.

He acknowledged that many people dislike the idea implied by the sacramental view, in their understanding at least, that the giving of the Spirit is postponed until water-baptism is administered. He responded by pointing out that in the New Testament, there was no such postponement, as baptism takes place immediately upon confession of faith.[66] One example is the baptism of the Philippian jailer. Beasley-Murray notes,

> An Apostle who has endured a flogging in the evening, and earthquake at midnight, rescues his captor from suicide, then baptises him at about 1 a.m. before he sits down to a square meal has a different idea of the relationship of baptism to the Christian life from the minister who says to a convert: "We are hoping to arrange a baptismal service in three months' time and we shall be pleased to include you." . . . To the Apostle becoming a Christian and getting baptised were inseparable experiences.[67]

Beasley-Murray did contend that some instruction should take place before baptism so that the person understands, at least to some extent, the significance of baptism.[68] However, a person should be baptized as soon as his response to the gospel is clear.[69]

---

65. Beasley-Murray, *Baptism in the New Testament*, 276.
66. Beasley-Murray, "Sacraments," 4.
67. Beasley-Murray, "Baptism and the Sacramental View," 9.
68. Beasley-Murray, "Child and the Church," 21.
69. Beasley-Murray, "Child and the Church," 23.

POSSIBLE MISUNDERSTANDINGS ACKNOWLEDGED AND ADDRESSED

The Spirit Is Active Before Baptism

Beasley-Murray acknowledged that there are some apparent difficulties with his position, but if they be properly understood, they are not difficulties at all. The first is that the work of the Spirit in the life of the baptized person does not appear in Scripture to be limited to baptism. Both Paul and Luke recognized the Spirit as being at work before, during, and after baptism. Beasley-Murray suggests, "We must beware of exaggerating distinctions in the various stages of what the New Testament writers probably saw as a unitary process."[70] He is not troubled, then, by the work of the Spirit in the life of a person before baptism. He concedes that the turn which takes place in baptism is enabled by the Spirit, but continues to maintain that baptism is also the time at which the Spirit is given.[71]

At one point, Beasley-Murray cites a claim by C. H. Dodd that would alleviate some of the tension. Dodd argued that the Spirit enables the turn which takes place in baptism, not through an "inner witness," but through the outward expression of the gospel in the corporate life of the church. This view allows for the work of the Spirit in the life of a person preceding baptism, without claiming that the Spirit is given to that individual before baptism. Beasley-Murray, however, disagrees with Dodd's view. Unfortunately, he does not offer much in response to Dodd on this particular point. Instead, he takes up a different point made by Dodd and addresses that one.[72] The exact relationship of the Spirit to the unbaptized person, therefore, is not fully explained. It is clear, however, that Beasley-Murray understands that in some sense the Spirit is at work before, in, and after baptism.

Christopher Ellis has argued along the same lines:

> God is not restricted by the sacraments as the only means whereby he may graciously work in the lives of men and women. Any theology that is developed concerning baptism as a means of grace must make room for this inconvenient, yet gloriously inspired, belief in the freedom of God.[73] The more we see bap-

---

70. Beasley-Murray, *Baptism in the New Testament*, 96.
71. Beasley-Murray, *Baptism in the New Testament*, 121.
72. Beasley-Murray, *Baptism in the New Testament*, 244.
73. Ellis, "Baptism and the Sacramental Freedom of God," 35.

tism as the focus of a redemptive process, the less important become the questions of where and how God is at work.[74]

Baptism Is Not Mechanical

A second potential misunderstanding is that this view of baptism may appear to be mechanical, as though the water itself inevitably guarantees the presence of the Spirit.[75] Beasley-Murray acknowledged that many Baptists have resisted a sacramental view of baptism for this exact reason, rightly wanting to emphasize the need for personal faith.[76] In response, Beasley-Murray claims that while a sacramental view could be interpreted as mechanical, that does not mean it should be interpreted in that way. In fact, the New Testament stresses throughout that it is the name of Christ, his resurrection, the Spirit, or the Word of God that makes the baptized person new, not the water itself.[77]

The necessity of faith, which rules out the possibility of an *ex opere operato* understanding of baptism,[78] is seen clearly in his discussion of Col 2. His understanding of that passage is governed by the phrase "through faith." It is not baptism *per se* that unites us to Christ and saves. It is God who saves. Baptism depicts the saving acts of God in Christ and objectifies the faith of the one trusting in Christ for salvation.[79] In fact, for Beasley-Murray, baptism is presented in the New Testament in a way that only makes sense if it involves the faith of the one baptized.[80]

In his view, 1 Pet 3:21 is further evidence that baptism should not be understood as mechanical. That verse attests in the plainest manner that the sacraments in the primitive Church were neither merely outward rites nor efficacious by their simple performance. On the contrary the

---

74. Ellis, "Baptism and the Sacramental Freedom of God," 38.

75. In fact, this was one of the criticisms of the sacramental resurgence, which will be discussed below.

76. Beasley-Murray, *Baptism Today*, 83.

77. Beasley-Murray, *Baptism in the New Testament*, 265. Beasley-Murray admits that Heb 10:22 is an exception to this rule.

78. Beasley-Murray identifies an *ex opere operato* interpretation of baptism with a "magical" understanding of the rite. "Any sacrament which confers grace *ex opere operato* (i.e., purely by virtue of its administration and apart from faith in the recipient) is magical." ("Child and the Church," 10).

79. Beasley-Murray, "Second Chapter of Colossians," 477.

80. Beasley-Murray, "Authority," 64.

external element of baptism is diminished in significance here. The sacrament of baptism is effective by virtue of its being the supreme moment when God, through Christ the Mediator, deals with a man who comes to Him on the basis of the redemptive acts of Christ the Mediator.[81] Beasley-Murray's position then, is that "neither the action nor the water is primarily what matters, it is rather the unity by faith with the Christ who died and rose again."[82]

God Is Not Bound by the Sacraments

A third potential difficulty with the position that the Spirit is given in baptism is the fact that a number of passages in the New Testament record the Spirit being given apart from baptism.[83] Cornelius and his friends, for example, received the Holy Spirit before baptism in Acts 10. The Samaritans in Acts 8 appear to receive the Spirit after baptism, though it is possible they had already received the Spirit and simply lacked the common manifestation of the Spirit until that time.[84] The disciples in the beginning of Acts also received the Spirit without baptism. According to Beasley-Murray this was because of their unique experience in history. They were already disciples of the Lord, witnesses of his resurrection, and ambassadors in the world. Everything that baptism signified had already been realized in them.[85] These facts demonstrate that God can give, and in fact has given, the Spirit apart from baptism. He is free to bestow His Spirit with or without baptism.[86] He is not bound to the sacraments,[87] nor is he bound by the formulations of doctrines, helpful as those doctrines may be.[88]

The pattern that Beasley-Murray argues for, then, is admittedly not the only pattern in the New Testament.[89] Still, the giving and receiving of the Holy Spirit apart from baptism is not the pattern that should be

---

81. Beasley-Murray, *General Epistles*, 55.
82. Beasley-Murray, *Resurrection of Jesus Christ*, 25.
83. Beasley-Murray argues that the differences in the pattern are due to the differences between the situation ("Holy Spirit," 30)
84. Beasley-Murray, *Baptism Today*, 58.
85. Beasley-Murray, *Baptism in the New Testament*, 107.
86. Beasley-Murray, *Baptism in the New Testament*, 120.
87. Beasley-Murray, "Authority," 69; Beasley-Murray, "Holy Spirit," 30.
88. Beasley-Murray, *Baptism in the New Testament*, 301.
89. Beasley-Murray, *Baptism Today*, 57.

followed.[90] The accounts of water-baptism and Spirit-baptism being separated are exceptional, and should not be viewed as normative either in the New Testament period or today.[91] John Polhill agrees, and calls the giving of the Spirit apart from baptism "most unusual," but points out that it is consistent with the fact that "a group demonstration of the Spirit invariably accompanies a new breakthrough in missions in Acts."[92] Fitzmeyer addresses this "unusual" sequence in his commentary on Acts 10, which records the household of Cornelius receiving the Spirit apart from baptism. Fitzmeyer explains, "One should not ask how they might have received the Spirit without having been baptised; that would be to miss the point of the Lucan story. Gentiles are baptised, because that is part of the process by which one becomes a Christian. Luke is interested in the complex of faith, baptism, and reception of the Spirit."[93]

An Account of New Testament Baptism

If the first key to unlocking Beasley-Murray's baptismal thought is a proper understanding of faith-baptism, the second, and equally important, key is the recognition that Beasley-Murray's intention was to describe the meaning of baptism as it was understood and practiced in the New Testament. His goal was not to explain the meaning of baptism as it was practiced in his own day, which was, in his view, significantly different from the way it was practiced in the early church.

In an article published in the *Baptist Times*, Beasley-Murray wrote,

> But if the question was put, "Do you believe that baptism is a means of grace?" I would answer: "Yes, and more than is generally meant by that expression." In the Church of the Apostles (*please note the limitation*) the whole height and depth of grace is bound up with the experience of baptism. For *to the New Testament writers* baptism was nothing less than the climax of God's dealings with the penitent seeker and of the convert's return to God (italics mine).[94]

---

90. Beasley-Murray, *Baptism in the New Testament*, 301.
91. Beasley-Murray, *Baptism in the New Testament*, 108.
92. Polhill, *Acts*, 264.
93. Fitzmeyer, *Acts of the Apostle*, 467.
94. Beasley-Murray, "Spirit Is There," 8.

He emphasized the same limitation when discussing Acts 2:38. He claims, "For Peter was an Apostle of Christ, not a modern preacher anxious to put baptism in its place, as it were."[95]

Some of the critics of the sacramental resurgence failed to make this distinction, and rejected his claims because they seemed inconsistent with modern day experience. Beasley-Murray pointed out the misunderstanding and reminded the critics that his concern was to put forth his understanding of baptism in the New Testament:

> The teaching of these scriptures seems to me to be unambiguous. It militates unreservedly against the reduced baptism championed of late by so many correspondents in this paper. I would ask, however, for it to be carefully observed that this teaching relates to baptism in the apostolic Church, not to baptism in the average modern Baptist church. Where baptism is sundered from conversion on the one hand, and from entry into the church on the other, this language cannot be applied to it; such a baptism is a reduced baptism. The objectors to the views that some of us have sought to expound have transferred the theology applying to apostolic baptism to that which they have known and still foster in their churches and hence have charged us with rabid sacramentarianism. This is an unfortunate misunderstanding. My concern, along with my colleagues, is to put before Baptists the picture of ideal baptism, as it is portrayed in the apostolic writers, in the hope that we may strive to recover it or get somewhere near it. To insist on keeping our impoverished version of baptism would be a tragedy among a people who pride themselves on being a people of the New Testament.[96]

In a separate letter published in the *Baptist Times* Beasley-Murray again pointed out the distinction between baptism as it was practiced and understood in his day and baptism as it was practiced and understood in the New Testament. He responded to a person who asked whether his own baptism had made him a Christian. Beasley-Murray answered, "The correspondent, therefore, who asked 'Was I baptised to become a Christian?' has a clear answer: 'No, you were not; but if you had had anything to do with Paul you would have been.'"[97] Anthony Cross has summed up the distinction well. He writes, "The contributors and defenders of *Christian*

---

95. Beasley-Murray, "Spirit Is There," 8.
96. Beasley-Murray, "Spirit Is There," 8.
97. Beasley-Murray, "Baptism and the Sacramental View," 9.

Baptism were deliberating on the theology of New Testament baptism, where baptism was part of conversion, and not on the contemporary situation as it prevailed among twentieth-century Baptists where baptism had been separated from conversion."[98]

This distinction was important when some people understood him to imply that those who separated baptism from conversion, such as paedobaptists and many modern day Baptists, could not be saved. Beasley-Murray responded by asking,

> Need I point out that an exposition of what God has willed baptism to be says not a word as to what God does when baptism is misapplied or absent? That the Churches have lost immeasurably and suffered corruption through the loss of believer's baptism cannot be denied. . . . Yet the Spirit is undeniably there, in those Churches, as well as in a Church that practices believer's baptism, and we rejoice in their true riches.[99]

This position is consistent with his claim that God is not bound by the sacraments. Conversion-baptism is the biblical norm. Yet God is free to graciously save even when conversion-baptism is not practiced.

BEASLEY-MURRAY AND THE BAPTIST TRADITION

Beasley-Murray's understanding of baptism brought him into conflict with his own Baptist tradition. The primary point at which Beasley-Murray disagrees with the majority of the Baptist tradition is that he believes baptism is more than a mere symbol. In fact, some of his critics accused him of teaching something that was contrary to historic Baptist beliefs.[100] The accusation, however, was not entirely true. As noted earlier, there was a strand of sacramental thought running throughout the Baptist tradition. Nevertheless, from the seventeenth century on, the dominant Baptist view had been that baptism is only symbolic. John

---

98. Cross, *Baptism and the Baptists*, 234.
99. Beasley-Murray, "Baptism and the Sacramental View," 9.
100. John, "Christian Baptism," 6; Baker, "Baptist Sacramentalism."

Smyth,[101] John Bunyan,[102] Thomas Patient,[103] Abraham Booth,[104] John Gill,[105] Joseph Kinghorn,[106] Will Gadsby,[107] Charles Spurgeon,[108] *The London Confession*,[109] *The Faith and Practice of Thirty Congregations*,[110] *The Somerset Confession*,[111] and *The Orthodox Creed*[112] all favor a symbolic view of baptism. I. G. Matthews has summed up the traditional Baptist view by stating, "Baptism is considered only an outward sign of an inner experience, a symbol in which the individual pledges himself to a new life. All agree that it should be administered only to those who have made a personal confession of faith in the Lord Jesus."[113]

According to Beasley-Murray, many Baptists hold to a purely symbolic view of baptism because of a materialistic view of man which claims that a physical person cannot carry out any action with spiritual consequences.[114] He points out that Christ's work on the cross is evidence that acts in the physical body can in fact have spiritual consequences.[115] Nevertheless, Baptists have tended to argue that baptism is a mere symbol. One concern that Beasley-Murray and others have with that view is that it may lead to baptism being thought of as meaningless. Beasley-Murray claimed that if baptism is merely symbolic, the result is "a rite with virtually no content—and what is that but ritualism?"[116] He

---

101. Smyth, *Short Confession of Faith*, 101.

102. Bunyan, "Peaceable Principles and True"; Bunyan, "Confession of My Faith"; Bunyan, "Differences in Judgment"; Calhoun, *Grace Abounding*, 184; Harrison, *John Bunyan*, 55.

103. White, "Open and Closed Membership," 330–34.

104. Booth, *Apology for the Baptists*, 18, 45, 47.

105. Gill, *Body of Practical Divinity*, 339, 626–27.

106. Kinghorn, *Baptism*.

107. Gadsby, "Gadsby's Catechism."

108. Spurgeon, "Baptism—A Burial," 618; Spurgeon, *Spurgeon on Baptism*, 14; Spurgeon, "Baptismal Regeneration," 324; Spurgeon, "Baptism Essential to Obedience," 606–7; Briggs, *English Baptists*, 48.

109. *London Confession*, 46.

110. Lumpkin, *Baptist Confessions of Faith*, 182.

111. Lumpkin, *Baptist Confessions of Faith*, 209.

112. George and George, *Baptist Confessions*, 113.

113. Matthews, "Point of View of the Baptists," 221.

114. Beasley-Murray, "Holy Spirit, Baptism, and the Body of Christ," 180.

115. Beasley-Murray, "Holy Spirit, Baptism, and the Body of Christ," 180.

116. Beasley-Murray, *Baptism Today*, 85.

also agreed with C. T. Craig's claim that if baptism is a mere symbol, it is a "superfluous addition which supplies nothing important."[117] Others expressed the same concern about the symbolic view. As early as 1812, Abraham Booth believed that some Baptists considered baptism "a nonessential, an external rite, an indifferent thing, a shadow, a mere outward form, comparing it with the antiquated rite of circumcision."[118] Joseph Kinghorn also expressed concern that baptism had become meaningless for many Baptists.[119]

This view continued to be expressed in the twentieth century. In a letter to the *Baptist Times*, W. M. Delf wrote, "In baptism we confess and express our faith . . . this is therefore greatly more than a dramatic representation. Where the latter is thought to be the full meaning, it would explain why so many Baptists regard the ordinance as optional."[120] S. W. Ford agreed, arguing that by separating baptism from conversion, non-sacramentalists render baptism meaningless.[121]

Not everyone agreed that a symbolic view necessarily renders baptism meaningless. In fact J. D Hughey Jr. stated that he was not aware of the phrase "mere symbol" being used in any confession or serious theological work. He suggested abandoning the term as a term of reproach.[122] Karl Barth, who held a non-sacramental view of baptism, explained why the symbol of baptism is still meaningful.

> Baptism is no dead or dumb representation, but a living and expressive one. Its potency lies in the fact that it comprehends the whole movement of sacred history and that it is therefore *res potentissima et efficacissima*. All that it intends and actually effects is the result of this potency. It exercises its power as it shows to a man that objective reality to which he himself belongs (and of which it is a sign) in such a way that he can only forget or miss it *per nefas*; in such a way, at all events, that he becomes by its marks himself a marked man, by its portraiture one who is himself portrayed.[123]

---

117. Beasley-Murray, *Baptism Today*, 24.
118. Booth, *Apology for the Baptists*, 174.
119. Kinghorn, *Baptism*, 9.
120. Delf, "Christian Baptism," 6.
121. Ford, "Christian Baptism," 6.
122. Hughey, "New Trend in Baptism," 7.
123. Barth, *Teaching of the Church*, 16.

For Beasley-Murray, however, if baptism is a mere symbol, then it is meaningless. With that said, Beasley-Murray does not deny that baptism is to some extent symbolic. For example, it symbolizes the washing of sins and the putting off of the old self and the putting on of Christ.[124] He refers to baptism as a "representing" of the baptized person's union with Christ in his burial.[125] Baptism also "witnesses" certain eschatological realities, such as the resurrection of the dead and victory over evil.[126] Anthony Cross claims that this point was essential to Beasley-Murray's view:

> It is important to recognise that Beasley-Murray nowhere dismisses or diminishes the importance of the symbolic nature of baptism. What he wants to do is avoid, on the one hand, the merely symbolic interpretation so characteristic of Baptists, especially since the mid-nineteenth century, and, on the other hand, a magical understanding of the rite.[127]

A. C. Underwood made the same point. He argued that sacramental Baptists stand for a via media, rejecting both an *ex opere operato* understanding and a *nuda signa* understanding of baptism. Instead, they consider it to be a means of grace for those who accept it in faith.[128] Alec Gilmore, editor of *Christian Baptism*, concurred, stating clearly in the *Baptist Times* that *Christian Baptism* rejects an *ex opere operato* understanding of baptism, but does consider baptism to be more than a symbol.[129]

In Beasley-Murray's view, the fundamental mistake many Baptists have made regarding baptism is that they have given more weight to certain traditional Baptist theological convictions than to the biblical text itself. For Beasley-Murray, Scripture should always be the final authority, and any doctrine or tradition must be tested against it. He points out that this approach to Scripture and tradition is part of the Baptist tradition. Yet many Baptists, at least in Beasley-Murray's opinion, have ignored that part of the tradition and have failed to listen to Scripture above what other Baptists have said. They have looked at Scripture "through spectacles manufactured by trusted Baptist opticians."[130] This mistake has

---

124. Beasley-Murray, *Baptism Today*, 24.
125. Beasley-Murray, *Baptism in the New Testament*, 133.
126. Beasley-Murray, *Baptism in the New Testament*, 162.
127. Cross, "Faith-Baptism," 10.
128. Underwood, "Baptist," 225.
129. Gilmore, *Christian Baptism*, 6.
130. Beasley-Murray, *Baptism Today*, 90.

led to wrongly accepting the Baptist tradition concerning the meaning of baptism. Ironically, then, when Beasley-Murray disagrees with most Baptists, he sees himself as being faithful to the Baptist tradition as it relates to authority and the means of developing doctrine, though that very faithfulness puts him at odds with the Baptist tradition as it relates to the content of a particular doctrine.

In this way, Baptist principles require Baptists to test their own tradition against Scripture. If Baptists are proved wrong in some area on biblical grounds, Baptist principles would require Baptists to change. "The day when Baptists deliberately choose to follow the tradition of their Fathers in preference to the testimony of the Word of God will be a day when everything for which they have ever stood will be repudiated."[131] Beasley-Murray goes against his tradition, then, not because he does not value tradition, but because he feels compelled to do so by the weight of the evidence in Scripture.[132]

One difficulty with Beasley-Murray's claim is that it does not account for the symbolic view of some early Baptists.[133] They were in fact willing to contradict their own tradition in favor of being faithful to Scripture, which is exactly what Beasley-Murray attempts to do and encourages others to do. Without denying the influence of one's own tradition on a person, it is possible, despite Beasley-Murray's suggestions, that some contemporary Baptists continue to follow the pattern of their forefathers, not by blindly accepting the positions of those forefathers, but by continuing to conclude from their own reading of Scripture that a person is united to Christ apart from baptism.

BEASLEY-MURRAY AND THE PAEDOBAPTIST TRADITION

Beasley-Murray's understanding of the meaning of baptism is also at odds with the paedobaptist tradition. Whereas Baptists have typically separated water-baptism from Spirit-baptism by claiming that Spirit-baptism

131. Beasley-Murray, "I Still Find Infant Baptism Difficult," 226.
132. Beasley-Murray, *Baptism in the New Testament*, 263.
133. Examples of seventeenth-century Baptists who held a symbolic view include John Smyth and Thomas Patient, as well as the authors of *The London Confession* (1644), *The Faith and Practice of Thirty Congregations* (1651), *The Somerset Confession* (1656), and *The Orthodox Creed* (1679). The Baptist tradition will be discussed in more detail below.

precedes water-baptism, paedobaptists separate the two by claiming that Spirit-baptism comes after water-baptism. It is the same fundamental mistake, but with a different conclusion. For paedobaptists, this means that faith need not be present in baptism. Faith is necessary for a person to be united to Christ, but that takes place independently of the baptismal event. This is precisely the point at which Beasley-Murray disagrees.

Beasley-Murray's primary premise is that faith and baptism must not be separated. He knew he was going against not only Baptists, but also most of the church throughout history. He acknowledged that Origen claimed that the practice of infant baptism can be traced back to the apostles, and that the majority of the church has assumed he was right.[134] Beasley-Murray disagreed on biblical grounds. He pointed out that while most of the church assumes infant baptism has its origin in apostolic practice, most biblical scholars do not share that assumption. Since the early nineteenth century, it has been recognized that the New Testament does not explicitly support infant baptism.[135] For Beasley-Murray, the New Testament data is the most important factor.

Many of the passages which indicate that faith is necessary for baptism have been addressed above. However, at times Beasley-Murray addresses the issue directly. Commenting on 1 Pet 3:21, he claims the verse makes it clear that baptism is not efficacious by its mere performance, but requires a response from the baptized to the grace of God.[136] He makes the same point when commenting on Matt 28:18–20. In reference to that passage, he claims that even if it is granted that a person becomes a disciple by or through baptism, it is still true that baptism immediately involves discipleship, which must include a confession of faith in response to the gospel.[137] Because of these passages, and others that indicate the same relationship between faith and baptism, Beasley-Murray disagrees with the paedobaptist tradition concerning the candidates and meaning of baptism.

Those disagreements forced Beasley-Murray to consider how Baptists should relate to those in the paedobaptist tradition. Beasley-Murray acknowledged that Baptists commonly experience difficulties related to baptism in ecumenical conversations. For him, addressing these issues

---

134. Beasley-Murray, *Baptism in the New Testament*, 306.
135. Beasley-Murray, *Baptism in the New Testament*, 307.
136. Beasley-Murray, *General Epistles*, 55.
137. Beasley-Murray, "Authority," 63.

and making progress in them is important. Addressing theological differences is not always an easy process. The days of the direct, polemical arguments among the Reformers are long gone. More recent ecumenical theologians, such as Beasley-Murray, have been more concerned about "the pain of inflicting wounds on Christian colleagues," even more than receiving wounds from others.[138] Nevertheless, if progress is to be made, people on both sides must be honest, and must be willing to listen to each other.

On the part of Baptists, they must be willing to lay aside their "confessional pride" and be willing to listen to and learn from others who have valid insights into the meaning of baptism. On the part of paedobaptists, they must be willing to listen to and learn from Baptists.[139] There are three specific issues that must be addressed. First, should infant baptism be considered valid baptism? Second, should people who were baptized as infants and who have since confessed faith in Jesus be allowed to join a Baptist church? Third, if such people are allowed to join a Baptist church, should they be encouraged to submit to believer baptism?

On the issue of the validity of infant baptism, Beasley-Murray changed his position over time. Early in his career, he denied that infant baptism is valid baptism. In *Baptism in the New Testament* he was clear in affirming that infant baptism is not valid baptism, and that at the time few English Baptists thought it was.[140] He took the same position in his essay, "Baptists and the Baptism of Other Churches." While he claimed that in general Baptists do not call into question the standing of fellow Christians who have not been baptized as believers,[141] he was led to "a highly unpopular conclusion: *Infant baptism is not the baptism of which the New Testament documents speak.*"[142] Infant baptism is, rather, a new sacrament which has been invented.[143] Consequently, we do not have one baptism in the church, but two, one for infants and the other for believers.[144] In support of that view, he quotes the French Reformed scholar, F. J. Leenhardt, a paedobaptist who said of infant baptism, "We are in

---

138. Beasley-Murray, *Baptism in the New Testament*, 387.
139. Beasley-Murray, *Baptism Today*, 112.
140. Beasley-Murray, *Baptism in the New Testament*, 92.
141. Beasley-Murray, "Baptists and the Baptism," 261.
142. Beasley-Murray, "Baptists and the Baptism," 267.
143. Beasley-Murray, "Baptists and the Baptism," 267.
144. Beasley-Murray, "Baptists and the Baptism," 268.

the presence of a new sacrament. . . . Truly a new sacrament has been invented!"[145] He also quotes the Anglican N. P. Williams, who said of the confession "We acknowledge one baptism unto the remission of sins,"

> When we repeat this clause in the Creed as part of the Eucharistic Liturgy, what we affirm is our belief in baptism as anciently administered to adults, for the washing away of actual sins, and as still administered, habitually in the mission field to converts from heathenism, and rarely in Christian countries.[146]

Consequently, he refused to apply it to infant baptism.[147] Beasley-Murray's conclusion in that essay is that infant baptism and believer baptism are different rites with different meanings.[148]

In 1967 he expressed his wish that the practice of infant baptism be abolished. He suggested that in the meantime Baptists should consider infant baptism another baptism.[149] In 1980 he once again claimed that infant baptism is not a valid baptism. "If infant baptism cannot comprehend the significance of baptism as expounded in Gal 3:25, Col 2:12, 1 Pet 3:21, it may be held to be a *different* baptism."[150]

Not everyone agreed with Beasley-Murray. Oscar Cullmann argued that the claim that infant baptism and adult baptism are two different baptisms results from a wrong understanding of the meaning of baptism.[151] Beasley-Murray's fellow British Baptist Neville Clark opposed (re)baptism on the grounds that an incomplete or defective baptism is not a "no baptism."[152] *Baptism, Eucharist and Ministry* claimed that infant baptism and believer baptism are two forms of the same baptism,[153] stating, "Churches are increasingly recognizing one another's baptism as the one baptism into Christ."[154]

By the end of his career, Beasley-Murray changed his position and argued that infant baptism is valid baptism. His new position was that

---

145. Beasley-Murray, "Baptists and the Baptism," 268.
146. Williams, *Ideas of the Fall*, 554.
147. Williams, *Ideas of the Fall*, 554.
148. Beasley-Murray, "Baptists and the Baptism," 270.
149. Beasley-Murray, "I Still Find Infant Baptism Difficult" 236.
150. Beasley-Murray, "Authority," 70.
151. Cullmann, *Baptism*, 29.
152. Clark, "Theology of Baptism," 325.
153. World Council of Churches, *Baptism, Eucharist and Ministry*, 4–5.
154. World Council of Churches, *Baptism, Eucharist and Ministry*, 6.

infant baptism can be, and often is, understand as part of an initiation rite which includes catechesis and conversion. Consequently, he writes,

> I make the plea that churches which practice believer's baptism should consider acknowledging the legitimacy of infant baptism, and allow members of paedobaptist churches the right to interpret it according to their consciences. This will carry with it the practical consequence of believer-baptist churches refraining from baptising on confession of faith those who have been baptised in infancy.[155]

The second ecumenical issue to be addressed is whether believing paedobaptists should be allowed into membership in Baptist churches. Beasley-Murray argues that they should be allowed to join, a position known as the open-membership position. Beasley-Murray's reasoning is that while baptism is the normal means of entering the church, "God is not bound to the sacraments in the imparting of his grace."[156] God accepts those who profess faith in Christ, even apart from baptism, and therefore the church should too. This is not meant to imply that baptism is without consequence, but is meant to recognize the reality that there are Christians who have not been properly baptized.[157] It is an acknowledgement that the true church is larger than the Baptist tradition.[158] It should not, however, be taken as a statement about the theology of baptism, but should be seen, rather, as an act of charity, a "compromise in a complex ecclesiastical situation."[159] Some paedobaptists felt that what Beasley-Murray saw as an act of charity was actually patronizing and wished he would welcome others more gladly.[160]

One important qualification of Beasley-Murray's open-membership position is that it should only be applied in the case of infant baptism, not when there has been no sort of baptism at all.[161] Alec Gilmore agreed, arguing that churches should practice open-membership "in the sense that they are open to all who have been baptised and have come to faith in the Christian Church, and not open to all believers regard-

---

155. Beasley-Murray, "Problem of Infant Baptism," 13–14.
156. Beasley-Murray, "Authority," 69.
157. Beasley-Murray, "Authority," 69.
158. Beasley-Murray, *Baptism Today*, 88.
159. Beasley-Murray, *Baptism in the New Testament*, 392.
160. "Open Membership Churches," 6.
161. Beasley-Murray, *Baptism Today*, 88.

less of baptism."[162] Robert Walton held the same position. In his view, an unqualified open-membership despises baptism and is the result of viewing baptism as a "mere symbol."[163] If baptism is indeed a sacrament, then Baptist churches sin seriously by not requiring it and actually stop up a channel of divine blessing. Christians have no right to "play fast and loose" with the sacraments.[164] However, Walton goes on to argue that if a person has been baptized as an infant and has since professed faith in Christ, that person should be admitted into membership. He claims, "Thus, because Christendom is divided, we could accept as members those, who, baptised as infants, have, in Confirmation, expressed in another though less scriptural form, the essential requirement of personal acceptance and personal faith in Christ and His benefits which is sacramentally expressed in Believers' Baptism."[165]

Historically, not all Baptists have been satisfied with a qualified open-membership approach. Abraham Booth, for example, considered qualified open-membership as an implicit affirmation of the validity of infant baptism.[166] For the closed membership group, the primary concern was obedience to Christ. As they saw it, baptism as a believer by immersion was a matter of obeying what Jesus had commanded. Their conclusion was that allowing people who had not been baptized as believers to join a church amounted to condoning sin. The result of such tolerance would be to have a church in which people were free to consciously disobey the Lord. From that perspective, it was Jesus who had set the terms, and no individual or church was free to disregard the teaching of Jesus.

This position was articulated clearly by the Particular Baptist pastor Thomas Patient. He wrote to a church who had joined with another church that practiced paedobaptism, claiming, "If you admit one that walks in disobedience to the ordinance of baptism whether through ignorance or error, you may admit all manner of disobedience into your society upon the same ground, which is a total destroying the end of church fellowship, which is to bring up every member to a visible subjection to all the laws of Christ their King, or else cast them out of that

---

162. Gilmore, *Baptism and Christian Unity*, 78.
163. Walton, *Gathered Community*, 165.
164. Walton, *Gathered Community*, 166.
165. Walton, *Gathered Community*, 166–67.
166. Booth, *Apology for the Baptists*, 85.

society as old leaven."[167] In his book, *God's Oracle and Christ's Command*, John Griffiths states, "where there is not a uniting in the rudiments of religion there can be no safe communion."[168] He went on to emphasize, though, that the fundamental issue was obedience to Christ: "You possibly may say, it's our want of love to you which hinders our communion with you, but let not such thoughts possess you, for it's our love to the truth of Christ, and the order he hath prescribed that will not permit us, as the case stands with you."[169]

The third ecumenical issue is (re)baptism, which has to do with whether those baptized as infants should be baptized after confessing faith in Jesus. Beasley-Murray's position on this issue changed during the course of his career. In 1963 he claimed that Baptists should not require (re)baptism, but should provide it when requested.[170] In 1966 he suggested that (re)baptism should not be administered. The reason is that baptism should mark the beginning of the Christian life, and once that life has begun, the time for baptism has passed.[171] In 1967 he claimed that those baptized as infants should submit to (re)baptism as believers.[172] In 1980 he returned to the view that people should not be (re)baptized, since nowhere in the New Testament were saints baptized, only converts.[173] Clearly, over the course of his career, Beasley-Murray struggled with the best way forward.

INITIAL RESISTANCE TO THE SACRAMENTAL RESURGENCE

The sacramental view of baptism for which Beasley-Murray argued gained some traction, as seen in the direct evaluations of his work and in the arguments of the scholars examined in this book. The sacramental view was not universally accepted, however. Fowler has summarized five lines of criticism that the authors of *Christian Baptism* faced.[174] First, the

---

167. As cited by White, "Open and Closed Membership," 331.
168. As cited by White, "Frontiers of Fellowship," 254.
169. White, "Frontiers of Fellowship," 254.
170. Beasley-Murray, *Baptism in the New Testament*, 392.
171. Beasley-Murray, *Baptism Today*, 168.
172. Beasley-Murray, "I Still Find Infant Baptism Difficult," 236.
173. Beasley-Murray, "Authority," 70.
174. Fowler, *More Than a Symbol*.

critics argued that the sacramental view denies the "faith alone" character of salvation.[175] Second, they argued that the book teaches baptismal regeneration.[176] Third, they argued that the authors misrepresented key scriptural text.[177] Fourth, they argued that the sacramental view excludes the unbaptized from salvation and the church. Fifth, they argued that the sacramental view is contrary to historic Baptist theology.

One of the main forums for public debate concerning baptism was the *Baptist Times*. A number of articles appeared attacking the sacramental view of baptism which was on the rise. For example, in response to the claim that baptism in the New Testament is part of the conversion experience, Dr N. Beattie wrote, "Surely not! The inner work on the heart by the Holy Spirit causing the new birth is certainly an operation which does not depend for its completion on the subsequent physical act of immersing the body in water."[178] He also claimed that the sacramental view panders "to the popular superstition that something done to us, or for us, or by us, is essential or demanded, so that we might be saved."[179] Robert Clark, who also wrote a letter to the *Baptist Times*, agreed. He criticized *Christian Baptism* for teaching baptismal regeneration. He asked, "Aren't those who trust in the Lord Jesus and Saviour and who are born again of the Holy Spirit partakers of the divine nature, and in possession of the divine life, before they are baptised?"[180] In another letter he wrote, "Baptism is a real means of blessing to the child of God who comes to it in obedience to the risen Lord. The Holy Spirit is there, but not to effect or consummate regeneration, not to complete forgiveness; He is there to bless and empower the regenerated and forgiven believer."[181]

S. B. John wrote multiple letters to the *Baptist Times* on this topic. In one, he considers the views of *Christian Baptism* to be "strange." He writes, "I was not baptised that I might become a Christian, but because I was a Christian by my faith in Christ." To make baptism part

---

175. Hughey, "New Trend in Baptism," 7; Carter, Letter to *The Baptist Times*, 6; Jaeger, Letter to *The Baptist Times*, 6. John, "Christian Baptism," 6

176. Clark, Letter to *Baptist Times*, 6; John, Letter to *Baptist Times*, 6

177. Hughey, "New Trend in Baptism," 6.

178. Beattie, "Christian Baptism," 6

179. Beattie, "Christian Baptism," 6

180. Clark, "Christian Baptism," *Baptist Times*, Aug. 13, 1959, 6; See also Clark, "Christian Baptism," *Baptist Times*, Oct. 8, 1959, 6.

181. Clark, "Christian Baptism" 6.

of conversion is "to wound the Gospel at its very heart."[182] In another letter he claimed that *Christian Baptism* was contrary to historic Baptist beliefs. He also claimed that it taught an *ex opere operato* understanding of baptism. He refers to Spurgeon and suggests that Spurgeon would not be happy that the principal of the college he founded was teaching such things, which John considered to be "heresy."[183] S. F. Carter also wrote a letter in which he put forth Acts 16:30–32 as evidence that baptism is not required for forgiveness. He quotes Spurgeon, who stated that he was saved and forgiven before his baptism.[184]

Anthony Cross believes that much of the reaction against the resurgence was a result of anti-Catholic feelings.[185] Beasley-Murray was convinced, I think rightly, that it was due at least in part to misunderstanding. The critics thought that the leaders of the resurgence were describing current baptismal practice, when in fact they were describing the situation in the New Testament and were calling Baptists back to that biblical ideal. He took the lead in defending the resurgence by trying to clarify the misunderstanding.

Despite the resistance, the leaders of the sacramental resurgence were quite successful. Fowler points out that after the resurgence in the middle of the century, the literature assumes a sacramental understanding of baptism, rather than defending it.[186]

CONCLUSION

Beasley-Murray produced a significant amount of work on the meaning of baptism. He wrote books, essays, and articles in which he argued that in the New Testament baptism and faith are held together as part of a person's response to the gospel. Because baptism was a confession of faith, it was the time and place in which a person was united to Christ and received all the benefits that are included in that union. Though he was knowingly going against the majority of Baptists in history and in his own day, he was not alone. Others before him, and some around the same time, made the same argument. He was not the only sacramental

182. John, "Christian Baptism" 6.
183. John, "Christian Baptism," 6.
184. Carter, Letter to *The Baptist Times*, 6.
185. Cross, *Baptism and the Baptists*, 117.
186. Fowler, *More Than a Symbol*, 8.

voice in the debate, then. He did become, however, a leading voice. He made an argument that elicited a range of responses, both positive and negative. The remaining chapters will demonstrate that Beasley-Murray's work continued to play a role in shaping the baptismal debate among Baptists even after the initial wave of responses.

PART 2

George Beasley-Murray
and Southern Baptists

3

Southern Baptist Contextual Factors

THE PREVIOUS CHAPTER PRESENTED Beasley-Murray's argument for a sacramental understanding of baptism and briefly demonstrated that his work helped shaped the debate about the meaning of baptism during the time he was publishing. The next four chapters will argue that Beasley-Murray's work has also played a key role in influencing the baptismal debate among Southern Baptists since that time. The present chapter will examine some of the contextual factors related to the baptismal debate among Southern Baptists. The three subsequent chapters will analyze the role of Beasley-Murray's work in the work of three Southern Baptist scholars who have written about baptism.

THREE FACTORS

Certain trends throughout the history of the Southern Baptist Convention provide some context for the reception of Beasley-Murray's work by Southern Baptist scholars. This section will present three specific contextual factors that should be taken into account when considering the debate about the meaning of baptism among Southern Baptists. The three factors are the lingering effects of the Campbellite movement, the lack of sacramentalism in Southern Baptist history, and the Southern Baptist focus on the inerrancy debate around the time that Beasley-Murray published his two books on baptism.

While there may be other contextual factors that could be examined, I have chosen to limit the focus to these three for several reasons. First, I consider these three to be highly significant factors. Second, I have attempted to distinguish factors that provide broad context from factors that are particularly prominent in the work of an individual scholar. Third, examining three contextual factors is sufficient to accomplish the purposes of this chapter.

There are two purposes for devoting a chapter to Southern Baptist contextual factors. The first reason is to demonstrate that, though Beasley-Murray has significantly shaped the baptismal debate, there are other factors that have influenced the debate as well. The second reason is that, when taken together with the later chapter concerning BUGB contextual factors, it will demonstrate that Beasley-Murray has affected the debate in various contexts. Scholars operating within varying contexts that include different histories, movements, and trends, have taken his work seriously and have appropriated his work in a significant way.

THE CAMPBELLITE CONTROVERSY

The first factor to consider is the legacy of the Campbellite movement. According to James Tull, Alexander Campbell was "one of the most controversial figures in Baptist history"[1] and "one of the most influential religious leaders on the American frontier in the first half of the nineteenth century."[2] Tull writes, "Although he was within the Baptist fellowship for only a relatively brief period of time, his influence upon Baptist life and thought . . . is worthy of consideration."[3] One of the more controversial aspects of Campbell's teaching was his view on baptism. Specifically, he claimed that baptism was for the remission of sins. In his book, *Christian Baptism*, he states, "were it not for an imaginary incongruity between the means and the end, or the thing done and the alleged purpose or result, no one could, for a moment, doubt that the design of baptism was 'for the remission of sins.'"[4] He goes even further in his claim that the remission of sin is "the only purpose" for which baptism was ordained.[5] He writes,

1. Tull, *Shapers of Baptist Thought*, 103.
2. Tull, *Shapers of Baptist Thought*, 101.
3. Tull, *Shapers of Baptist Thought*, 101.
4. Campbell, *Christian Baptism*, 249.
5. Campbell, *Christian Baptism*, 250.

"We are not commanded to be baptized for faith, for repentance, for justification, for regeneration, for sanctification, for adoption, for the Holy Spirit, for eternal life."[6]

According to Tull, Campbell's views on baptism have been offensive to many people, "most of all, quite likely, to the Baptists."[7] It appeared to some as though Campbell was making baptism, together with faith and repentance, necessary for salvation.[8] Indeed, Andrew Broaddus labeled Campbell's view as "baptismal regeneration."[9] Tull claims that it is understandable that many would conclude that Campbell did in fact make baptism necessary for salvation.[10] He points to one of Campbell's favorite illustrations in which he drew an analogy between baptism and the naturalization of a foreigner. Tull summarizes the analogy: "Baptism, like naturalization, is an oath of allegiance by which an alien becomes a citizen. Although the formal oath does not effect a change in the disposition of the person, it does change his state."[11]

Whatever may be ambiguous about Campbell's view of baptism, Tull concludes, it is clear that he believed that baptism with the Spirit coincided with water-baptism.[12] W. E. Garrison, whom Tull considers to be "an authoritative interpreter of Campbell," denies that Campbell's position was that of baptismal regeneration, since Campbell did not believe that baptism in itself was redemptive.[13] Edwin Dargan believed Campbell himself was not always perfectly clear about his position, yet concludes that Campbellites "do teach a necessary connection between baptism and salvation."[14]

Campbell's views provoked strong reactions from many Baptists. In 1825 the Redstone Baptist Association excluded 13 churches for holding the views espoused by Campbell.[15] Shortly after, Tate's Creek Association in Kentucky excluded 16 churches for the same reason. In 1828 The Beaver Association in Pennsylvania removed the Mahoning Association

6. Campbell, *Christian Baptism*, 253.
7. Tull, *Shapers of Baptist Thought*, 112.
8. Tull, *Shapers of Baptist Thought*, 112.
9. Garrett, *Baptist Theology*, 256.
10. Tull, *Shapers of Baptist Thought*, 113.
11. Tull, *Shapers of Baptist Thought*, 113.
12. Tull, *Shapers of Baptist Thought*, 114.
13. Tull, *Shapers of Baptist Thought*, 113.
14. Dargan, *Ecclesiology*, 321.
15. Tull, *Shapers of Baptist Thought*, 118.

from fellowship for its Campbellite views. These are but a few early examples of a larger, longer reaction by Baptists to Campbellite views.[16] Baptist J. B. Jeter, who knew Campbell personally and published a refutation of Campbell's views—a refutation which many Baptists considered to be unanswerable—concluded that Campbell's arguments and writing likely indicated that Campbell had a "screw loose in his mental machinery," or put another way, "he labored under an idiosyncrasy which gradually developed into mental derangements."[17]

According to E. Robert-Thomson, though Campbellism existed beyond America, it was there that Campbellism had its "strongest foothold."[18] Garrett, who considers the Campbellite controversy to be "one of the major controversies in Baptist history,"[19] claims the Campbellites may have left a greater impact on Southern Baptists than their northern counterparts.[20] Robert-Thomson has asserted that many Southern Baptists remained opposed to union with those in the Campbellite tradition, due to continued suspicion that the latter promoted baptismal regeneration.[21]

Some interpret the Southern Baptist reaction to Campbellism as an over-reaction. Tull argues that the Baptist reaction to Campbell's view of baptism led to an impoverishing of their own understanding of the baptismal rite. He states, "Campbellism strengthened by reaction the Baptist tendency to interpret baptism as a 'mere symbol,' thus further robbing baptism of its biblical meaning as a profoundly significant symbol and experience."[22] Timothy George agrees. He believes Southern Baptists have stressed what baptism is not and have been left only with a "mere symbol."[23] He claims that "the majority of Southern Baptists would find the [word] 'sacramental' . . . unhelpful and even deplorable."[24] George argues that many Baptists have arrived at this view by reacting to Roman

---

16. Tull, *Shapers of Baptist Thought*, 118.
17. Tull, *Shapers of Baptist Thought*, 124.
18. Robert-Thomson, *Baptists and Disciples of Christ*, 161.
19. Garrett, *Baptist Theology*, 249.
20. Garrett, *Baptist Theology*, 257.
21. Robert-Thomson, *Baptists and Disciples of Christ*, 184.
22. Tull, *Shapers of Baptist Thought*, 127.
23. George, "Southern Baptists," 50.
24. George, "Sacramentality of the Church," 311.

Catholic and Campbellite sacramentalism, and he believes that those who have done so have "overdone it."[25]

Given the strong reaction by Southern Baptists against Campbell's views, it is significant that some people have considered Beasley-Murray's view of baptism to be similar to that of Alexander Campbell. Herbert Bird, though not a Baptist, made this connection. In his review of *Baptism in the New Testament*, he states, "In fact, it seems fair to say that the baptismal doctrine that surfaces here is more closely related to (though by no means identical with) the views of Alexander Campbell and the Church of Christ."[26] Dale Moody recalled that when Beasley-Murray lectured in Southern Baptist Theological Seminary in 1959, "I heard a devout Bible student call him a 'refined Campbellite,' a very evil estimate in these parts!"[27]

THE LACK OF SACRAMENTALISM IN SOUTHERN BAPTIST HISTORY

The anti-sacramentalism seen in the Southern Baptist reaction to the Campbellite movement is also evident in the work of Southern Baptist scholars throughout the Convention's history. From the beginning of the Southern Baptist Convention through 1962—the year that Beasley-Murray published *Baptism in the New Testament*—works on baptism by Southern Baptists overwhelming favored a symbolic view of baptism. Though there are occasional suggestions that God uses baptism in some way, the literature during that period emphasizes baptism as a symbol and an act of obedience.

Nineteenth century Southern Baptist theologian J. L. Dagg argued for a symbolic view of baptism and denied that there is any saving efficacy in the mere rite.[28] He emphasized baptism as an act of obedience, stating, "every disciple of Christ who wishes to walk in the ways of the Lord, meets this duty at the entrance of his course."[29] He goes on, however, to claim that baptism is more than a mere act of obedience. He writes, "Though it is an outward ceremony, it is important, not only as an act

---

25. George, "Southern Baptists," 50.
26. Bird, "Baptism in the New Testament," 390–94.
27. Moody, "Baptism in the New Testament," 233.
28. Dagg, *Manual of Theology*, 72.
29. Dagg, *Manual of Theology*, 71.

of obedience, but as expressing a believer's separation from the world, and consecration to God, in a manner intelligible and significant, and well adapted to impress his own mind and the minds of the beholders."[30] Dagg considers baptism to be an important symbol that has an effect on the one baptized, as well as those who observe the baptism. He does not, however, explicitly refer to any divine activity in baptism.

Writing early in Southern Baptist life, J. R. Graves, the leader of the Landmark movement, gave much attention to baptism.[31] Timothy George defines Landmarkism as the belief that there is an unbroken line of Baptist churches extending back to Jesus himself, or possibly even to John the Baptist.[32] According to the Landmark tradition, the only true church is a Baptist church, and therefore the only true baptism is that which is properly administered in a Baptist church. Though much of Graves's work focused on the relationship between baptism and church membership, Graves also put forth a view of the meaning of baptism. In doing so, he emphasized the human action in baptism and said nothing of divine activity. Graves opens his book, *The Relation of Baptism to Salvation*, by quoting three verses: "Why call ye me Lord, Lord, and do not the things I command you?" "Ye are my friends if ye do whatsoever I command you." "If a man loves me, he will keep my words—commandments."[33] For Graves, baptism is representative of all future obedience.[34] His emphasis on baptism as a human act of obedience is characteristic of the symbolic view of baptism.

Writing in 1882, J. M. Pendleton, another leader of the Landmark movement, agreed with Graves that baptism is the first public act of obedience.[35] He also agreed that baptism is only a symbol. He claimed, "No symbol can produce that which it symbolizes."[36] The thing must precede the symbol.[37] While acknowledging that the washing away of sins is associated with baptism, he argues that the "real" washing results from faith

---

30. Dagg, *Manual of Theology*, 72.

31. Landmarkism became very influential among Baptists. According to Chad Hall, by the late 1980s, over 250,000 Baptists openly adhered to Landmark theology (Hall, "When Orphans Became Heirs," 126

32. George, "Southern Baptists," 44.

33. Graves, *Relation of Baptism to Salvation*, 5.

34. Graves, *Relation of Baptism to Salvation*, 23.

35. Pendleton, *Distinctive Principles of Baptists*, 171.

36. Pendleton, *Distinctive Principles of Baptists*, 116.

37. Pendleton, *Distinctive Principles of Baptists*, 116.

in Christ, and the washing associated with baptism is "symbolic."[38] According to Robert Baker, these Landmark convictions had a significant impact on the Southern Baptist Convention.[39]

B. H. Carroll was a Texas pastor who, according to Ken Hemphill, "cast a shadow across the developing Southern Baptist Convention, and his influence remains to this day."[40] In a sermon on baptism preached at the First Baptist Church of Waco, Texas in 1893, Carroll claimed that in Matt 28:19–20, the order of the obligations given is itself part of the command.[41] First, we are to make disciples, which involves preaching the gospel and leading people to faith and repentance. Only after a person has repented of his sins is the person ready to be baptized.[42] Carroll offered four purposes of baptism. First, it is a public profession of faith in Jesus.[43] Second, it is an expression of subjection to Jesus.[44] Third, it symbolizes purification from sin.[45] Fourth, it represents union with Christ in his death and resurrection.[46] For Carroll, then, the significance of baptism lies in what it represents, not in what it accomplishes. As James Spivey summarizes, for Carroll, "the proper design is symbolic, with no trace of baptismal regeneration. Salvation precedes baptism, not vice versa."[47]

Edwin Dargan pastored several Baptist churches, taught at The Southern Baptist Theological Seminary, served as editorial secretary of the Sunday School Board, and served as President of the Southern Baptist Convention.[48] Dargan asserted that baptism "is not spiritually efficacious in any sense, but is symbolic and declarative."[49] He denied that baptism effects "any spiritual change in the subject," but instead symbolizes a change that has already taken place.[50]

38. Pendleton, *Distinctive Principles of Baptists*, 117.
39. Baker, *Southern Baptist Convention*, 208.
40. Carroll, *Baptists and Their Doctrines*, vii.
41. Carroll, *Baptism*, 2.
42. Carroll, *Baptism*, 6.
43. Carroll, *Baptism*, 13.
44. Carroll, *Baptism*, 13.
45. Carroll, *Baptism*, 14.
46. Carroll, *Baptism*, 16.
47. Spivey, "Benajah Harvey Carroll," 175.
48. Biographical information accessed: at http://www.sbhla.org/downloads/795-203.pdf.
49. Dargan, *Ecclesiology*, 204.
50. Dargan, *Ecclesiology*, 205.

James Boyce helped found The Southern Baptist Theological Seminary, served as a professor and as a President of the seminary, served as President of the Southern Baptist Convention, and in 1899 published a systematic theology, *The Abstract of Principles*. Boyce did not have a section on ecclesiology in his systematic theology, and only dealt with baptism in an extended footnote. In that footnote, Boyce claims that baptism can be "instrumental" in salvation, but it does not convey grace. It is an act of obedience for those who have been saved.[51] In *A Brief Catechism of Bible Doctrine*, Boyce asserts that baptism is a profession for those who have already experienced those things which baptism represents.[52]

W. T. Conner is considered by Garrett to be "the leading theologian among Southern Baptists during the second quarter of the twentieth century."[53] Conner, too, held to a symbolic view. He argued that baptism does not convey grace.[54] It is a symbol of the washing away of sins, the believer's death and resurrection with Christ, and the death and resurrection of Christ himself.[55]

W. O. Carver, who taught New Testament and missions at The Southern Baptist Theological Seminary, was concerned about what he considered a mechanical interpretation of baptism. He went so far as to state, "At the heart of the evils of ritual is the concept of the 'sacrament.'"[56] He affirmed that God works through the materials of the symbols of baptism and Lord's Supper, claiming that they are useful for "spiritual meditation and for the development of spiritual insight."[57] However, attaching any "magical significance" to physical objects leads to an understanding of the "sacraments" that is "deceitful, corrupting, and destructive of genuine experience of God."[58] William Smith, who wrote his doctoral dissertation on Carver, concludes that Carver held to a symbolic view of baptism.[59]

---

51. Boyce, *Abstract of Systematic Theology*, 333–34. See also Boyce, *Brief Catechism of Bible Doctrine*.
52. Boyce, *Brief Catechism of Bible Doctrine*.
53. Garrett, *Baptist Theology*, 449.
54. Conner, *Christian Doctrine*, 274.
55. Conner, *Christian Doctrine*, 278–79.
56. Carver, "Introduction," 10.
57. Carver, "Introduction," 10.
58. Carver, "Introduction," 10.
59. Smith, *Critical Investigation*, 70–71.

E. Y. Mullins is considered by Herschel Hobbs to be "probably the Southern Baptists' greatest theologian."[60] Mullins was emphatic that baptism is an ordinance, not a sacrament. In his view, baptism does not convey grace.[61] He highlighted the importance of being baptized as an act of obedience, stating that every believer is under obligation to submit to the command to be baptized.[62]

According to David Dockery, Herschel Hobbs, "by any account, was one of the most influential and shaping leaders in Southern Baptist life in the twentieth century."[63] In addition to being a pastor, Hobbs was chairman of the 1963 "Baptist Faith and Message" Committee, served on multiple boards, had a weekly radio program for eighteen years, and served as President of the Southern Baptist Convention.[64] Hobbs said of baptism and the Lord's Supper, "they are not sacramental but symbolic in nature."[65] He denied that there is grace to be found in baptism which cannot be found elsewhere.[66] In defense of the position that baptism is not necessary for salvation, Hobbs pointed out that Jesus did all that was necessary for salvation, yet baptized no one.[67] He also noted that Paul was sent to the Corinthians not to baptize but to preach the gospel.[68] He states, "The New Testament abounds in instances of and statements about salvation with no reference to baptism."[69] After a thorough explanation of what baptism is not, Hobbs states what baptism is. "While baptism is not necessary for salvation, it is an act of obedience (Matt 28:19) by which we show that our faith for salvation is in the death, burial, and resurrection of Jesus Christ and that we have died to sin, the old life had been buried, and we are raised to a new life in Christ."[70]

These works on baptism, and the positions for which they argue, provide a large part of the historical background for the reception of Beasley-Murray's work. While there are hints of baptism being more than

60. Hobbs, "People of the Book," 12.
61. Mullins, *Baptist Beliefs*, 67.
62. Mullins, *Baptist Beliefs*, 68.
63. Dockery, "Herschel H. Hobbs," 216.
64. Dockery, "Herschel H. Hobbs," 216, 218–19.
65. Hobbs, *Fundamentals of Our Faith*, 114.
66. Hobbs, *Fundamentals of Our Faith*, 118.
67. Hobbs, *Fundamentals of Our Faith*, 118.
68. Hobbs, *Fundamentals of Our Faith*, 118.
69. Hobbs, *Fundamentals of Our Faith*, 119.
70. Hobbs, *Fundamentals of Our Faith*, 118.

a mere symbol, particularly in the work of Dagg and Carver, even then there is no thorough argument for divine activity in baptism. By the time Beasley-Murray argued for a sacramental understanding of baptism, then, there simply was little to no precedent for such an understanding of baptism within the Southern Baptist literature.[71]

Nevertheless, at least some Southern Baptist scholars were willing to consider Beasley-Murray's proposals. Two reviews of *Baptism in the New Testament* by Southern Baptists shed some light on the reception of Beasley-Murray's work. In a 1963 review, Dale Moody stated that it would be a very false impression to suggest that Beasley-Murray defends "what Baptists have always believed."[72] However, he acknowledged Beasley-Murray's "profound grasp of biblical theology and careful exegesis"[73] and claimed that Southern Baptists would benefit from it.[74] In an article published five years later, Moody was again affirming of Beasley-Murray's view, suggesting that "Southern Baptists tend to dismiss his dynamic sacramentalism all too hastily."[75]

In his review of *Baptism in the New Testament*, Bill Hull claimed the sacramental resurgence, of which Beasley-Murray was a part, was a "significant new development in the study of New Testament baptism"[76] and "a new understanding of baptism."[77] Hull offered what he thinks should be the Southern Baptist response to Beasley-Murray's view. He believed that there was much more right with Beasley-Murray's view than there was wrong.[78] "I must state emphatically that the reservations which have been expressed should be interpreted as reflecting difference of *degree* rather than of *kind*."[79] He argued that whereas Beasley-Murray made baptism a unique sacrament of the gospel, an integral part of personal conversion, and a central concern in the ecumenical movement, baptism

---

71. There is some precedent for a sacramental view within the larger Baptist tradition. See Fowler, *More Than a Symbol*. This section, however, is focused specifically on the Southern Baptist tradition.

72. Moody, "Baptism in the New Testament," 233.

73. Moody, "Baptism in the New Testament," 234.

74. Moody, "Baptism in the New Testament," 232.

75. Moody, "Baptism in the New Testament," 21.

76. Hull, "Baptism in the New Testament," 3.

77. Hull, "Baptism in the New Testament," 4.

78. Hull, "Baptism in the New Testament," 11.

79. Hull, "Baptism in the New Testament," 11.

is a given "a more modest place in the Bible."[80] In short, Beasley-Murray "overstated his case."[81] Southern Baptists, he claimed, have been right to emphasize a personal relationship with Christ and to keep baptism as a secondary issue.[82] At the same time, he pointed out that baptism should be considered more important than it was by most Southern Baptists of his day.[83] Instead of simply dismissing Beasley-Murray, Southern Baptists should accept "his clarion call to infuse the Christian pilgrimage from its very beginning with the gracious and dynamic activity of God."[84]

These two reviews indicate that there was a sense that Beasley-Murray was saying something new, at least for Southern Baptists. They also indicate that there was an openness by some to listen to what he was saying.

THE INERRANCY CONTROVERSY

A third factor to be considered when examining the baptismal debate among Southern Baptist scholars is the theological climate of the Southern Baptist Convention at and shortly after the time that Beasley-Murray published some of his major works on baptism. While Beasley-Murray was one of many British Baptists contributing to a prolonged debate about the meaning of baptism, the theological focus of Southern Baptists was elsewhere at that time, namely, on the nature of the Bible. Though specific interpretations of Scripture, academic freedom, and the proper governance of the Convention were all considerations in the controversy, the debate focused on whether the Bible is inerrant.

According to the editors of *Is the Bible a Human Book*, published in 1970, the nature of the Bible had been "the topic of lively discussion" for a decade. "This discussion, in fact, is so lively today that it can be called a debate."[85] From his perspective in 1993, Larry McSwain claimed that the inerrancy controversy was a twenty-five year process.[86] Not only was the debate long, it was also divisive and was considered by many to be the

---

80. Hull, "Baptism in the New Testament," 11.
81. Hull, "Baptism in the New Testament," 11.
82. Hull, "Baptism in the New Testament," 12.
83. Hull, "Baptism in the New Testament," 12.
84. Hull, "Baptism in the New Testament," 12.
85. Ward and Green, *Is the Bible a Human Book*, 5.
86. McSwain, "Swinging Pendulums," 262.

most significant debate possible. Harold Lindsell considered inerrancy to be "the most important theological topic of this age."[87] James Draper contended that the issue of authority, including the debate over inerrancy, was "the key issue among Southern Baptists."[88] James Leo Garret describes the inerrancy controversy as a "prolonged, intense, and divisive controversy"[89] and concludes, "it is not difficult to identify inerrancy as the paramount doctrinal issue in the controversy that dominated Southern Baptist life during the last two decades of the twentieth century."[90]

On one side, often referred to as the "moderate" or "progressive" side, the focus on inerrancy was driven by a desire to be honest about the nature of the Bible as they saw it. In his essay, "Could God Trust Human Hands?," James Flamming appears to suggest that an affirmation of inerrancy is a denial of the "human characteristics" of the Bible, a denial which makes us look "foolish."[91] Additionally, Humphreys notes that some "progressives" believed that emphasizing the human quality of the book allows us to study the Bible critically, and therefore better understand and apply its message.[92]

On the other side, often referred to as the "conservative" or "fundamentalist" side, the debate was driven primarily by two convictions. The first is that "a perfect God would not inspire imperfect Scriptures."[93] The doctrine of inerrancy, then, was directly related to the doctrine of God. The second motivating conviction was that a loss of inerrancy would lead to an improper methodology, which would further lead to wrong theological conclusions. Lindsell referred to the denial of inerrancy as a "disease" that leads to disbelief in other cardinal doctrines.[94] He urged Southern Baptists to act before the "infection" spreads.[95] Clark Pinnock argued, "The problem of revelation and inspiration is momentous, and central to every theological question. The authority of Scripture is the watershed of theological conviction, and its importance to a sound

---

87. Lindsell, *Battle for the Bible,* Preface.
88. Draper, *Authority,* 9.
89. Garrett, *Baptist Theology,* 491.
90. Garrett, *Baptist Theology,* 493.
91. Flamming, "Could God Trust Human Hands?" 18.
92. Humphreys, *The Way We Were,* 100.
93. Humphreys and Wise, *Fundamentalism,* 44.
94. Lindsell, *Battle for the Bible,* 167.
95. Lindsell, *Battle for the Bible,* 167.

methodology is incalculable."⁹⁶ He believed, "The battle for the plenary inspiration of the Bible is part of the larger struggle for authentic biblical religion."⁹⁷ About Southern Baptists and their commitment to inerrancy, W. A. Criswell claimed, "If our preachers, evangelists, pastors, churches, and institutions are true to that expression of faith, we shall live. If we repudiate it, we shall die."⁹⁸

Controversy began to erupt in the late 1950s. In 1959, Eric Rust presented a paper at a pastor's conference in which he claimed that the biblical story of Noah was a parable, a claim which proved to be quite controversial.⁹⁹ During 1958–1959, a controversy developed at the Southern Baptist Theological Seminary which resulted in the dismissal of twelve professors. Different interpretations of the controversy have been offered, but theological differences, including a more "progressive orientation" and what was viewed by some as an "uncritical adoption of historical-critical methods" by the professors, were significant factors.¹⁰⁰ In 1960, the Baptist Standard published the Convention message of president Ramsey Pollard in which he stated, "If you don't believe the miracles and the Word of God, get out of our Seminaries!"¹⁰¹

Much of the debate stemmed from certain interpretations of passages in the book of Genesis. In the 1972 Southern Baptist Convention presidential address, Carl Bates pointed out, "Twice in the past ten years we have fought the battle of Genesis."¹⁰² The first of those battles was over a book published by a Southern Baptist professor. In 1961 Ralph Elliot, professor at Midwestern Baptist Theological Seminary, published *The Message of Genesis*, which promoted a view of some of the Genesis stories as parables or symbols.¹⁰³ In Nancy Ammerman's view, the publication of Elliot's book was "the first sign that alien ideas might have found their

---

96. Pinnock, *Biblical Revelation*, 11.
97. Pinnock, *Biblical Revelation*, 228.
98. Criswell, *Why I Preach*, 159.
99. Sutton, *Baptist Reformation*, 6.
100. Garrett, *Baptist Theology*, 457–58
101. Sutton, *Baptist Reformation*, 7.
102. Shurden, "Problem of Authority," 219.
103. Garrett, *Baptist Theology*, 458.

way inside the gates."[104] From July 1961 to June 1962, Baptists newspapers were "filled" with debate about the Elliot controversy.[105]

In 1962 about one hundred Southern Baptists met to develop a plan for securing more conservative trustees for Midwestern Baptist Theological Seminary.[106] Part of that plan involved passing resolutions at the annual conference. That year the messengers to the annual Southern Baptist Convention adopted a resolution which read, "We reaffirm our faith in the entire Bible as the authoritative, authentic, infallible Word of God . . . our historic position."[107] After the convention and the appointment of new trustees, Elliot was dismissed from the faculty of the seminary.[108]

The second battle of Genesis resulted from what is often called the Broadman Commentary controversy. In 1970 the Broadman Press released Volume 1 of the Broadman Bible Commentary. The Genesis commentary was written by G. Henton Davies, Principal of Regent's Park College, Oxford, England. In his commentary, Davies denied that God told Abraham to sacrifice his son. Many in the Southern Baptist Convention disapproved of Davies's claims. Baptist papers contained articles critical of Davies, as well as some articles defending him.[109] Before the 1970 annual convention, a group of pastors met for an "Affirming the Bible Conference." During the convention, the messengers voted to halt the distribution of the commentary and have it rewritten. The Sunday School Board withdrew the volume from distribution, but asked Davies to do the rewriting. At the 1971 Convention, the messengers voted to have someone other than Davies rewrite the commentary.[110]

Even with the Broadman Commentary controversy having been settled, the debate about the nature of the Bible continued. In fact, the debate became so intense that in his 1976 book, *The Battle for the Bible*, Harold Lindsell criticized Robert Alley, Howard Colson, William Hull, The Christian Index, the Arkansas Baptist News, and the Sunday School Board, and then concluded, "the time must come when there will be

---

104. Ammerman, *Baptist Battles*.
105. Shurden, "Problem of Authority," 220.
106. Garrett, *Baptist Theology*, 460.
107. Criswell, *Why I Preach*, 159.
108. Garrett, *Baptist Theology*, 461.
109. Garrett, *Baptist Theology*, 486–87.
110. Garrett, *Baptist Theology*, 486–87.

a showdown."[111] The showdown began three years later at the annual meeting which, according to Garrett, marked the formal beginning of what is known as "the conservative resurgence" or "the fundamentalist takeover."[112] Fisher Humphreys also sees this date as significant, claiming that Southern Baptists have been engaged in controversy since 1979.[113] The resurgence included numerous meetings, committee reports, study conferences, efforts to elect successive presidents of the convention who affirmed biblical inerrancy, and working through the Convention's leadership structure to remove perceived liberal professors at the seminaries and replace them with conservative professors.[114]

One result of the ongoing controversy was that around the time Beasley-Murray published his works on baptism, little scholarly work on baptism was produced by Southern Baptists. In 1964 Warren Carr published *Baptism: Conscience and Clue for the Church*.[115] In 1967 Dale Moody published *Baptism: Foundation for Christian Unity*.[116] However, in a 1968 article, "Baptism in recent research," Moody claimed that some of the most solid recent study on baptism had been done by British Baptists.[117] He also mentions several continental scholars who had contributed to the debate.[118] According to Moody, Southern Baptists had not been very productive in baptismal theology.[119]

By contrast, beginning in the 1960s, Southern Baptists published numerous books on the nature of the Bible.[120] Several of the authors indicated that the reason for their books was the controversy within the

111. Lindsell, *Battle for the Bible*, 91–104.
112. Garrett, *Baptist Theology*, 493.
113. Humphreys, *Way We Were*, 2.
114. Garrett, *Baptist Theology*, 491–506; Sutton, *Baptist Reformation*, 343.
115. Carr, *Baptism*.
116. Moody, *Baptism*.
117. Moody, "Baptism in Recent Research," 20.
118. Moody, "Baptism in Recent Research," 21.
119. Moody, "Baptism in Recent Research," 21.
120. Pinnock, *Defense of Biblical Infallibility* (1967); Pinnock, *New Reformation* (1968); Criswell, *Why I Preach* (1969); Pinnock, *Biblical Revelation: The Foundation of Christian Theology* (1971); Pinnock, *Scripture Principle* (1984); Ward and Green, *Is the Bible a Human Book* (1970); Ally, *Revolt Against the Faithful* (1970); Henry, *God, Revelation, and Authority* (1976); Lindsell, *Battle for the Bible* (1976); Lindsell, *Bible in the Balance* (1979); Bush and Nettles, *Baptists and the Bible* (1980); Dilday, *Doctrine of Biblical Authority* (1982); Draper, *Authority* (1984); Lewis, *Revelation, Inspiration, Scripture* (1985).

Convention. One of the early books on the subject was W. A. Criswell's *Why I Preach That the Bible is Literally True*. Though not a polemical work, he does imply that there were circumstances which called for a book on inerrancy. He was invited to write the book, and did so even during "a time of tremendous pressure," and while serving as the President of the Southern Baptist Convention.[121] Eleven years later, Bush and Nettles published a book on the nature of the Bible because "the controversial issues surrounding the various ideas about biblical authority have recently been thrust into the forefront of theological discussions among Southern Baptists as well as other denominations."[122]

While Beasley-Murray and other British Baptists were writing books on baptism, then, Southern Baptists were busy writing books on the nature of the Bible. In terms of the works that were being published, they were not engaging much with the baptismal literature being produced by their British counterparts.

CONCLUSION

The three Southern Baptist scholars under consideration in this project belong to a tradition that has a history of reacting strongly against a sacramental view of baptism. Furthermore, given the fact that for the first 115 years of the Southern Baptist Convention, scholars overwhelmingly argued for a symbolic view of baptism, the momentum of the Convention was in a decisively anti-sacramental direction. During much of the time that British Baptists were publishing works that challenged the prevalent Southern Baptist position, Southern Baptists were occupied with another issue.

While all three Southern Baptist scholars under consideration share this context, they have not all responded to it in the same way. As we will see, their positions on baptism are not uniform. Nevertheless, these factors have impacted the debate among Southern Baptists. The next three chapters will consider some factors unique to each scholar and will assess the extent to which Beasley-Murray has been instrumental in shaping the debate.

---

121. Criswell, *Why I Preach*, 7.
122. Bush and Nettles, *Baptists and the Bible*, 15.

4

Thomas Nettles

THIS CHAPTER WILL ADDRESS the role of Beasley-Murray in the baptism-related works of Thomas Nettles. After a brief biographical sketch of Nettles, we will examine Nettles's understanding of the meaning of baptism. We will then compare Nettles's view with Beasley-Murray's view and will consider some possible reasons for their differences. The next section will analyze Nettles's use of other sources, including Beasley-Murray. We will end by showing that Beasley-Murray's work is a factor in the way that Nettles develops his argument.

A BIOGRAPHICAL SKETCH OF THOMAS NETTLES

Nettles was born in 1946 in Brandon, Mississippi.[1] He was raised in First Baptist Church of Brandon, where, in his own estimation, he was influenced by a godly pastor who was committed to the Scriptures and by other godly leaders in the church. At age 11, Nettles decided he wanted to be a Christian and was baptized. In the years that followed, however, Nettles struggled with assurance of his salvation. After his first year of studies at Southwestern Baptist Theological Seminary, Nettles concluded

---

1. Biographical information is taken from an interview with Nettles (Zaspel, "Thomas J. Nettles Retires"), a presentation given by Nettles ("Salvation and Ministry Testimony"), and his profile page from The Southern Baptist Theological Seminary website, which was deleted after his retirement.

that he had never been converted. He confessed faith in Jesus and was baptized. Nettles continued his education at Southwestern, where he earned an MDiv and a PhD.

At Southwestern, Nettles studied theology with Boyd Hunt, who introduced Nettles to the works of Charles Hodge, B. B. Warfield, James Boyce, and J. L. Dagg. Although Hunt often disagreed with those theologians, Nettles came to agree with much of their theology, and he acknowledges their influence on his own theology. He also claims that Charles Spurgeon, J. I. Packer, John Stott, Clark Pinnock and Francis Schaeffer were significant influences on his theological development. The Reformers had an impact not only on his theology, but also his methodology. He states, "Calvin, Luther, Zwingli and the Anabaptists not only informed me theologically in many areas, but studying them convinced me that historical study opened wide the windows for the investigation of all important questions."[2]

Beginning in 1965, Nettles served on the staff of four churches in Texas, Mississippi, and Louisiana. He taught at Southwestern Baptist Theological Seminary, 1976–1982; Mid-America Baptist Theological Seminary, 1982–1988; Trinity Evangelical Divinity School, 1988–1997; and The Southern Baptist Theological Seminary, 1997–2014,[3] where Beasley-Murray also taught. He is also the author or editor of nine books, along with numerous journal articles and scholarly papers.

THOMAS NETTLES'S VIEW OF BAPTISM

"Baptist View"

Nettles addresses the theology of baptism in two of his works. The first is "Baptist View: Baptism as a Symbol of Christ's Saving Work," which is an essay Nettles contributed to the book *Understanding Four Views on Baptism*. The book includes essays on the Baptist view, the Reformed view, the Lutheran view, and the Christian Churches/Churches of Christ view. Each essay is followed by responses from the other three contributors.

In his essay, Nettles begins his discussion of baptism by recounting a story about a former student. He describes a time a student wrote to him about a recent experience. While working on an assignment, the student

---

2. Interview with Nettles, at Zaspel, "Thomas J. Nettles Retires."
3. Nettles has retired from full-time teaching.

realized that he had not been saved. He wrote, "In the process of reading through the material, I cried out to God, and he saved me."[4] Nettles asks rhetorically, "When he comes to me for advice, what shall I tell him? That he is not yet saved because he is not yet baptized?"[5] As his question suggests, Nettles goes on to argue for understanding baptism as something subsequent to, and separate from, conversion.

Nettles defines baptism as "the immersion in water of a believer in Jesus Christ performed once as the initiation of such a believer into a community of believers, the church."[6] He makes clear from the beginning that in his view baptism contains no "saving efficacy."[7] The main reason he arrives at this conclusion, and the key to understanding his baptismal theology, is that he sees in the Scriptures "a distinction between faith and baptism,"[8] not only conceptually, but also temporally. He points to a number of passages in the Bible that he believes make this distinction. One is Acts 8. He claims that Philip's ministry recorded in Acts 8, specifically Acts 8:12, "assumed that believing the message about the kingdom of God and the name of Jesus Christ preceded baptism."[9] Not everyone draws the same conclusion from the Acts 8 passage. Bock agrees that belief precedes baptism, but does not separate them to the extent that Nettles appears to. The response of faith, Bock argues, "leads *immediately* to baptism" (italics mine).[10]

Nettles cites 1 Cor 1:14 and 4:15 in support of this view. He takes these verses to indicate that Paul became their father "in their response through faith to the gospel he preached. They were begotten not by baptism but by the preached word."[11] He also understands Jesus' command in Matt 28:19–20 to indicate a separation of faith and baptism. He argues that the order of the participles suggests Jesus' followers are to first make disciples, and then baptize those disciples.[12] It is "an order that his

---

4. Nettles, "Baptist View," 25.
5. Nettles, "Baptist View," 25
6. Nettles, "Baptist View," 25.
7. Nettles, "Baptist View," 25
8. Nettles, "Baptist View," 33.
9. Nettles, "Baptist View," 30.
10. Bock, *Acts*, 328.
11. Nettles, "Baptist View," 33.
12. Nettles, "Baptist View," 34.

disciples have no right to alter."[13] Other commentators, such as France[14] and Morris,[15] agree that the order is important, but in their commentaries say nothing of the relationship between faith and baptism, focusing instead on the fact that teaching should follow baptism.

Nettles also refers to Rom 16:25 as evidence, which states that believers were established by the gospel and the proclamation of Jesus, and not by baptism.[16] Nettles concludes,

> If Paul were not sent to baptize, but nevertheless those to whom he preached were established by his gospel and if his preaching of the "revelation of the mystery" subdued nations to the "obedience of faith" (Rom. 1:5 NASB), he cannot have seen faith as incomplete without baptism. He certainly does not minimize baptism in its proper place as an expression of the relationship established by faith, but he views it as separate from faith and adding nothing to that which can be gained by faith only.[17]

Being separate from faith, baptism, for Nettles, cannot be the occasion or the means of salvation. In response to John Castelein's view that baptism is the occasion of salvation, Nettles claims that "Scripture represents all spiritual obedience as subsequent to and consequent on the new birth."[18] Unless a person is already born again, he would not desire to be obedient by being baptized.[19] Salvation, for him, must precede baptism. He writes, "For this reason, baptism follows regeneration, follows faith, and does not form a constituent element in either. All faith flows from regeneration; all obedience flows from faith. Baptism is an act of obedience to Christ that testifies to the prior existence of the regenerating work of the Spirit that has produced faith in Christ."[20]

For Nettles, the significance of baptism is not that it is the occasion of salvation, but that it is a symbol and a picture of salvation.[21] Baptism pictures Christ giving his life as a ransom; it pictures the baptized per-

---

13. Nettles, "Baptist View," 34.
14. France, *Gospel of Matthew*, 1116.
15. Morris, *Gospel According to Matthew*, 746–47.
16. Nettles, "Baptist View," 34.
17. Nettles, "Baptist View," 34
18. Nettles, "Baptist Response," 146.
19. Nettles, "Baptist Response," 146.
20. Nettles, "Baptist Response," 147.
21. Nettles, "Baptist Response," 25, 26.

son's testimony that the work of Christ allows him to be accepted by God; it pictures the baptized person's awareness that he was dead in his sins and is now alive in Christ.[22] The symbolic nature of baptism is also seen in his explanation of Acts 2:38. Though his primary point in that section is that only those who believed Peter's message about Jesus were baptized, he also touches on the meaning of baptism when he states that "baptism signified all that is involved in repentance for the forgiveness of sins." It indicated their acceptance of the message.[23] He is arguing that repentance takes place prior to baptism, and the act of baptism represents, or "signifies" that change that has already taken place. In other words, baptism "bears witness" to that which a sinner receives by faith.[24]

Nettles also points to Gal 3:27 as evidence that baptism is not the occasion of salvation.[25] He argues that in that passage Paul is rejecting the necessity of a religious ceremony, in this case circumcision, to complete the saving work of Christ. For Nettles, it is unthinkable that Paul would encourage them to replace that ceremony with a new one, namely baptism. Instead, baptism was a "physical representation" of their union with Christ through faith. It "illustrates" the union with Christ that has already taken place.

Nettles acknowledges that there are some passages of Scripture which can be, and sometimes are, interpreted in a way which indicates that a person is united to Christ and forgiven in baptism. He brings up a number of those passages and offers interpretations which are consistent with a symbolic understanding of baptism. One such passage is Acts 22:16, which can be understood to mean that Paul's sins were washed away in baptism. Nettles argues that Paul would not have understood his sins to be washed away in baptism. Rather, his baptism identified him with Jesus. The washing away of sins in that verse is connected to calling on Jesus' name, not the act of baptism.[26] He does not, however, provide any exegetical support for his claim, which would strengthen his argument.

He also deals with a category of passages which refer to washing or cleansing, and, if interpreted to be references to baptism, may be used as

---

22. Nettles, "Baptist Response," 26.
23. Nettles, "Baptist Response," 29.
24. Nettles, "Baptist Response," 31.
25. Nettles, "Baptist Response," 32–33.
26. Nettles, "Baptist Response," 31.

support of a sacramental view of baptism. Indeed, they have often been interpreted in such a way. As Knight notes, "A considerable number of commentators have associated 'washing' with baptism."[27] Chrysostom and Augustine both saw a reference to baptism in the "washing" in Titus 3:5.[28] On Eph 5:26, Thielman notes that throughout the history of the church "the vast majority" of interpreters have taken "washing" as a reference to baptism.[29] Wood is one example of that interpretation, stating, "There seems to be little or no doubt that the reference is to baptism."[30] Bruce understands washing to be a reference to Christian initiation, of which baptism is a "central part."[31]

Nettles, however, contends that "washing" and "cleansing" do not have to be, and in fact should not be, read as references to baptism. He writes, "For example, the assumption that the 'washing of rebirth' (Titus 3:5) refers to baptism is purely gratuitous. This text and several others that mention washing, cleansing, and water (e.g., Eph. 5:26; John 3:3–8) form a part of every sacramentalist's discussion of the operations of grace within baptism. None of them, however, even mentions baptism."[32] Fee argues along the same lines, pointing out that while it is possible that the term "may have carried with it an indirect allusion to baptism," Paul is not here concerned with the rite of baptism, as evidenced by the fact that Paul wrote, "you were washed" and not "you were baptized."[33] Nettles believes that the concepts of washing and cleansing in many of those passages refer to the power of the word of God to apply the work of Christ to cleanse a person of sin.[34] A number of recent commentators, including MacArthur,[35] Mare,[36] Thielman,[37] Towner,[38] and Knight,[39] agree, understanding "washing" to be a metaphor for spiritual cleansing.

27. Knight, *Pastoral Epistles,* 350.
28. Gorday, *New Testament IX,* 304.
29. Thielman, *Ephesians,* 383.
30. Wood, "Ephesians," 77.
31. Bruce, *Epistles to the Colossians,* 388.
32. Nettles, "Baptist Response," 74.
33. Fee, *First Epistle to the Corinthians,* 246–47.
34. Nettles, "Baptist Response," 147.
35. MacArthur, *1 Corinthians,*143.
36. Mare, "1 Corinthians," 223.
37. Thielman, *Ephesians,* 384.
38. Towner, *Letters to Timothy and Titus,* 781.
39. Knight, *Pastoral Epistles,* 342.

There is another category of passages which are certainly about baptism and appear to indicate that baptism saves. Nettles's explanation is that the Bible speaks of things that save in three ways. First, some passages speak of God's immediate work in salvation.[40] Second, some passages speak of certain "means that operate in various ways congruent with the rational and moral nature of salvation."[41] For example, "The mind and heart must consent to truth divinely revealed. . . . Confession naturally flows from the heart of the regenerate person. . . . Paul told Timothy that in his faithful stewardship of the ministry he would save both himself and his hearers."[42] Those means, then, are said to save because they are responses to God's saving acts or are used by God to save people. Third, some passages speak of "the symbols of his passion that Jesus commanded his church to observe. This involves concrete pictures—fit symbols—to express and call to mind the divine mercy in salvation."[43] Nettles concludes, "It is within the sphere of this third group of Bible passages that we understand Peter's statement that 'this water symbolizes baptism that now saves you also.' . . . As a clear symbol of the saving reality, baptism stands as a perpetual witness to the historical substance of salvation and because of that connection is said to save us."[44]

Though Nettles claims that baptism should be placed in the third group of passages—those which use salvation language in reference to symbols—he does not provide a reason for placing it in that category. This is especially significant in light of the second group that Nettles identifies—passages which use salvation language in reference to the means of salvation. According to Nettles's own categories and explanation, it seems that baptism could be placed in that second group, allowing for a sacramental understanding of baptism. Nettles, however, chooses to place baptism in the third group, which leads to a symbolic view of baptism.

Richard Pratt addresses Nettles's decision to place baptism in the third group instead of the second. Pratt points out that Nettles acknowledges that the Bible sometimes uses salvation language to refer to the means of salvation. He questions why Nettles does not include baptism

---

40. Nettles, "Baptist View," 36.
41. Nettles, "Baptist View," 36.
42. Nettles, "Baptist View," 37.
43. Nettles, "Baptist View," 37.
44. Nettles, "Baptist View," 37–38.

in this category, pointing out, "He does not explain why baptism does not fall into this category; he only asserts it."[45]

Not the Only Baptist View

Nettles's essay in *Understanding Four Views on Baptism* is titled "Baptist View." He is tasked with explaining the way Baptists understand baptism and to interact with scholars in three other traditions who understand baptism differently. The title and article both imply that there is a single Baptist view of baptism. Nettles is not alone in his suggestion that he represents the Baptist viewpoint. Charles Quarles, for example, states, "Baptists insist that baptism is a mere symbol of our union with Christ."[46]

However, given that there is no single creed or statement of faith to which all Baptists adhere, there is not a single or official Baptist view of the meaning of baptism. It is true that the vast majority of literature produced by scholars within the Southern Baptist tradition—Nettles's own tradition—has argued for a symbolic view of baptism,[47] and that there has for some time been a consensus among Southern Baptist scholars that the majority of Southern Baptists hold to a symbolic view of baptism.[48] It is also true, however, as Fowler has shown, that there has been a sacramental strand running throughout Baptist life since the beginning of the Baptist tradition,[49] and since the early twentieth century a number of British Baptist scholars have argued for a sacramental understanding of baptism. Some Southern Baptists, including Timothy George and Thomas Schreiner, understand baptism to be more than a symbol as well. These facts alone—to say nothing of other Baptist traditions—demonstrate that while there may be a majority view among Baptists, there is not a single Baptist view.

---

45. Pratt, "Reformed Response," 45.
46. Quarles, "Ordinance or Sacrament," 48.
47. See the discussion of the Southern Baptist tradition in the previous chapter.
48. Tull, *Shapers of Baptist Thought*, 127; George, "Southern Baptists," 50; Moody, "Baptism in the New Testament," 233; Hull, "Baptism in the New Testament," 4.
49. Fowler, *More Than a Symbol*.

Nettles, the Sacramental View, and Idolatry

The Baptists is Nettles's three-volume work on the Baptist movement. In the third volume, Nettles addresses some of the debate concerning the meaning of baptism. First, he deals with the "Baptismal Regeneration Controversy" in England in the 1860s, focusing primarily on Charles Spurgeon's role in it. In the words of Nettles, Spurgeon "sought to prove, and passionately so, that [baptismal regeneration] was a false doctrine calculated to damn sinners through false assurance."[50] Nettles himself does not at this point deal with this issue theologically. He merely provides an historical account of a controversy that Spurgeon was involved in.

However, he later makes a case for believer baptism. He states, "Baptism of none but professing believers more precisely coincides with the full biblical witness in several ways."[51] First, it is in line with the New Testament examples of baptism. Every instance of baptism in the New Testament involves professed believers.[52] He refers to one household baptism but does not offer any evidence to support the claim that all in the household were believers. Second, believer baptism is consistent with the biblical teaching that baptism is meant to be a manifestation of a repentant heart and is meant for disciples only.[53] Third, believer baptism incorporates in "a more consistent manner" doctrines such as effectual calling, sanctification, assurance, and good works.[54]

Nettles also addresses the meaning of baptism. He claims that regeneration, repentance, faith and justification are all "depicted" in baptism, and refers to baptism as "a rich symbol" of God's gracious gift of salvation to the sinner.[55] He acknowledges that there are Baptists who have a different understanding of baptism. He points out that since the early twentieth-century some Baptists—including theologians, New Testament scholars, and historians—have argued for a sacramental view of baptism.[56] He notes, "The historians and historical theologians argue that this is an early commitment embodied in seventeenth-century

---

50. Nettles, *The Baptists*, 49.
51. Nettles, *The Baptists*, 309.
52. Nettles, *The Baptists*, 309.
53. Nettles, *The Baptists*, 309.
54. Nettles, *The Baptists*, 309.
55. Nettles, *The Baptists*, 309–10.
56. Nettles, *The Baptists*, 310.

confessions and theologians."[57] New Testament scholars and theologians argue that New Testament baptism is inseparable from turning to God in faith.[58] He refers specifically to Beasley-Murray and H. Wheeler Robinson as examples of scholars who are part of the movement that argued for a sacramental understanding of baptism.[59]

Concerning the sacramental view, Nettles writes, "This movement toward sacramentalism has a corrupting influence on Baptist ecclesiology and soteriology. As to salvation, one's focus must now be divided between the historic work of Christ on the cross and the present event of baptism. This is real idolatry."[60] He continues,

> Also, the transforming event of human experience shifts from the hearing of the word of truth under the efficacious and transforming power of the Spirit, to the doing of an event enacted by the church. In this scheme, the church changes from a transformed community, that receives other transformed sinners into the benefits of its fellowship and Spirit-granted gifts, into a community that grants transformation by its practice of sacraments, baptism and communion.[61]

Elsewhere, Nettles insists that salvation is "gained by faith only" and suggests that a sacramental view of baptism implies an insufficiency of faith for salvation.[62]

The perceived inconsistency between the sacramental view of baptism and salvation by grace through faith is arguably the primary theological reason that Nettles holds to a symbolic view of baptism and rejects the sacramentalism argued for by Beasley-Murray. As Pratt states,

> Nettles argues for a symbolic view of baptism in large measure because he sees it as the way to safeguard other central teachings of the Scriptures. He holds NT doctrines such as sola fide and sola gratia very firmly. Sinners are justified by faith alone and saved by divine grace alone. It is important to safeguard these doctrines, but we must be careful to do so in biblical ways. Nettles concludes from these sure biblical doctrines that this

---

57. Nettles, *The Baptists*, 310.
58. Nettles, *The Baptists*, 311.
59. Nettles, *The Baptists*, 311.
60. Nettles, *The Baptists*, 311.
61. Nettles, *The Baptists*, 311.
62. Nettles, *The Baptists*, 34.

baptism can only be symbolic, as if this were the only logical way of keeping salvation by grace through faith intact.[63]

Though it has not been common to label the sacramental view "idolatry" as Nettles does, the related claim that the sacramental view attributes to baptism what should only be attributed to God is not limited to Nettles. After the ecumenical document "Baptism, Eucharist, and Ministry" was published,[64] some responses expressed concern that "the text makes baptism itself the subject of the action: 'baptism makes,' 'constitutes,' 'initiates,' 'gives,' 'has,' 'anticipates.' Not a few responses claim that the language of the text goes too far in the direction of a mechanical understanding of baptism, suggesting 'efficacious power' which—some fear—tends towards a 'magical' view of the sacrament."[65] According to one report, the Baptist Union of Great Britain in particular took issue with BEM's claim that baptism "is," "gives," "initiates," "unites," and "effects."[66] This could be read to mean that the actual performance itself achieves things that should only be attributed to God. "The language is at best hyperbole and at worst objectionable."[67] Charles Quarles argues along similar lines. He believes that those who espouse a sacramental view of baptism teach that baptism imparts salvation. According to a sacramental view, he argues, water-baptism forgives and justifies.[68]

Beasley-Murray dealt with the same accusation in the aftermath of *Christian Baptism* being published. In *The Baptist Times*, for example, Dr. N. Beattie wrote, "The inner work on the heart by the Holy Spirit causing the new birth is certainly an operation which does not depend for its completion on the subsequent physical act of immersing the body in water."[69] S. B. John wrote, "To make baptism part of conversion is to wound the Gospel at its very heart."[70]

Despite the accusations, Beasley-Murray insisted that the New Testament stresses throughout that it is the name of Christ, his resurrection, the Spirit, or the Word of God that makes the baptized person new, not

---

63. Pratt, "Reformed Response," 44.
64. "Baptism, Eucharist and Ministry."
65. "Baptism, Eucharist and Ministry," 42.
66. Thurian, *Churches Respond to BEM*, 70.
67. Thurian, *Churches Respond to BEM*, 70.
68. Quarles, "Ordinance or Sacrament," 47.
69. Beattie, "Christian Baptism," 6.
70. John, "Christian Baptism," 6.

the water itself.[71] Others have agreed with Beasley-Murray that a sacramental understanding of baptism is in fact compatible with salvation by grace through faith. John Calvin was aware of the danger of putting too much emphasis on baptism. He suggested that when sacraments are thought to be mechanical, people are led to "repose in the appearance of a physical thing rather than in God himself."[72] He did not believe, however, that this danger should cause us to deny that baptism is more than a mere symbol. He writes,

> Surely, forasmuch as the blood of Christ is the only means whereby our sins are washed away, and as it was once shed to this end, so the Holy Ghost, by the sprinkling thereof through faith, doth make us clean continually. This honour cannot be translated unto the sign of water, without doing open injury to Christ and the Holy Ghost; and experience doth teach how earnestly men be bent upon this superstition. Therefore, many godly men, lest they put confidence in the outward sign, do overmuch extenuate the force of baptism. But they must keep a measure, that the sacraments may be kept within their bounds, lest they darken the glory of Christ; and yet they may not want their force and use.[73]

Specifically in response to Nettles, John Castelein, a member of the Churches of Christ, agrees that there is no saving efficacy in the water itself, but argues that "there is saving efficacy, by God's grace, in actions that actualize the obedience of faith."[74] He concludes, "There should be no divorcing of professing Jesus with one's mouth, embracing him as Lord in one's heart, and surrendering one's body to him in immersion."[75] Clark Pinnock, one of Nettles's main theological influences,[76] also believes that a sacramental view is compatible with justification by faith, claiming, "The Spirit is normally given with water in response to faith. This makes baptism a sacrament and a means of grace."[77]

---

71. Beasley-Murray, *Baptism in the New Testament*, 265. Beasley-Murray admits that Heb 10:22 is an exception to this rule.

72. Calvin, *Institutes*, 1289.

73. Calvin, *Commentary Upon the Acts of the Apostles*, 302.

74. Castelein, "Christian Churches/Churches of Christ Response," 52.

75. Castelein, "Christian Churches/Churches of Christ Response," 52–53.

76. Interview with Nettles, at Zaspel, "Thomas J. Nettles Retires."

77. Pinnock, *Flame of Love*, 124.

Nettles does acknowledge that Beasley-Murray's intention is not to commit idolatry. In fact, Nettles understands the purpose of the literature arguing for a sacramental view to be "convincing, not only Baptists, but non-Baptists, that baptism of those professing faith in Christ is the event in which God unites a believer with Christ by the Spirit."[78] In his own estimation, then, the view of the sacramentalists is that salvation is something God does and is received by faith. Baptism is the event, or occasion, in which such salvation takes place. Nettles even quotes Beasley-Murray's claim that "New Testament baptism is inseparable from turning to God in faith, on the basis of which God justifies, gives the Spirit, and unites to Christ."[79] Again, it is God who justifies.

Anthony Cross, whose work will be considered in a later chapter, has responded to Nettles's charge of idolatry. He writes, "It is not idolatry; and would not be even if this was what they were saying—which it is not. None of the Baptist sacramentalists separate baptism from faith; rather they repeatedly emphasize that what they are discussing is New Testament baptism, that is, faith-baptism. To suggest otherwise, as Nettles does, is simply to misread and misrepresent them."[80]

Nevertheless, for Nettles, the principle is clear. He writes, "Let me state as a principle, that any attribution of saving efficacy that we make to a material substance, or our partaking of a material substance in which the focus of attention is on that act as saving (or sanctifying) has the tendency toward idolatry in that it gives to a creature what belongs to God alone."[81]

NETTLES'S APPROPRIATION OF THE WORK OF BEASLEY-MURRAY

Nettles and Beasley-Murray agree on a number of points related to the meaning of baptism. They agree that baptism is a confession of faith in Jesus as Lord.[82] They also agree that baptism pictures a believer's union with Christ in his death and resurrection.[83]

78. Nettles, *The Baptists*, 311.

79. Nettles, *The Baptists*, 311; the statement is made in Beasley-Murray, "Baptism and the Sacramental View."

80. Cross, *Recovering the Evangelical Sacrament*, 173.

81. Thomas Nettles, personal email, January 31, 2015.

82. Nettles, "Baptist View," 30; Beasley-Murray, "John 3:3–5," 29.

83. Nettles, "Baptist View," 26; Beasley-Murray, *Baptism*, 133.

There are, however, some significant differences between Nettles and Beasley-Murray. Perhaps the most fundamental difference concerns their respective understandings of the relationship between faith and baptism. Nettles argues for a clear separation of faith and baptism. Beasley-Murray, on the other hand, argues that faith and baptism, though distinct, should be held together.[84] Another disagreement concerns the interpretation of passages which associate baptism with salvation. Nettles believes that the Bible sometimes uses salvation language in connection with the symbols that point us to the reality of salvation, and baptism is one of those symbols.[85] Beasley-Murray, on the other hand, believes that baptism is in fact a means of saving grace due to the fact that baptism is an expression of saving faith.

These two differences lead to different conclusions regarding the meaning of baptism. Nettles understands baptism to be a symbol of realities already present due to the previous exercise of faith. Beasley-Murray understands baptism—at least baptism in the New Testament—to be the means of expressing faith in response to the gospel, and therefore the occasion in which a person is united to Christ.

Possible Factors Contributing to Nettles's Disagreement with Beasley-Murray

Nettles has read at least some of Beasley-Murray's work on baptism and appears to consider that work to be important, yet he has not been persuaded by Beasley-Murray's argument. In addition to the theological assumptions discussed above—namely, that sacramentalism and justification by faith are mutually exclusive, and that baptism is connected to salvation in the Bible because it is a symbol of salvation—there are two additional significant factors that may have led him to reject Beasley-Murray's argument.

One factor that is worth noting is Nettles's own experience. Nettles was baptized at age 11 but not converted until he was in seminary.[86] In his own life, then, there was a separation of baptism and faith. He personally experienced a baptism—at least the actions of a baptism—without being united to Christ. Though he does not state it explicitly, the sacramental

---

84. Beasley-Murray, "Authority," 66.
85. Nettles, "Baptist View," 37–38.
86. Nettles, "Salvation and Ministry Testimony."

connection between baptism and conversion may to some extent seem inconsistent with his own experience.

Personal experience has been a factor for the way other people have appropriated Beasley-Murray. At the time he was publishing works on baptism, some people rejected his conclusions because those conclusions were inconsistent with their own experiences.[87] Beasley-Murray recognized that the experience of any given individual may not be consistent with a sacramental view of baptism, but maintained that our understanding of the meaning of baptism should be determined by the New Testament and not by personal experience.[88]

A second factor to consider in Nettles's position on baptism is his theological influences. Several of the scholars that Nettles lists as significant theological influences have written about baptism, including non-Baptists Charles Hodge and John Stott, and Baptists Charles Spurgeon, J. L. Dagg, James Boyce, and Clark Pinnock. These scholars represent different positions concerning the meaning of baptism.

Charles Hodge affirms that it is faith which unites a person to Christ, and it is consequently by faith that a person is justified.[89] He also argues that the sacraments are "real means of grace" which "convey the benefits of [Christ's] redemption to his people,"[90] and claims that their efficacy does not reside in the elements used or the actions themselves but rather in the blessing of Christ and the work of his spirit.[91]

Stott also holds to a sacramental view of baptism. In *The Cross of Christ*, Stott refers to the Lord's Supper and baptism as "sacraments of the gospel" and "sacraments of grace."[92] He claims that our death to sin took place "at our baptism,"[93] and that baptism "unites us with Christ."[94] Though Nettles disagrees with those claims, there are some similarities between Nettles and Stott, both in terms of the theology and the terminology related to baptism. For example, like Nettles, Stott emphasizes salvation by faith alone. He states, "This emphasis is needed to safeguard

---

87. Beasley-Murray, "Baptism and the Sacramental View," 9.
88. Beasley-Murray, "Spirit Is There," 8.
89. Hodge, *Systematic Theology*, 104–5.
90. Hodge, *Systematic Theology*, 499.
91. Hodge, *Systematic Theology*, 500.
92. Stott, *Cross of Christ*, 253.
93. Stott, *Cross of Christ*, 270.
94. Stott, *Romans*, 173.

the glory of Christ as Savior" and to "safeguard the genuineness of faith itself."[95] He refers to baptism as "a public token of their repentance"[96] which "dramatises the central truths of the good news,"[97] and claims that in baptism justification is "outwardly symbolised."[98] He also contends, "Baptism does not by itself secure what it signifies."[99] In some cases, such as Rom 6, "dynamic language" is used which "attributes to the visible sign the blessing of the reality signified."[100] Nettles makes the same argument in his essay on baptism.[101] Though he does not attribute the argument to Stott's influence, he does acknowledge Stott as a theological influence, making it at least possible that, even though they disagree about much related to the meaning of baptism, Stott has influenced Nettles in that area.

Clark Pinnock is another of Nettles's influences that holds a sacramental view of baptism. Pinnock claims, "Baptism is the moment when the Spirit is imparted and when people open themselves to the gifts of the Spirit. . . . The Spirit is normally given with water in response to faith. This makes baptism a sacrament and a means of grace."[102] He continues, "Baptists seldom make the link between water and Spirit-baptism, but see water-baptism as a human response only. A sharp line is often drawn between baptism in water and in Spirit. The former is viewed not as a sacrament but as a response to what God has done in Christ, the true sacrament."[103]

Three of Nettles's other influences are also Baptists who, like Nettles, hold a symbolic view of baptism. Charles Spurgeon is one of those. When preaching on Mark 16:16, which refers to faith and baptism, Spurgeon asserts, "Faith is the one indispensable requisite for salvation."[104] It is connected to certain benefits because it represents them. It is an "outward symbol and representation."[105] This is the same position which Nettles espouses. J. L. Dagg also argued for a symbolic view of baptism. Though

---

95. Stott, *God's Words*, 132–33.
96. Stott, *Message of Acts*, 78.
97. Stott, *Cross of Christ*, 253.
98. Stott, *Basic Christianity*, 136.
99. Stott, *Romans*, 173.
100. Stott, *Romans*, 174.
101. Nettles, "Baptist View," 37.
102. Pinnock, *Flame of Love*, 124.
103. Pinnock, *Flame of Love*, 125.
104. Spurgeon, *Spurgeon on Baptism*, 324.
105. Spurgeon, *Spurgeon on Baptism*, 326.

he did believe that baptism can have an effect on the one baptized,[106] he denied that there is any saving efficacy in the mere rite[107] and instead emphasized baptism as an act of obedience.[108] James Boyce is another of Nettles's influences who argued for a symbolic view of baptism. Like Nettles, Boyce emphasized that salvation is offered upon the condition of repentance and faith only.[109] He believed that such repentance and faith were separate from baptism. In *A Brief Catechism of Bible Doctrine*, Boyce asserts that baptism is a profession for those who have already experienced those things which baptism represents.[110] According to Nettles, Boyce believed that the usefulness of baptism in sanctification had "nothing to do with anything intrinsic to the elements or even the act, but only with the truth remembered and contemplated at the time of [its] enactment."[111] Like Nettles, Boyce disagreed with those who regarded baptism as a "sacrament," "sign," or "seal."[112]

According to Nettles, he has been influenced by scholars from different traditions and with differing points of view concerning the meaning of baptism. Though Nettles does not credit any of them with specifically having influenced his baptismal theology, and it cannot be determined with certainty to what extent any scholar is responsible for Nettles holding the view he does, there are some similarities between his view of baptism and the views of his theological influences. In general, then, and possibly in the area of baptism, Nettles's theology has been influenced more by the people in this section than it has by Beasley-Murray.

Nettles's Use of Other Sources

In his essay "Baptist View," Nettles only cites other sources six times, and all six references are in a short section which demonstrates that the word *baptizo* literally means "immerse." To help make his point he refers to *Strong's Exhaustive Concordance*, *A Greek-English Lexicon*, Chrysostom,

---

106. Dagg, *Manual of Theology*, 72.
107. Dagg, *Manual of Theology*, 72.
108. Dagg, *Manual of Theology*, 71.
109. Boyce, *Brief Catechism of Bible Doctrine*.
110. Boyce, *Brief Catechism of Bible Doctrine*.
111. Nettles, *James Petigru Boyce*, 433.
112. Nettles, *James Petigru Boyce*, 433.

Luther, Calvin, and George Beasley-Murray.[113] The Beasley-Murray reference is to his article "Baptism and the Sacramental View." He quotes Beasley-Murray's claim that "even when [baptizo] became a technical term for baptism, the thought of immersion remains."[114] In the remainder of the essay, in which Nettles argue for a symbolic understanding of baptism, he does not cite any other authors.

He does, however, refer to the Bible often. In the essay, which is sixteen pages, he refers to specific biblical texts ninety times. Though he does at times provide some literary context, in the essay itself, he does not engage in any detailed exegesis of the passages to which he refers. This approach is quite different from that of Beasley-Murray, who provided thorough, detailed exegesis of numerous passages related to baptism. Beasley-Murray also interacts with many other scholars, including both Baptists and non-Baptists. This may be due to the fact that Nettles approaches the issue of baptism as an historian, not as a New Testament scholar or a theologian.

In his section on the meaning of baptism in *The Baptists*, Nettles again makes his case with very few references to other scholars. He refers to three other people, and all three references are in one paragraph in which Nettles provides a brief description of the sacramental resurgence. He cites Stanley Fowler, H. Wheeler Robinson, and George Beasley-Murray as scholars who argued for a sacramental understanding of baptism in the twentieth century. He quotes Beasley-Murray's claim that "New Testament baptism is inseparable from turning to God in faith, on the basis of which God justifies, gives the Spirit, and unites to Christ."[115] Nettles does not interact with any of the arguments made by the people to whom he refers. He merely establishes their position and then responds to it. In his response, which includes his argument for a symbolic view, Nettles does not refer to any other scholars or to any Scripture. That Nettles only refers to Beasley-Murray twice, then, may be explained in part by the fact that Nettles refers to very few people at all in his writing on baptism. He primarily explains his own views, and refers to Scripture far more than to scholars.

---

113. Nettles, "Baptist View," 26.

114. Nettles, "Baptist View," 26.

115. Nettles, *The Baptists*, 311; the statement is made in Beasley-Murray, "Baptism and the Sacramental View."

CONCLUSION

The ways in which Nettles appropriates Beasley-Murray indicate that Nettles considers the work of Beasley-Murray to be significant. Nettles assumes that Beasley-Murray's conclusion regarding the word "baptizo" carries weight, which implies that both he and his readers have confidence in Beasley-Murray's exegesis and historical understanding regarding that word.

In *The Baptist*, Nettles provides Beasley-Murray as one of two representatives of the biblical scholars/theologians who promoted a sacramental understanding of baptism in the sacramental resurgence.[116] The other is H. Wheeler Robinson, who, as discussed in an earlier chapter, is generally considered to be the earliest advocate of the sacramental resurgence. Though a number of Baptists followed Robinson in making a case for a sacramental view of baptism, the only other one with whom Nettles chooses to engage is Beasley-Murray. Although Nettles has not been convinced by Beasley-Murray's argument, he does not ignore it. He considers it to be representative of a movement that "is producing a serious body of literature."[117] In fact, for Nettles, Beasley-Murray's position deserves examination in a work on significant developments in the Baptist tradition and merits a serious response. A symbolic view cannot simply be taken for granted among Baptists. The sacramental view is a serious part of the debate, even among those who do not share that view, and Beasley-Murray remains a significant voice in the debate.

---

116. Nettles cites Fowler as well but appears to place him after the resurgence and not part of it (*The Baptists*, 311).

117. Nettles, *The Baptists*, 311.

5

Timothy George

THIS CHAPTER WILL CONSIDER the impact of George Beasley-Murray's work on Timothy George's argument for his understanding of the meaning of baptism. We will begin with a biographical sketch of George, which will provide some context for his writings on baptism. It will also demonstrate his influence within the Southern Baptist Convention. We will then consider George's understanding of baptism. Next, we will compare George's baptismal thought to Beasley-Murray's baptismal thought. The next section will examine the role of the Reformers in George's work on baptism. Finally, we will consider the role of Beasley-Murray in George's work on baptism.

A BIOGRAPHICAL SKETCH OF TIMOTHY GEORGE

Timothy George was born in Chattanooga, Tennessee in 1950.[1] He attended a small Baptist church in his community. He became a Christian in that church at age 11 and soon after began preaching. Throughout his life, he has been significantly influenced by numerous Baptists in a variety of ways. He has benefitted from being part of Baptist life, including the work of the Home Mission Board which allowed him to serve as a church planter in Boston. He writes, "I was a Baptist before I knew what being

---

1. Biographical information in this paragraph is from Timothy George, "Is Jesus a Baptist?"

a Baptist was all about, because I came to know Jesus Christ through the witness of the people of God called Baptist. And in all my years of study, I have never found a more persuasive or more compelling way of trying to be a faithful, biblical Christian."[2]

George studied at Harvard Divinity School, where he earned two degrees, an MDiv and a ThD. In 1979, he began teaching historical theology at The Southern Baptist Theological Seminary in Louisville, Kentucky.[3] In 1988 George left that seminary to be the founding dean of Beeson Divinity School in Birmingham, Alabama, a position he still holds today. While Beeson is an interdenominational seminary, it produces many Southern Baptist ministers. Between 2001 and 2013, just over 44 percent of its students identified themselves as Southern Baptist,[4] giving George significant influence in the convention through the pastors, missionaries and lay leaders he helps train.

In addition to teaching, George has served a number of local churches. In May 1970, he was ordained at Brainerd Baptist Church in Chattanooga, Tennessee. He then served as pastor of Fellowship Baptist Church (1970–1971) and First Baptist Church of Chelsea, Massachusetts (1972–1975). He served as the associate pastor of Metropolitan Baptist Church in Cambridge, Massachusetts (1975–1979). Since that time, he has served as interim pastor for several churches.[5]

He has also served in a number of positions within the Southern Baptist Convention. He has served on the Southern Baptist Convention Advisory Committee on Calvinism (2012–present), the Southern Baptist Convention Reconciliation Committee (1998), the Southern Baptist Convention Theological Study Committee, co-chair (1992–1994), the Southern Baptist Convention/Roman Catholic Conversations Committee (1996–2003), and served on the Board of Trustees for LifeWay Christian Resources (1993–1998).[6]

George has several personal connections to Beasley-Murray. They first met when George was a doctoral student at Harvard and

2. George, "Is Jesus a Baptist?" 91.//
3. George, "Sacramentality of the Church," 22.//
4. Data obtained from the office of Ministry Leadership Development, Placement and Assessment through an email on April 25, 2013.//
5. Information concerning George's pastoral experience was obtained from his research associate through an email on May 6, 2013.//
6. Information concerning George's denominational involvement was obtained from his research associate through an email on February 15, 2013.

Beasley-Murray was visiting New England.[7] Later, while George was teaching at Southern, Beasley-Murray became a colleague and friend. During that time, Beasley-Murray invited George to sit in on the International Lutheran-Baptist Dialogue, which was one of George's first introductions to ecumenical dialogue. Once at Beeson Divinity School as the founding dean, George invited Beasley-Murray to teach a course on the Gospel of John.

TIMOTHY GEORGE'S VIEW OF BAPTISM

Baptism Involves Both Grace and Faith

Despite the lack of sacramentalism in the Southern Baptist tradition, George himself argues that baptism is more than a mere symbol. For him, it is a meeting of divine grace and human faith. In response to the "attenuated meaning" given to baptism in many Baptist churches, he points instead to the Reformation principles of *sola gratia* and *sola fide* to help show the significance of baptism. Even though many of the Reformers still argued for infant baptism, in the seventeenth century a view of baptism emerged among Baptists which held together these two Reformation emphases in believer baptism, which are relevant to both the subject of baptism and the meaning of baptism.[8] The necessity of faith limits baptism to believers and helps us understand the meaning of baptism. The presence of grace in baptism makes it more than a symbol.

Divine Activity in Baptism

To speak of divine grace in baptism is to speak of the presence and activity of God in baptism. George believes that God is active in the life of the convert during and through the rite of baptism. At times, George affirms this divine activity without specifying what the activity is or how it operates. For instance, in "The Sacramentality of the Church," George claims, "The dominical sacraments of baptism and the Lord's Supper also have a heraldic function in the economy of salvation. They are 'the visible words of God' proclaiming in visual, tactile and olfactory ways what

---

7. A description of George's personal connection to Beasley-Murray was provided by George in a personal email, January 7, 2016.

8. George, "Reformed Doctrine," 246.

the preacher has declared audibly in the exposition of holy scripture."[9] George does not at this point explain what the visible words accomplish, other than the proclamation of truth. However, since proclamation is an activity, and it is the words of God which are being proclaimed, then George's claim allows for the possibility that God is active in the baptismal event, and the event itself is the very means by which God acts. In the same article, George refers to "the *opus operatum* of the sacraments."[10] While he does not describe what is accomplished in baptism, he does affirm that something is accomplished.

In his article, "Faith-based Bathing," George is more specific regarding divine activity in baptism. He claims that the church receives "many wonderful gifts through baptism."[11] Through baptism, God blesses, nourishes, and sanctifies his body.[12] He may also "confirm the faith of the believer."[13] Though George is more specific here than elsewhere in his writings, he is still not precise in explaining exactly what God accomplishes in baptism. He does not indicate what is involved in the blessings, nourishment, or confirmation that God provides. He is clear, however, that God is active in baptism.

Human Faith in Baptism

While George affirms divine activity in the rite of baptism, he rejects an *ex opere operato* understanding of baptism. In his view, baptism involves not only divine activity, but also the human response of faith. Faith in response to the promises of God is necessary for a person to receive the "many wonderful gifts" mentioned above, namely, blessing, nourishing, sanctification and sealing. George claims, "It is the Holy Spirit who imparts faith to the believer and thus makes effective the *opus operatum* of the sacraments."[14] The effectiveness of baptism, then, depends upon both divine grace—including the work of the Holy Spirit—and the faith of the one baptized.

---

9. George, "Sacramentality of the Church," 28.
10. George, "Sacramentality of the Church," 29.
11. George, "Faith-Based Bathing," 62.
12. George, "Faith-Based Bathing," 62.
13. George, "Faith-Based Bathing," 62.
14. George, "Sacramentality of the Church," 29.

In "Faith-based Bathing," George again affirms the necessity of faith in baptism. Faith is necessary, he argues, because of the very nature of baptism. "Baptism," he writes, "is our profession of faith."[15] He puts the same idea a different way, stating, "baptism signifies an earnest pledging of ourselves to God (1 Pet 3:21)."[16] In another place he refers to baptism as "the solemn profession of a redeemed sinner."[17] In other words, baptism is an expression of faith in the promises of God. Understanding baptism in such a way not only affects George's view of the meaning of baptism, it also has implications for understanding the proper subjects of baptism. If baptism is an expression of the faith of the person being baptized, then only those capable of making such a profession of faith should be baptized. After pointing out that in the Bible baptism is closely related to "personal faith and repentance," George concludes, "This is the primary reason why many Christians (and I am among them) think baptism should be administered only to those persons who have repented of their sins and believe the gospel."[18]

George holds that position because he believes that some of the passages in the New Testament which provide the clearest insight into the meaning of baptism conjoin baptism with faith as "integral parts of the same reality."[19] One such passage is Gal 3:27. In his commentary on Galatians, George refers to that verse as "one of the most important references to this important Christian ordinance in all of Paul's writings."[20] According to George, Paul is emphatic that salvation is by grace alone through faith alone. For believers, "baptism is recalled as the concrete moment in their own life in which they for their part confirmed, recognized, and accepted their investing with Christ from above."[21] Again, for George baptism is an expression of faith in the promises of God, promises which are sealed upon the conscience of a person in the rite of baptism.

In his article, "The Reformed Doctrine of Believers' Baptism," George deals extensively with the meeting of divine grace and human faith in baptism. He demonstrates that the Reformation principles of *sola*

---

15. George, "Faith-Based Bathing," 62.
16. George, "Faith-Based Bathing," 62.
17. George, "Foreword," xvii.
18. George, "Faith-Based Bathing," 62.
19. George, "Reformed Doctrine," 246.
20. George, *Galatians*, 275.
21. George, *Galatians*, 277.

gratia and *sola fide* were both associated with baptism by the Reformers. For example, the Anglican catechism asks, "What is required of persons to be baptized?" and answers, "Repentance, whereby they forsake sin, and faith, whereby they steadfastly believe the promises of God made to them in that sacrament."[22] He also points to the First Helvetic Confession, which states, "We therefore by being baptised do confess our faith."[23] Both the catechism and the confession acknowledge a connection between personal faith and baptism.

George claims that although Luther still argued for infant baptism, he saw this connection between faith and baptism more clearly than any other mainline Reformer.[24] In fact, Luther challenged an *ex opere operato* understanding of the sacraments, arguing that "without faith there is no sacrament."[25] Nevertheless, Luther still held that when an infant is baptized, he is changed and cleansed by inpoured faith. A number of scholars have pointed out the apparent inconsistency between Luther's affirmation of the necessity of faith on the one hand, and his defence of infant baptism on the other. As George notes, both Gottschick and von Harnack have critiqued Luther on this point. D. J. Gottschick has questioned the difference between "inpoured faith" and "the various schemes of *gratia infusa* against which Luther inveighed so heavily."[26] Adolf von Harnack states, "In the doctrine of the sacraments Luther abandoned his position as a reformer, and was guided by views that brought confusion into his own system of faith."[27] George agrees with their critique and argues that holding together divine grace and human faith in baptism should lead to the practice of believer baptism. Despite his differences with Luther, however, he appreciates the fact that Luther maintained "the biblical connection between faith and baptism."[28]

---

22. George, "Reformed Doctrine," 247.

23. George, "Reformed Doctrine," 247.

24. George, "Reformed Doctrine," 247.

25. George, "Reformed Doctrine," 47 quoting Luther's *The Holy and Blessed Sacrament of Baptism*.

26. George, "Reformed Doctrine," 247; referencing Gottschick, *Die Lehre Reformation von der Taufe*, 14.

27. George, "Reformed Doctrine," 247; referencing von Harnack, *History of Dogma*, 248.

28. George, "Reformed Doctrine," 248.

The Purpose of Baptism

In George's view, though baptism "models" justification, it does not mediate justification.[29] The reason is that baptism with the Holy Spirit precedes water-baptism. Water-baptism is a confession and "public witness" to Spirit-baptism.[30] George explains, "The objective basis of faith is not the ordinance of baptism but rather that to which baptism bears witness, namely, the whole Christological-soteriological 'event' summarized in the phrase 'God sent his Son' (4:4), together with the gift of the Holy Spirit who through the preaching of the gospel has awakened faith in the elect."[31] George immediately acknowledges that this may raise a question concerning baptism. "With all this in mind, the question naturally arises: If one has already received the gift of the Spirit and has trusted Christ for salvation, then why be baptized with water at all?"[32]

For George, the most basic answer to this question is that Jesus commanded us to be baptized,[33] though he does provide other purposes of baptism. Some of those purposes have been discussed above. God uses baptism to bless, nourish, sanctify, and to seal his promises. Beyond those direct activities of God in the life of the person baptized, baptism has other purposes. One is that we are identified with Christ in our baptism.[34] Indeed, George claims that the most important role of baptism is to identify us with Jesus and with other believers.[35] Drawing from Huldrych Zwingli, he compares baptism to the white cross sewn onto the uniform of a Swiss soldier. That symbol identified the soldier with the Swiss cause. In the same way, baptism marks us as people who identify with the cause of Christ.[36]

One implication of being identified with Christ and his cause is that believers leave behind their old way of life and enter into a new way of life. George makes this claim explicitly and repeatedly in his writing. In "The Reformed Doctrine of Believers' Baptism," he states that the "basic New Testament meaning" of baptism is that it is "the decisive transition

---

29. George, *Galatians*, 278.
30. George, *Galatians*, 278.
31. George, *Galatians*, 278.
32. George, *Galatians*, 278.
33. George, *Galatians*, 279.
34. George, *Galatians*, 279.
35. George, "Faith-Based Bathing," 62.
36. George, "Faith-Based Bathing," 62.

from an old way of human life to a new way."[37] He makes a nearly identical statement in the "Foreword" to *Believer's Baptism*.[38] There he says that in baptism "a specific renunciation is made," meaning, a renunciation of the former way of life.[39] In his commentary on Galatians he makes the same point but puts it differently. There he claims that in the New Testament, baptism always implies a "no" to one's former way of life and a "yes" to Jesus.[40]

In George's view, this new way of life is closely connected to belonging to a new people. As baptism marks our identification with Christ, it also marks our identification with Christ's people. Or put another way, as baptism marks a new way of life, it also marks an entrance into a new community. George claims that the most important role of baptism is to identify us with Jesus and with other believers.[41] The two go together. George argues that for Paul, baptism was a sign not only of personal faith but also of the new community that belongs to Christ.[42] In one of George's clearest statements on this subject, he writes,

> We need to affirm that while baptism is not a magical rite which washes away our sins, it is nonetheless a very important, sacred and serious act of incorporation into the visible community of faith. Not only are we saying something to God in baptism, but God is also saying and doing something for us in baptism. We can do this in a way that respects the integrity of our own theological tradition and yet incorporates the richness of what Paul meant in the New Testament when he talked about being baptized into Christ and putting on Christ as a significant act of Christian identification.[43]

While George associates baptism with being identified with Christ and the church, and holds that it is a "very important" rite,[44] he also maintains that baptism is not necessary for salvation. The reason is that although baptism is a means of grace, God is not bound by the ordinary

---

37. George, "Reformed Doctrine," 243.
38. George, "Foreword," xvii.
39. George, "Foreword," xvii.
40. George, *Galatians*, 276.
41. George, "Faith-Based Bathing," 62.
42. George, *Galatians*, 276.
43. George, "Southern Baptists," 50.
44. George, "Southern Baptists," 50.

means of grace.[45] We have a responsibility to be baptized in obedience to the Lord, but he is free to give grace apart from the act of baptism. George makes this point at length in his essay, "The Sacramentality of the Church." In a section titled, "The Sovereignty of the Holy Spirit," he writes,

> In describing the visible church as "not primary but secondary, functional and instrumental," the BWA statement reflects the conviction, rooted in the Augustinian and Calvinist traditions, that the church and its sacraments never become eminent subjects of causality, that God the Holy Spirit remains sovereign even over the means he has chosen to draw men and women unto himself. Christ neither shares his glory nor gives his lordship to anyone else, not even to the church. The wind of the Spirit blows wherever it pleases (cf., Jn 3.8). This means that the church is the body of Christ, created and continually renewed by the awakening power of the Holy Spirit. It is the Holy Spirit who imparts faith to the believer and thus makes effective the *opus operatum* of the sacraments. The sacraments are thus seals of assurance and may not be dispensed with without spiritual detriment. But while *we* are bound to the sacraments, God is not. By no means should we disparage the external means of grace God has given to the church in its earthly pilgrimage, but neither should we be surprised when by his Spirit God works in ways that go beyond our understanding but a touch less—*etiam extra ecclesiam*![46]

Practical Concerns

In two places, George addresses some practical concerns about the practice of baptism, specifically among Southern Baptists. In his essay, "The Southern Baptists," he discusses five pastoral problems related to baptism that Southern Baptists face.[47] The first is the legacy of Landmarkism, which was discussed in Chapter 3. George does not offer any solution but notes that baptism reception is an increasingly difficult issue for Baptists in an ecumenical age.

---

45. George, "Faith-Based Bathing" 62.
46. George, "Sacramentality of the Church," 29–30.
47. George, "Southern Baptists," 44–51.

The second pastoral problem is the proper age for baptism. Since World War II the average age for baptism in Southern Baptist churches has declined. George states that while Southern Baptists do not practice infant baptism, many do practice "toddler" baptism, which is a break from Baptist tradition and the practice of other Baptists in Europe.

The third pastoral problem is the practice of (re)baptism. In using this term, George is not referring to the baptism of people who come from different traditions, but to the baptism of people who have come to believe that despite having been baptized, they never had a genuine conversion experience. George does not disparage this practice entirely but warns that it might lead to baptism becoming a rite of rededication rather than a rite of initiation into the Christian community.

The fourth pastoral problem is the baptismal rite itself. George believes that Baptists have attenuated the rite of baptism due to an emphasis on the symbolic nature of baptism. He offers several suggestions for overcoming this "liturgical loss." First, Southern Baptists should emphasize the period of catechesis. He would like to see an extended time of instruction before baptism. Second, make baptism once again a profession of faith, ideally including an audible profession in the baptistery. Third, emphasize the Trinitarian nature of baptism. Fourth, practice the laying on of hands in connection with baptism. Fifth, baptize outdoors if possible.

The fifth pastoral problem concerns baptismal theology. George states,

> Southern Baptists and Baptists in general have stressed the negative aspect of sacramentalism. We have stressed that baptism does not wash away sins, that it is "merely" a symbol. We have done this largely in reaction to Roman Catholic and Campbellite sacramental views. But I think we have overdone it. We need to affirm that while baptism is not a magical rite which washes away our sins, it is nonetheless a very important, sacred and serious act of incorporation into the visible community of faith.[48]

He concludes with the assertion that baptism should be more directly related to the church covenant. We should keep in mind the communal implications of baptism, including the new "radical lifestyle" to which the baptized person is called.[49]

---

48. George, "Southern Baptists," 50.
49. George, "Southern Baptists," 51.

George also addresses numerous practical concerns in the foreword of *Believer's Baptism*. There, he offers several suggestions for reforming the baptismal rite.[50] First, baptism should be restored to its place as a central liturgical act and not merely tagged on at the beginning or end of the main service. Second, baptism should include prayer, the reading of Scripture and the personal confession of the one being baptized. Third, if possible, baptism should be done outdoors. Baptism symbolizes the trauma of death and resurrection, and that symbolism is lost when the baptistery is "too neat and convenient."[51] Fourth, baptism should be related to the discipline and covenantal commitments of the congregation. Fifth, Baptist churches must have a proper theology of children. While no one is saved through biological connections, children of believing parents do stand in "a special providential relationship to the people and promises of God."[52]

GEORGE AND ECUMENISM

George's willingness to dissent from the traditional Southern Baptist position may be due in part to George's ecumenical approach to theology. In affirming the ecumenical efforts of some evangelicals, George states, "For too long, ecumenism has been left to Left-leaning Catholics and mainline Protestants."[53] George, however, has been part of an ecumenical "official consultation"[54] known as Evangelicals and Catholics Together.[55] He participated in a symposium that brought together scholars and church leaders among evangelicals, pentecostals, fundamentalists, Roman Catholics, and mainline Protestants. The presentations at the symposium were later published as *Pilgrims on the Sawdust Trail*, which George edited.[56] George's ecumenism is also evident in the fact that the school he leads operates "in an intentionally interdenominational and explicitly evangelical manner."[57] The faculty of Beeson are from a variety of traditions,

50. George, "Foreword," xvii–xviii.
51. George, "Foreword," xvii.
52. George, "Foreword," xviii.
53. George, "Catholics and Evangelicals," 16.
54. Rausch, *Catholics and Evangelicals*, 122–48
55. George, "Evangelicals and Catholics Together," 34–35.
56. George, *Pilgrims on the Sawdust Trail*.
57. "Interdenominational Spirit."

including Baptist, Anglican, Presbyterian, Lutheran, Episcopalian, and American Methodist Episcopalian.[58] George believes that dialogue with other traditions allows us to learn from each other. He states,

> We believe that how we act and relate to one another within the Body of Christ is no less important than the theology we profess and the beliefs we champion. Indeed, they are inextricably linked, for true revival and spiritual awakening will only come in the context of repentance, humility, and forgiveness. We hope for the miracle of dialogue, not a raucous shouting at one another, nor a snide whispering behind each other's backs, but a genuine listening and learning in the context of humane inquiry and disciplined thought.[59]

George has attributed his openness to other traditions in part to Beasley-Murray. He states,

> But my experience at Southern Seminary taught me that one could be deeply committed to the Baptist heritage and also committed to Christian unity throughout the body of Christ. At its best, Southern Seminary has a history of being both evangelical and ecumenical. This was the emphasis of George Beasley-Murray, Carl F. H. Henry, and James Earl Massey, three great teachers of the church who became my friends and mentors—all of whom I first met at Southern Seminary.[60]

GEORGE AND THE REFORMERS

The Reformers are another influence on George's baptismal thought. In the works surveyed for this chapter, George refers to the Reformers 17 times. Of the Reformers, he refers to Luther most (eight times), then Zwingli (seven times), and finally Calvin (two times). The reason for the extensive interaction with the Reformers has to do with George's overall approach to theology. George describes himself as an historical theologian "with a special concern for Reformation theology," who finds his "theological bearings within the Reformed tradition, with a preference for Calvin over Zwingli, but with many good lessons learned from Dr

---

58. biographical information about faculty members found at http://www.beesondivinity.com/facultyandstaff.
59. Dockery and George, "Preface," xiv.
60. "The SBJT Forum Interview," 112.

Martinus of Wittenberg."[61] According to Garrett, "George's more systematic expressions of theology grew out of his expertise in historical theology."[62]

Such an approach to theology is consistent with George's formal training by Harvard professor George Huntston Williams. George acknowledges Williams's influence on his own theology. George writes, "As a participating member of the Harvard community for 53 years, George Williams had an incalculable effect on several generations of students." That George counted himself among those students is evident when he claims that Frank H. Littell, colleague and friend of Williams, "speaks for so many of us: 'On the landscape of my life, George was a major landmark.'"[63]

George Williams was a generalist in church history, but did give special attention to the Reformation period.[64] Williams believed that church history as a discipline "conveys religious insight" and is therefore a valid theological discipline.[65] For Williams, the historian should not be an idle observer of history, including the developments around him.[66] Rather, we study church history in order that we might intervene in history with the necessary insight.[67] In fact, George claims that Williams's greatest contribution was his ability to discern "underlying patterns of meaning" in the past, which can be used to interpret and shape the present.[68]

George has adopted this same approach, especially with regards to the theology of the Reformers. In fact, he claims that biblical Christianity and Reformation theology are "the wellsprings of the evangelical tradition."[69] This belief directly affects how George approaches theological issues. The concluding chapter of *Theology of the Reformers* is titled "The Abiding Validity of Reformation Theology." In it, George claims that "the Reformation has an enduring significance for the church of Jesus Christ."[70] Consequently, "We must ask not only what it meant but also

---

61. George, "Sacramentality of the Church," 22.
62. Garrett, *Baptist Theology*, 697.
63. George, "Keeping Truth Alive," 4–6.
64. George, "Keeping Truth Alive," 4–6.
65. George, "George Huntston Williams," 16.
66. George, "George Huntston Williams," 20.
67. George, "George Huntston Williams," 20–21.
68. George, "George Huntston Williams," 33.
69. Raush, *Catholics and Evangelicals*, 124.
70. George, *Theology of the Reformers*, 309.

what it means. How can the theology of the reformers challenge and correct and inform our own efforts to theologize faithfully on the basis of the Word of God?"[71]

This approach is seen in George's discussion of the Lord's Supper. In "The SBJT Forum: The Lord's Supper," George was one of several scholars who was asked to respond to the question, "What advice would you give to pastors regarding the celebration of the Lord's Supper in our churches?"[72] In only the second paragraph of his response, George refers to the Reformation. After summarizing the different views of Luther and Zwingli, George asserts, "John Calvin forged a middle way between Zwingli's minimalism and Luther's literalism."[73] Nearly a third of his response is spent explaining the views of the Reformers. An additional portion of his response is spent explaining historic Baptist views, including an extended quote by Spurgeon, who, though not a Reformer, is a significant figure in church history.[74]

We see this same methodology in his essay on the priesthood of all believers. Nearly one third of the essay is a section titled "Priesthood of Believers—The Reformation Model."[75] After explaining the teachings of Luther and Calvin, he states of the doctrine of the priesthood of all believers, "It is a precious and irreducible part of our Reformation heritage and our Baptist legacy." His practice of drawing from the Reformers is also on display in an article titled, "What Baptists Can Learn From Calvin," in which George provides five theological principles that Baptists can learn from Calvin.[76]

George takes the same approach to baptism. He explicitly states that his understanding of baptism "is rooted in both the historic Baptist tradition *and the leading principles of Reformation theology*" (italics mine).[77] In *Theology of the Reformers*, he claims that for some traditions which affirm believer baptism, including the Southern Baptist Convention, the meaning of baptism has become attenuated, which he considers to be problematic. George's solution is to encourage such traditions to learn from the Reformers. He writes,

71. George, *Theology of the Reformers*, 309.
72. "The SBJT Forum: The Lord's Supper," 94.
73. "The SBJT Forum: The Lord's Supper," 100.
74. "The SBJT Forum: The Lord's Supper," 101.
75. George, "Priesthood of All Believers" 85–93.
76. George, "What Baptists Can Learn," 19–21.
77. George, "Reformed Doctrine," 243; George, "Foreword," xvi.

> As a corrective to the casual role assigned to baptism in much contemporary church life, we can appropriate two central concerns from the Reformation doctrines of baptism: From the Anabaptists we can learn the intrinsic connection between baptism and repentance and faith; from the mainline reformers (though more from Luther and Calvin that Zwingli) we can learn that in baptism not only do we say something to God and to the Christian community but God also says and does something for us, for baptism is both God's gift and our human response to that gift.[78]

His corrective, then, for what he sees as a fault in Southern Baptist baptismal theology involves going straight to the Reformers.

The influence of Calvin in particular is evident in George's work even when Calvin is not explicitly referenced. His influence is seen both in the similarity of the language they use in reference to baptism and in their understanding of that language. Borrowing from Calvin, George refers to baptism as a sign and seal. Calvin himself defined a sacrament as "an outward sign by which the Lord seals on our consciences the promises of his good will toward us in order to sustain the weakness of our faith."[79] He likens the sacraments to the seals which are attached to government documents. The seal itself is meaningless if the document has nothing written on it. But when the seal is added to an actual writing, it confirms what is written.[80] George shares that understanding of the sacraments.[81] In light of George's admission that he has been significantly influenced by Calvin,[82] these similarities suggest that Calvin has played an important role in George's development of a baptismal theology.

GEORGE'S APPROPRIATION OF THE WORK OF BEASLEY-MURRAY

George's writings that are surveyed in this chapter contain four references to Beasley-Murray. Those four references are found in two of George's works. In this case, however, Beasley-Murray's significance cannot be

---

78. George, *Theology of the Reformers*, 318.
79. Calvin, *Institutes*, 1277.
80. Calvin, *Institutes*, 1280.
81. George, "Sacramentality of the Church," 29.
82. George, "Sacramentality of the Church," 22.

determined simply by the number of times he is cited. Understanding his role in George's work requires a careful examination of each reference.

One of the references is in the article, "The Reformed Doctrine of Believers' Baptism." He cites Beasley-Murray approvingly in his discussion of the discontinuity of the old and new covenants. While many paedobaptists argue for infant baptism on the basis of the continuity of the covenants, Beasley-Murray argued that "the difference between the two administrations is 'cataclysmic' and must be taken into account when thinking about the relationship between circumcision and baptism."[83] George concludes that a failure to recognize the diversity, as well as the continuity, of the covenants leads to a "truncated view of redemptive history."[84] Though he does not say so explicitly, given the context, he also implies that it leads to a wrong understanding of baptism. Here, George draws upon Beasley-Murray in regards to a hermeneutical principle that supports George's argument for believer baptism.

The second work in which George references Beasley-Murray is his commentary on Galatians. In his discussion of Gal 3:27, he refers to Beasley-Murray three times. The ways in which George interacts with Beasley-Murray are varied. The purpose of one reference is to support an exegetical observation. It comes in George's discussion of the phrase "put on." He cites Beasley-Murray in support of his observation that in Rom 13 and Eph 6 the verb for "put on" is an imperative, while in Gal 3 it is an indicative.[85] The purpose of another reference is to support an historical claim, namely, that many early Christians practiced baptism in the nude.[86]

In terms of the ways in which George has appropriated Beasley-Murray's argument concerning the meaning of baptism, the third reference in his commentary on the Gal 3 passage is the most significant. In a footnote, George points out a difference between himself and Beasley-Murray. The fundamental difference is that George believes that conversion precedes baptism, while Beasley-Murray maintains that the biblical norm—though not always the case in modern-day churches—is that conversion and baptism are parts of the same event.

---

83. George, "Reformed Doctrine," 250.
84. George, "Reformed Doctrine," 250.
85. George, *Galatians*, 279.
86. George, *Galatians*, 280.

George argues that water-baptism is a confession and public witness to, and follows, Spirit-baptism. He writes, "For the New Testament believer's baptism with (or 'in' or 'by'; cf. 2 Cor 12:13) the Holy Spirit is antecedent to baptism with water, the latter being a confession and public witness to the former."[87] George appears to again make a distinction between those two events when he points out, "in the opening verse of Gal 3, when Paul reminded the Galatians of the very beginning of their Christian experience, he did not say, 'Were you baptized?' but rather, 'Did you receive the Spirit?'"[88] The same distinction is apparent when he raises the question, "If one has already received the gift of the Spirit and has trusted Christ for salvation, then why be baptized with water at all?"[89] As discussed above, George still maintains that there are reasons for being baptized with water. He denies, however, that one of those reasons is to receive the Holy Spirit.

Beasley-Murray, on the other hand, directly denies that in the New Testament conversion took place before baptism.[90] Even more directly, he claims that in the New Testament "baptism was conversion."[91] One specific passage Beasley-Murray points to is Gal 3:26–27. Commenting on those verses, Beasley-Murray notes, "It is faith which receives Christ in baptism."[92] By responding in faith a person is united to Christ. One way Scripture speaks about this reality is to say that a person puts on Christ. Gal 3:27, for example, uses that language and connects the putting on of Christ to baptism. Beasley-Murray insists that the flow of thought in that passage demands the conclusion that the putting on of Christ takes place in baptism, not before.[93] He also insists that the reception of Christ and the gift of the Spirit are inseparable.[94] He concedes that the Spirit is at work in a person's life before baptism but continues to maintain that baptism is also the time at which the Spirit is given.

---

87. George, *Galatians*, 278.
88. George, *Galatians*, 278.
89. George, *Galatians*, 278.
90. Beasley-Murray, *Baptism in the New Testament*, 277.
91. Beasley-Murray, *Baptism in the New Testament*, 93.
92. Beasley-Murray, "Authority," 64.
93. Beasley-Murray, *Baptism in the New Testament*, 148.
94. Beasley-Murray, "Holy Spirit, Baptism, and the Body of Christ," 179.

In his commentary on Gal 3:27, George brings up this difference with Beasley-Murray and directly critiques Beasley-Murray's position. He states,

> G. R. Beasley-Murray also stresses the indissoluble alliance of faith and baptism arguing that this connection prevented Christianity from evaporating into "an ethereal subjectivism on the one hand and from hardening into a fossilized objectivism on the other" (*Baptism in the New Testament*, 151). While Beasley-Murray offers a helpful corrective to certain minimalist views of baptism, he goes too far in affirming that "baptism is the moment of faith in which the adoption is realized." As R. Fung has noted, this view leads logically to the conclusion that baptism by water is indispensible for incorporation into Christ.[95]

Beasley-Murray, however, denies that that is the only logical conclusion. He argues that while we are obligated to confess our faith in baptism, God is not bound by the sacraments.[96]

By affirming that baptism is more than a symbol and denying that it is coincidental with conversion, George has argued for a position in between those of his own Southern Baptist tradition on the one hand and George Beasley-Murray on the other. He is in agreement with those who have claimed that while there is much to be commended in Beasley-Murray's argument, he has overstated his case.[97]

However, since the time that George's Galatians commentary was published, George's view has become similar to Beasley-Murray's. In a personal email, George writes,

> Over the years, I have come more and more to see the wisdom in George's understanding of baptism. When I published my commentary on Galatians for the New American Commentary, I was still somewhat critical of George's "sacramental" interpretation of the ordinance of initiation. In subsequent years, my own views on the subject have more closely approximated his. I still believe that baptism is primarily *confession of faith*: the obedient answering of faith to the work of grace in the life of the believer. However, I have come to see much more clearly that in baptism not only do we say something to God (and to the watching community), but God also says and does something to/for us.

---

95. George, *Galatians*, 278.
96. Beasley-Murray, "Authority," 69; Beasley-Murray, "Holy Spirit," 30.
97. See Hull, "Baptism in the New Testament," 11.

Perhaps one day I will write a book on baptism to spell out more clearly this line of thought. As for now, I can say simply that the more I read George R. Beasley-Murray, the more he agrees with me, and I with him![98]

CONCLUSION

Others have shaped George's understanding of baptism more than Beasley-Murray has. Nevertheless, George's interaction with Beasley-Murray helps us see the continuing significance of Beasley-Murray's work in the baptismal debate among Baptists. Though George's baptismal theology shares much in common with that of Beasley-Murray, George, at least in his published works, stops short of Beasley-Murray's conclusion that in the New Testament Spirit-baptism and water-baptism coincide. This is no minor disagreement. In fact, it is a main point for both George and Beasley-Murray in their respective understandings of the meaning of baptism. However, it is precisely at this point of disagreement that we see the significance of Beasley-Murray's work. As established earlier in the section on the sacramental resurgence, Beasley-Murray is not the only Baptist scholar to argue that the dominant pattern in the New Testament is that water-baptism and Spirit-baptism coincide. Yet, as is the case with Nettles, when George wants to argue against that view, it is Beasley-Murray that he brings up and disagrees with. It is Beasley-Murray who becomes George's conversation partner on this significant point. This is one way, then, that Beasley-Murray has shaped the debate about a sacramental understanding of baptism. As suggested in George's email correspondence, it is also possible that his future works will indicate a more positive influence of Beasley-Murray on George's thinking about baptism.

98. Timothy George, personal email, January 7, 2016.

6

Thomas Schreiner

THIS CHAPTER WILL CONSIDER the role of George Beasley-Murray's baptismal thought in the work of Thomas Schreiner. We will begin with a biographical sketch of Schreiner, which will provide some context for his writings on baptism. We will then consider Schreiner's understanding of baptism. The next section will examine Schreiner's interaction with Beasley-Murray and will provide some explanation as to why Schreiner appropriates Beasley-Murray the way he does.

A BIOGRAPHICAL SKETCH OF THOMAS SCHREINER

Thomas Schreiner grew up as a Roman Catholic and was converted at the age of 17, mainly through the witness of a girl named Diane who is now his wife.[1] He received his bachelor's degree from Western Oregon University. He then earned both an MDiv and a ThM from Western Conservative Baptist Seminary.[2] In 1983 he earned a PhD in New Testament from Fuller Theological Seminary, where he studied under Donald A. Hagner.[3]

After graduation, Schreiner taught New Testament at Azusa Pacific University. He then taught New Testament at Bethel Theological

---

1. Taylor, "Interview with Tom Schreiner on Baptism."
2. Schreiner, Faculty Profile.
3. Taylor, "Interview with Tom Schreiner on NT Theology."

Seminary for eleven years.[4] Since 1997, he has served as James Buchanan Harrison Professor of New Testament Interpretation—the same position held by Beasley-Murray—and Professor of Biblical Theology at The Southern Baptist Theological Seminary.[5] He also serves as Preaching Pastor of Clifton Baptist Church.[6] In addition to his teaching responsibilities, Schreiner was editor of The Southern Baptist Journal of Theology, 1999–2003.[7] He has also had a prolific writing ministry. He has written or edited 10 books, published 25 articles, published 35 book reviews, and written 16 editorials for The Southern Baptist Journal of Theology.[8]

THOMAS SCHREINER'S VIEW OF BAPTISM

Baptism and Becoming a Christian

Schreiner addresses the issue of baptism in a number of places. He has written commentaries on three of the biblical books that mention baptism—Romans, Galatians and 1 Peter. There are sections on baptism in his books on Paul's theology and on the theology of the New Testament. He contributed a chapter on baptism in Paul's letters to *Believer's Baptism*, a book he co-edited. He has also given an interview on that book, in which he answers questions about baptism.

Schreiner defines baptism using the New Hampshire Confession of 1833: "We believe that Christian Baptism is the immersion in water of a believer, into the name of the Father, and Son, and Holy Ghost; to show forth, in a solemn and beautiful emblem, our faith in the crucified, buried, and risen Saviour, with its effect in our death to sin and resurrection to a new life."[9] Central to Schreiner's understanding of baptism is his belief that throughout the New Testament baptism is closely associated with conversion. He claims that in the New Testament baptism was applied "almost immediately" after a profession of faith.[10] He therefore agrees with Schnackenburg that, for Paul, baptism "is for every man the

---

4. Schreiner, Faculty Profile.
5. Schreiner, Faculty Profile.
6. Taylor, "Interview with Tom Schreiner on Baptism."
7. Taylor, " Interview with Tom Schreiner on NT Theology."
8. Schreiner's full bibliography can be accessed at Schreiner, Faculty Profile.
9. Taylor, "Interview with Tom Schreiner on Baptism."
10. Schreiner, "Baptism in the Epistles," 73.

regular means of becoming a Christian."[11] Schreiner is in agreement with Beasley-Murray's contention that in the New Testament Christians would not have conceived of becoming a Christian without baptism.[12] It was a given for Paul that all converts were baptized at conversion.[13]

That explains why, according to Schreiner, in Eph 4:4–6 Paul assumes that all believers have been baptized.[14] In his commentary on Rom 6, Schreiner argues that since unbaptized Christians were virtually nonexistent in the New Testament, the reference to baptism is a designation for Christians[15] and a reference to conversion.[16] In Schreiner's view, Paul refers to baptism in Rom 6 and Col 2 because that is the simplest and easiest way to recall the readers' conversion.[17] Or, put even more directly, baptism is a reference to conversion.[18]

Consistent with this connection between baptism and conversion, Schreiner places baptism in the larger context of redemptive history. For him, baptism is an initiation into the new age of redemption in fulfillment of the Old Testament era.[19] Commenting on Col 2:12 he says, "Baptism as the initiatory event in the lives of believers represents death to the old way of life and the birth of a new life."[20]

The Symbolism of Baptism

For Schreiner, part of the significance of baptism lies in its imagery. Baptism pictures death and resurrection. Submersion under water kills and therefore is associated with God's wrath in 1 Pet 3:20–21 and Mark 10:38–39.[21] He discusses this imagery in detail in his commentary on 1 Pet 3:21. There, he claims that the flood is a "type" or "pattern" of baptism, as is made clear by the statement, "baptism . . . now saves you," a

---

11. Schreiner, "Baptism in the Epistles," 68.
12. Schreiner, "Baptism in the Epistles," 69
13. Schreiner, *Paul*, 373.
14. Schreiner, "Baptism in the Epistles," 71.
15. Schreiner, *Romans*, 310.
16. Schreiner, *Romans*, 306.
17. Schreiner, "Baptism in the Epistles," 75.
18. Schreiner, *Romans*, 310.
19. Schreiner, "Baptism in the Epistles," 88.
20. Schreiner, "Baptism in the Epistles," 77.
21. Schreiner, "Baptism in the Epistles," 82.

statement that Schreiner finds "surprising."[22] He goes on to explain that the flood waters were an agent of death and that submersion under the water represents death, which Rom 6:3–5 suggests.[23] Put another way, the waters of the flood were "the agent of destruction." So too are the waters of baptism "waters of destruction." Believers, however, are rescued from that death by the resurrection of Jesus.[24] Since Christ has emerged from "the waters of death" through his resurrection, believers are delivered because they are baptized with Christ.[25] In his commentary on Rom 6, Schreiner claims even more explicitly that baptism symbolizes the believer's death and resurrection with Christ. He agrees with Moo that Paul is not emphasizing how we were united to Christ, but that we were united to Christ.[26] He writes, "The emphasis is not on baptism as the means of God's activity, although this is not excluded, but on the occasion of his work. Paul probably refers to baptism because it symbolizes dying and rising with Christ."[27]

According to Schreiner, baptism also symbolizes the washing away of the believer's sin. He mentions this symbolism twice in "Baptism in the Epistles." He claims that baptism pictures the washing a person receives when he enters the body of Christ.[28] He also states that baptism dramatically "represents" the washing away of sins.[29] In both instances, he emphasizes the symbolic quality of baptism.

Baptism and Union with Christ

In Schreiner's view, however, while baptism has a symbolic quality, it is more than a symbol. In fact, a major theme throughout Schreiner's writings on baptism is the connection between baptism and a person's union with Christ. In his commentary on Rom 6, he points out that according to C. E. B. Cranfield, there are four possible ways to interpret the phrase "died to sin": 1) in a forensic sense, meaning we died to sin in God's sight;

22. Schreiner, *1,2 Peter, Jude*, 193.
23. Schreiner, *1,2 Peter, Jude*, 194.
24. Schreiner, *1,2 Peter, Jude*, 194.
25. Schreiner, *1,2 Peter, Jude*, 194.
26. Schreiner, *Romans*, 310.
27. Schreiner, *Romans*, 310.
28. Schreiner, "Baptism in the Epistles," 83.
29. Schreiner, "Baptism in the Epistles," 93.

2) in a sacramental sense, meaning we died with Christ and are raised with Christ; 3) in a moral sense, meaning we mortify sin in our bodies; 4) as meaning we die to sin when we die physically.[30] Schreiner opts for the sacramental view: "we died to sin when we died with Christ in baptism."[31] He argues that the main theme of the passage is not baptism, but union with Christ. However, union with Christ becomes a reality for the believer through baptism.[32] Indeed, to be baptized into Christ is to be united to Christ, the one who brings salvation.[33] He summarizes his interpretation of Rom 6:1–11 by stating, "At baptism (i.e., conversion) the death of Christ becomes ours because we share the benefits of his death by virtue of our incorporation into him."[34]

Schreiner also understands Gal 3:27 to teach that baptism is associated with union with Christ. In his commentary on that verse he argues that at baptism believers are "plunged into" Christ.[35] He also states, "Believers are clothed with Christ since their baptism."[36] In another place, he takes Gal 3:27 to indicate that a believer's "new clothes" become his at baptism.[37] In the very next sentence he states, "At conversion believers have stripped off the old Adam and put on the new." According to his interpretation, then, this verse teaches that all believers are God's sons if they are "united with Christ by baptism."[38] In "Baptism in the Epistles," he claims that Gal 3:27 means that "in baptism believers are united with Christ."[39]

Col 2:12, according to Schreiner, also teaches that union with Christ takes place in baptism. When addressing the issue of whether Paul intends water-baptism to be an analogy for burial and resurrection, Schreiner agrees with Beasley-Murray, and others, in claiming that Paul did intend the analogy. To support the argument, he uses Beasley-Murray's

---

30. Schreiner, *Romans*, 305.

31. Schreiner, *Romans*, 305. It should be noted that at other times Schreiner indicates that he prefers not to use the term "sacramental" due to its implication that baptism itself saves. Schreiner's terminology will be discussed later in this chapter.

32. Schreiner, *Romans*, 306.

33. Schreiner, *Romans*, 307.

34. Schreiner, *Romans*, 310.

35. Schreiner, *Galatians*, 257.

36. Schreiner, *Galatians*, 256.

37. Schreiner, *Paul*, 260.

38. Schreiner, *Galatians*, 256.

39. Schreiner, "Baptism in the Epistles," 91.

exegesis of Col 2:12. Schreiner points out that it could refer to Christ himself, but he agrees with Beasley-Murray that the phrase indicates that believers are buried with Christ in baptism.[40] In "Baptism in the Epistles," he again brings up Col 2:12, and again claims it teaches that a person is both buried and raised with Christ in baptism.[41]

In "Baptism in the Epistles," Schreiner argues that in baptism, we become part of Christ and therefore heirs of the promises made to Abraham.[42] In *Paul*, he claims that baptism is also associated with being immersed in Christ[43] and that believers were clothed with Christ "at baptism."[44] He goes on to state, "In baptism . . . they have been transferred from the first Adam to the second, from the old era of redemptive history to the new."[45] He again refers to Rom 6 and Col 2 to make his point: "Rom 6 also emphasizes that in baptism believers are incorporated into Christ."[46] On Col 2:12 he comments, "Again Paul affirms that believers have been buried together with Christ in baptism."[47]

Baptism and the Forgiveness of Sins

For Schreiner, being united to Christ involves other blessings as well. Consequently, those blessings become the believer's in baptism, since that is the time of union with Christ. One of those blessings is the forgiveness of sins. Schreiner seems to interpret a number of New Testament references to washing as references to the forgiveness which takes place in baptism. In Titus 3:5, according to Schreiner, regeneration and renewal both come from the Spirit. It cannot be the case, then, that the water "magically transforms" people. However, he argues that "it is hard to believe that early believers would not think immediately of water-baptism when reading the words *washing* and *cleansing*."[48] At other times, Schreiner is more direct in his connection between baptism and forgiveness.

---

40. Schreiner, *Romans*, 309.
41. Schreiner, "Baptism in the Epistles," 77.
42. Schreiner, "Baptism in the Epistles," 77.
43. Schreiner, *Paul*, 375.
44. Schreiner, *Paul*, 375.
45. Schreiner, *Paul*, 375.
46. Schreiner, *Paul*, 375.
47. Schreiner, *Paul*, 376.
48. Schreiner, *Paul*, 374.

Discussing 1 Cor 6:11, he claims that Paul is thinking of his readers' "baptismal washing by which they were cleansed of their sins."[49] He also interprets Eph 5:25–27 to mean that forgiveness "belongs to believers at baptism."[50] In the same section, Schreiner states that baptism is "the occasion when sins were cleansed on the basis of Christ's death."[51] In his commentary on 1 Peter he acknowledges that some people might object that a person is forgiven before being baptized. He answers, "But Peter did not attempt here to distinguish between the exact moment when sins were forgiven and baptism. Baptism, like going forward in many Baptist churches today, is portrayed as the time when sins are forgiven and one becomes a believer."[52]

Baptism and the Reception of the Holy Spirit

Another blessing that comes with union with Christ, and therefore is associated with baptism, is the gift of the Holy Spirit. Schreiner consistently holds baptism and the reception of the Spirit together. However, he is inconsistent in precisely how he does so. At one point he claims that Spirit-baptism precedes water-baptism, but the two are still closely connected. He writes, "The Spirit is fundamental in Paul's theology, for *the reception of the Spirit preceded baptism in water*. Still, Paul linked washing with water and with the Spirit. Both occurred at conversion. The two ideas can be conceptually distinguished, but Paul often merges them together in his writings" (italics mine).[53] Here he indicates that while the two are held very closely together in Paul's writings, they do in fact occur at separate times.

Throughout the rest of his work on baptism, however, Schreiner claims that the Spirit is given at the time of baptism. He makes that case in various ways in various works. In *Paul*, he claims that the "washing" in 1 Cor 6:11; Eph 5:26; and Titus 3:5 are references to baptism. He believes the background to these passages is most likely Ezek 36:25–27, in which the sprinkling of clean water is "coterminous" with receiving a new Spirit.[54] The implication is that New Testament water-baptism is coter-

49. Schreiner, *Paul*, 220–21.
50. Schreiner, *New Testament Theology*, 374.
51. Schreiner, *New Testament Theology*, 374.
52. Schreiner, *1,2 Peter, Jude*, 197.
53. Schreiner, *Paul*, 375.
54. Schreiner, *Paul*, 374.

minous with the reception of the Spirit. At other times he moves beyond implications to a direct statement. He argues that 1 Cor 12:13 indicates water-baptism and the reception of the Spirit occur at the same time.[55] To emphasize the inextricable connection between baptism and the reception of the Spirit, Schreiner writes, "If one asked Paul, 'Are we baptized in water or in the Spirit at conversion?' His reply would be, 'Both.'"[56]

He discusses the connection between baptism and the reception of the Spirit again in *New Testament Theology*. There he argues that water-baptism and Spirit-baptism are closely associated in Paul because both occur at the initiation of the Christian life.[57] Though here he only claims that the two are associated and that both occur at the beginning of the Christian life, he goes on to make it clear that they take place at the same time. Commenting on 1 Cor 12:13, he points out that the verse shows the close connection between baptism and the Spirit, "demonstrating that the reception of water-baptism and reception of the Spirit occur *at the same time*" (italics mine).[58]

In "Baptism in the Epistles" Schreiner discusses extensively the connection between water-baptism and Spirit-baptism. Commenting on 1 Cor 12:13, he claims that Jesus baptizes believers with the Holy Spirit at the time of conversion.[59] However, he agrees with Beasley-Murray that Paul did not separate water-baptism from Spirit-baptism, since both are associated with "the transition from the old life to the new."[60] He sees the same connection in Rom 6:3–4, which he believes refers to both water-baptism and Spirit-baptism, since in Paul's writings, the two go together.[61] According to Schreiner, both were part of "the complex of saving events that took place at conversion."[62] Schreiner goes on to state his position explicitly, claiming believers "receive the Spirit when baptized."[63]

As Schreiner is aware, some scholars disagree with him on this point and separate water-baptism and Spirit-baptism to an extent that Schreiner believes is inconsistent with the New Testament. For example,

55. Schreiner, *Paul*, 373.
56. Schreiner, *Paul*, 374.
57. Schreiner, *New Testament Theology*, 479.
58. Schreiner, *New Testament Theology*, 728.
59. Schreiner, "Baptism in the Epistles," 72.
60. Schreiner, "Baptism in the Epistles," 72.
61. Schreiner, "Baptism in the Epistles," 74.
62. Schreiner, "Baptism in the Epistles," 75.
63. Schreiner, "Baptism in the Epistles," 86.

in his review of James D. G. Dunn's *The Theology of Paul the Apostle*, Schreiner argues that Dunn goes too far in separating water-baptism from Spirit-baptism. Schreiner states, "I find it hard to believe that the metaphor of washing did not naturally bring to mind actual water-baptism in Paul's day."[64] He notes that some scholars argue that the washing in 1 Cor 6:11, Eph 5:26, and Titus 3:5 refers to the Spirit and not to baptism. Schreiner maintains that such a position is "a classic case of 'either-or' exegesis where a 'both-and' solution fits better."[65]

Schreiner suggests that the distinction sometimes made between water-baptism and Spirit-baptism results from "modern experiences in which water-baptism often occurs significantly before or after conversion."[66] In Schreiner's view, that modern-day experience was not the New Testament experience. "When we recall that in Paul's day virtually all were baptized immediately after putting their faith in Christ, we grasp that both Spirit-baptism and water-baptism were part and parcel of the same complex of saving events that took place at conversion. . . . In the New Testament, when people were converted, they were baptized with the Spirit and with water, and confessed Jesus as Lord."[67] According to Schreiner, to separate water-baptism and Spirit-baptism is to be unfaithful to Paul's thought and teaching.[68]

Baptism and Initiation Into the Church

For Schreiner, one other implication of baptism being closely associated with conversion is that baptism serves as an initiation not only into Christ, but also into his body, the church. He makes this case in a number of places in his work on baptism. In *Paul*, Schreiner claims that although Paul would not have imagined people who had not received the Spirit being baptized, in Eph 4:5, Paul most likely had water-baptism in mind since that was "invariably the rite of entrance into the new community."[69] Baptism signaled that a person had joined the Christian church.[70] Bap-

---

64. Schreiner, "Theology of Paul the Apostle," 99.
65. Schreiner, *Paul*, 374.
66. Schreiner, "Baptism in the Epistles," 75.
67. Schreiner, "Baptism in the Epistles," 75.
68. Schreiner, *Romans*, 307.
69. Schreiner, *Paul*, 372.
70. Schreiner, *Paul*, 373.

tism, then, is associated with incorporation into the body of Christ and therefore "induction into the people of God."[71]

In *New Testament Theology* he states that baptism was "the initiation rite for the church."[72] As a result, Schreiner argues that the unity of the church is "realized at baptism, where believers are baptized into one body."[73] He claims that in light of the connection between baptism and membership in the church, churches that baptize infants compromise the purity of the church by allowing into membership some who are unregenerate.[74]

Baptism and the Work of Christ

While Schreiner maintains a close connection between baptism and conversion, he also emphasizes that baptism itself contains no saving power. He writes, "Peter did not succumb to a mechanical view of baptism, as if the rite itself contains an inherent saving power. Such a sacramental view was far from his mind."[75] Rather, the "saving power" of baptism is rooted in Jesus' resurrection.[76] He compares Peter's teaching to Heb 10:22, in which "there is no doubt that a cleansed conscience is due to the cross of Christ," and not the result of baptism itself.[77] Although Schreiner does believe baptism involves a commitment to Jesus by the one baptized, the focus is not on the promises that the baptized person makes, but on the death and resurrection of Christ. It is because of what Christ has done that believers can be confident their appeal for a clear conscience will be answered.[78]

Schreiner believes a misunderstanding of this point is the primary flaw of the "sacramental"—or mechanical—view of baptism. To his mind, such a view emphasizes baptism over the death and resurrection of Jesus.

---

71. Schreiner, *Paul*, 373.
72. Schreiner, *New Testament Theology*, 696.
73. Schreiner, *New Testament Theology*, 715.
74. Taylor, "Interview with Tom Schreiner on Baptism."
75. Schreiner, *1,2 Peter, Jude*, 194. Schreiner's use of the term "sacramental" will be discussed below.
76. Schreiner, *1,2 Peter, Jude*, 194.
77. Schreiner, *1,2 Peter, Jude*, 197.
78. Schreiner, *1,2 Peter, Jude*, 197.

The emphasis in Romans, for example, is not on baptism as a *means* of union with Christ, but on baptism as the *occasion* of that union.[79]

Baptism and Faith

Schreiner agrees with Beasley-Murray that some people lay too much stress on the objective nature of salvation, so that they fail to do justice to the subjective element.[80] He points to two passages in 1 Corinthians that, in his view, should caution us against emphasizing baptism over the work of Christ. In 1 Cor 10, he argues, Paul warned that baptism would not inevitably protect the Corinthians from judgment.[81] 1 Cor 1:13–17 rules out the possibility of baptismal regeneration since it indicates that baptism must be understood in light of the gospel and not vice versa.[82] Schreiner also argues against a mechanical view of baptism in his discussion of 1 Pet 3. He notes that some commentators argue that Peter speaks of "flesh" in a moral rather than physical sense, and concludes that Peter's meaning is that baptism does not involve the removal of sin. Schreiner claims that interpretation should be rejected, since elsewhere baptism is associated with the removal of sin.[83] He takes the statement as a rejection of any mechanical understanding of baptism and a reminder that the focus is not on the water itself but on "what is really happening in baptism."[84]

A significant part of what is really happening, according to Schreiner, is that the person baptized is expressing his faith in the work of Christ. He claims that baptismal regeneration was not addressed in the New Testament because the New Testament authors did not separate baptism from faith.[85] In his commentary on Galatians, he again places the emphasis on the faith expressed in baptism and not on the baptism itself. He writes, "Instead of focusing on baptism, however, Paul stresses that faith in Christ is what qualifies one to be a member of God's people."[86]

---

79. Schreiner, *Romans*, 309–10.
80. Schreiner, "Baptism in the Epistles," 81.
81. Schreiner, "Baptism in the Epistles," 81.
82. Schreiner, "Baptism in the Epistles," 92.
83. Schreiner, *1,2 Peter, Jude*, 195.
84. Schreiner, *1,2 Peter, Jude*, 195.
85. Schreiner, "Baptism in the Epistles," 92.
86. Schreiner, *Galatians*, 257.

In *Paul*, he states, "Paul does not view baptism alone as sufficient. All those who are baptized have exercised faith (Gal 3:26)!"[87] He also notes that in Col 2:12, baptism is linked with faith, prohibiting a "mechanical" understanding of baptism.[88] He acknowledges his agreement with Beasley-Murray that baptism is not only an objective event, but involves the appropriation of that event by faith.[89]

Schreiner acknowledges that for many people today the connection between baptism and conversion seems odd, because baptism and faith are so often separated. But that was not the case in the New Testament. In the New Testament era it was "unheard of" to separate baptism from faith in Christ, either by being baptized before faith was present, or by postponing baptism for an extended period of time after faith was present.[90]

Baptism and Sacramental Language

As discussed in the introduction, there is no agreed definition of the term "sacrament." The lack of a clear definition has left room for disagreement, not only concerning the meaning of baptism, but also concerning the language used to talk about baptism.[91] There is some agreement, though, that many Baptists do not prefer the term "sacrament" in reference to baptism. Christopher Ellis claims that the word "sacrament" has often been rejected by Baptists "because of assumptions about what others have been thought to believe about sacraments, rather than because there is no sacramental element in Baptist thinking about baptism."[92] As noted earlier, Timothy George claims that "the majority of Southern Baptists would find the [word] 'sacramental' . . . unhelpful and even deplorable."[93]

Schreiner is among that majority. Though his understanding of baptism is similar to others who use the term "sacrament," Schreiner himself disagrees with the use of that term in reference to baptism. He understands a "sacramental" view of baptism to be a view in which saving

---

87. Schreiner, *Paul*, 375.
88. Schreiner, *Paul*, 376.
89. Schreiner, "Baptism in the Epistles," 91.
90. Schreiner, "Baptism in the Epistles," 93.
91. Cross, "Faith-Baptism," 6.
92. Ellis, "Baptism and the Sacramental Freedom of God," 24.
93. George, "Sacramentality of the Church," 311.

grace is automatically conferred through baptism.[94] He associates a sacramental view with an *ex opere operato* view, in which baptism "saves by virtue of the action itself being performed."[95] This definition of a "sacrament" is evident in his commentary on 1 Pet 3. He states, "Peter did not succumb to a mechanical view of baptism, as if the rite itself contains an inherent saving power. Such a sacramental view was far from his mind."[96] Here he equates a "sacramental" view with a "mechanical" view. In his commentary on Rom 6 he writes, "The reference to baptism has been taken sacramentally, meaning that baptism itself communicates the power to overcome sin."[97] He continues, "A sacramental understanding is flawed because it emphasizes baptism rather than the historic and definitive death and resurrection of Christ."[98] Not everyone who uses the term "sacrament" agrees with Schreiner's definition of that term. Nevertheless, he avoids describing baptism as a sacrament in order to avoid suggesting that baptism is effective apart from faith in the saving work of Christ.

SCHREINER'S APPROPRIATION OF THE WORK OF BEASLEY-MURRAY

Schreiner's Exegetical Approach to Baptism

Of the three Southern Baptist scholars under consideration in this book, Schreiner interacts with Beasley-Murray the most. Of significance, however, is not only the number of references, but also the degree of similarity between Schreiner and Beasley-Murray. Nettles rejects Beasley-Murray's understanding of baptism as idolatry. George agrees with much of Beasley-Murray's view but stops short of agreeing with Beasley-Murray's claim that in the New Testament baptism is the time of conversion. Schreiner's view is the most similar to Beasley-Murray's. Though they disagree on the appropriate language to use, they share the same fundamental understanding of the meaning of baptism.

---

94. Schreiner, "Baptism in the Epistles," 69.
95. Schreiner, "Baptism in the Epistles," 70.
96. Schreiner, *1,2 Peter, Jude*, 194.
97. Schreiner, *Romans*, 309.
98. Schreiner, *Romans*, 310.

For both, baptism is an expression of faith in the death and resurrection of Jesus.[99] Schreiner and Beasley-Murray agree that in the New Testament faith and baptism are held together as part of the same reality,[100] and that consequently baptism was administered immediately after a confession of faith,[101] and was therefore much more closely connected to conversion than is often the case today.[102]

Schreiner is also in agreement with Beasley-Murray that baptism is the point at which a person is united to Christ.[103] Consequently, it is also the point at which a person becomes part of the body of Christ and receives the Holy Spirit. Schreiner and Beasley-Murray also agree that the requirement of faith for baptism precludes an *ex opere operato* understanding of baptism.[104] Salvation remains an act of grace which is received by faith—faith which is expressed in the act of baptism.

Another similarity between Schreiner and Beasley-Murray is that they both acknowledge that the practice of baptism in many modern-day churches is different from baptism in the New Testament. When they describe the meaning of baptism, they are describing baptism as they understand it in the New Testament. Beasley-Murray is explicit about this limitation of his baptismal theology.[105] Throughout Schreiner's work, this limitation is apparent in his repeated use of "in the New Testament" as a qualification of his statements. It is also evident when he contrasts a biblical view of baptism with "modern experience." The remainder of this section will offer some explanation for why Schreiner has appropriated the work of Beasley-Murray in the way, and to the extent, that he has.

The key to understanding Schreiner's appropriation of Beasley-Murray is the recognition that they both approach the subject of baptism as New Testament scholars. Nettles is a church historian. George is an historical theologian. Schreiner, however, shares Beasley-Murray's training and expertise in the field of New Testament scholarship. Schreiner earned his PhD in New Testament from Fuller Seminary, where he studied under New Testament scholar Donald Hagner. Hagner himself

---

99. Beasley-Murray, *Baptism in the New Testament*, 132.
100. Beasley-Murray, "Authority," 66.
101. Beasley-Murray, "Sacraments," 4.
102. Beasley-Murray, *Baptism Today*, 93.
103. Beasley-Murray, *Baptism Today*, 27–36.
104. Beasley-Murray, "Child and the Church," 10.
105. Beasley-Murray, "The Spirit Is There," 8.

emphasized the need for thorough exegesis of the biblical text as preliminary to theological formulations. In his article, "The Bible: God's Gift to the Church of the Twenty-First Century," he claims, "Theological interpretation can ill afford to bypass the hard work of exegesis."[106] He continues,

> There can be correction of bad exegesis by good exegesis. I think of the way in which, by means of better exegesis on both sides, Protestants and Catholics have drawn together in recent decades to a point that could hardly have been believed in a previous era. This is not the result of saying that the same text can mean different things to different people! When I teach Romans these days I use the Anchor Bible Commentary by Joseph Fitzmyer, a Jesuit, just because it provides such good exegesis. We are in large agreement on what Paul meant, and therefore on what the word of God says.[107]

The same emphasis on biblical exegesis is evident in Schreiner's work. Schreiner defines exegesis as "the method by which we ascertain what authors meant when they wrote a particular piece of literature."[108] In his view, the purpose of such exegesis is to gain a worldview based on and informed by the biblical text.[109] Like his mentor Hagner, Schreiner argues that exegesis is a necessary prerequisite to good theological formulations. He states, "Interpreters inevitably move from exegesis to theology, but it is imperative that such theologizing is truly rooted in exegesis."[110] He even expresses his wonder that exegesis is not "the consuming passion of pastors and students."[111] He continues, "Someone has rightly said that every Christian has a systematic theology. The question is this: Is the systematic theology faithful to the biblical text and logically rigorous, or is it contrary to the biblical text and logically in disarray?"[112]

This emphasis on exegesis leads Schreiner to focus much of his work on the study of specific passages of Scripture. In addition to commentaries on books of the Bible and articles about particular texts, Schreiner often interacts with biblical texts throughout his more thematic works.

106. Hagner, "Bible," 21.
107. Hagner, "Bible," 23.
108. Schreiner, *Interpreting the Pauline Epistles*, 7.
109. Schreiner, *Interpreting the Pauline Epistles*, 5.
110. Schreiner, *Interpreting the Pauline Epistles*, 1.
111. Schreiner, *Interpreting the Pauline Epistles*, 4.
112. Schreiner, *Interpreting the Pauline Epistles*, 5.

In *Paul*, he acknowledges that he interacts with other scholars, but then states, "My fundamental aim, however, is to explain the biblical text since students need to see that the primary sources are foundational for doing Pauline theology."[113] This approach is apparent in his essay, "Baptism in the Epistles." The essay is divided into four sections: 1) exegetical comments on the main baptismal texts, 2) comments on the mode of baptism and how baptism relates to washing and sealing, 3) the relationship of baptism to redemptive history, 4) the question of whether baptism should be confined to believers.[114] Schreiner's exegetical approach to theological topics is also seen in his references to Scripture in works, or sections of works, that are not primarily focused on a specific passage. In *Paul*, for example, Schreiner devotes approximately eight pages to baptism. In those eight pages there are 85 references to Scripture. In *New Testament Theology*, he devotes one page to baptism. That one page includes 20 references to Scripture.

As mentioned above, not all of Schreiner's work is devoted to the exegesis of particular passages. He does at times approach the Bible more thematically. He says of such an approach,

> Investigating each book separately, then, opens some fresh windows in doing NT theology, and a thematic approach inevitably omits some of the distinctives uncovered in the book-by-book structure. Nevertheless, I have chosen a thematic approach in this work because a thematic structure also has advantages. The coherence and unity of NT theology are explained more clearly if a NT theology is presented thematically.[115]

However, he adds the qualification that such an approach to New Testament theology should be "truly rooted in biblical theology."[116]

Schreiner's exegetical approach affects which scholars he engages. Of the 32 scholars that Schreiner references at least three times, 25 of those are New Testament scholars. 3 of the non-New Testament scholars have written commentaries with which Schreiner interacts. Many of those citations involve exegetical or interpretative issues related to a specific verse or passage.

---

113. Schreiner, *Paul*, 9.
114. Schreiner, "Baptism in the Epistles," 68.
115. Schreiner, *New Testament Theology*, 10.
116. Schreiner, *New Testament Theology*, 10.

Schreiner's Engagement with Beasley-Murray

Schreiner's exegetical approach to baptism is much like Beasley-Murray's approach. William Hull, in his review of *Baptism in the New Testament*, begins with "a surprising concession: most of the exegesis of the relevant passages is thorough and accurate."[117] He adds, "Even some biblical scholars still tacitly assume that 'Baptism in the New Testament' is nothing more than a correct exegesis of all passages that mention baptism."[118] Though Hull disagrees with some of Beasley-Murray's hermeneutical principles and theological conclusions, his assessment of Beasley-Murray's methodology is noteworthy. Beasley-Murray's pattern throughout *Baptism in the New Testament*, as well as many of his other works on baptism, is to engage in thorough exegesis of specific biblical passages before forming theological conclusions. Given the amount of literature he produced on baptism, along with the attention that literature received when it was published, Beasley-Murray's corpus on baptism is a significant resource for scholars who wish to exegete biblical passages related to baptism.

Schreiner has made extensive use of that resource. In "Baptism in the Epistles," Schreiner cites Beasley-Murray 14 times. In each instance, Schreiner agrees with Beasley-Murray's claims and arguments. Eight of the citations involve exegesis or interpretation of specific passages. For example, Schreiner agrees with Beasley-Murray that "en ho" in Col 2:12 refers to baptism, and therefore teaches that a person is both buried and raised with Christ in baptism.[119] He also agrees with Beasley-Murray that in Col 2:12 faith is indispensable for biblical baptism.[120] He agrees with Beasley-Murray that 1 Cor 1:17 indicates that Paul did not denigrate baptism but taught that baptism must be subordinate to the gospel.[121] He agrees with Beasley-Murray that the imagery in Rom 6 suggests baptism by immersion.[122] He agrees with Beasley-Murray that 1 Cor 6:11; Eph 5:26; and Titus 3:5 all relate to water-baptism. In fact Schreiner does not demonstrate this himself but refers to Beasley-Murray's argument for

---

117. Hull, "Baptism in the New Testament," 4.
118. Hull, "Baptism in the New Testament," 5.
119. Schreiner, "Baptism in the Epistles," 77.
120. Schreiner, "Baptism in the Epistles," 77.
121. Schreiner, "Baptism in the Epistles," 80.
122. Schreiner, "Baptism in the Epistles," 82.

this position.¹²³ He agrees with Beasley-Murray that Eph 5:25 can refer to both the bridal bath in Ezek 16 and to water-baptism.¹²⁴ He agrees with Beasley-Murray that both "regeneration" and "renewal" in Titus 3:5 point to the new life believers are given at conversion.¹²⁵ He agrees with Beasley-Murray that 1 Cor 7:14 cannot be rightly interpreted as a defence of infant baptism, since the context makes clear that the holiness of the child is commensurate with the holiness of the unbelieving spouse.¹²⁶

In the same essay, Schreiner cites Beasley-Murray approvingly in ways not directly related to exegesis or interpretation of a particular passage. For example, he cites Beasley-Murray's claim that in the New Testament Christians would not have conceived of becoming a Christian without baptism.¹²⁷ He agrees with Beasley-Murray that Paul did not separate water-baptism and Spirit-Baptism, and neither should we.¹²⁸ He agrees with Beasley-Murray that some people stress the objective nature of salvation to such an extent that they wrongly eliminate the necessity of subjective faith.¹²⁹ He agrees with Beasley-Murray that the parallels between Israel's experience, and baptism and the Lord's Supper, are meant to demonstrate that those rites do not magically protect Christians from judgments.¹³⁰ He agrees with Beasley-Murray that covenant theology often overemphasizes the continuity between the old covenant and the new covenant.¹³¹ Finally, he agrees with Beasley-Murray that baptism is not only an objective event but involves the appropriation of that event by faith.¹³²

In his commentary on Romans, Schreiner cites Beasley-Murray four times. Each citation has to do with the exegesis or interpretation of a specific passage, and in each instance Schreiner agrees with Beasley-Murray. He cites Beasley-Murray in support of the view that "eis christon" refers to union with Christ. The implication of this interpretation is

---

123. Schreiner, "Baptism in the Epistles," 83.
124. Schreiner, "Baptism in the Epistles," 84.
125. Schreiner, "Baptism in the Epistles," 85.
126. Schreiner, "Baptism in the Epistles," 95.
127. Schreiner, "Baptism in the Epistles," 69.
128. Schreiner, "Baptism in the Epistles," 72.
129. Schreiner, "Baptism in the Epistles," 78.
130. Schreiner, "Baptism in the Epistles," 81.
131. Schreiner, "Baptism in the Epistles," 86.
132. Schreiner, "Baptism in the Epistles," 91.

that those who are baptized are united with Christ.¹³³ He cites in agreement Beasley-Murray's view that in Rom 6 Paul was drawing a parallel between dying with Christ and immersion, and being raised with Christ and emersion.¹³⁴ He agrees with Beasley-Murray's claim that in Col 2 baptism symbolizes the believer's death and resurrection.¹³⁵ Finally, he again agrees with Beasley-Murray's view that in Col 2 "en ho" refers to baptism, and therefore is a reference to dying and being raised with Christ in baptism.¹³⁶

In *Paul*, Schreiner cites Beasley-Murray three times. Each citation has to do with the exegesis or interpretation of a specific passage, and in each instance Schreiner agrees with Beasley-Murray. Commenting on 1 Cor 12:13, Schreiner writes, "we see the close association between baptism and the Spirit, demonstrating that the reception of water-baptism and reception of the Spirit occur at the same time." He references Beasley-Murray in support of that claim.¹³⁷ Commenting on Titus 3:5 and 1 Cor 6:11, he notes that some scholars see an allusion to Ezek 16:8–14 rather than the baptism in Eph 5:26. He argues that there is no need to posit an either-or conclusion and cites Beasley-Murray who agrees.¹³⁸ Finally, once again he argues that Col 2:12 teaches that a person is both buried with Christ and raised with Christ in baptism, and again he cites Beasley-Murray who agrees.¹³⁹

Schreiner's one other reference to Beasley-Murray is in *New Testament Theology*. He notes the controversy concerning whether John the Baptist's baptism was influenced by proselyte baptism. He mentions Beasley-Murray as someone who argues that it was.¹⁴⁰

CONCLUSION

This chapter has demonstrated that Schreiner's baptismal theology has much in common with Beasley-Murray's, and that Schreiner has

---

133. Schreiner, *Romans*, 307.
134. Schreiner, *Romans*, 309.
135. Schreiner, *Romans*, 309.
136. Schreiner, *Romans*, 309.
137. Schreiner, *Paul*, 728.
138. Schreiner, *Paul*, 728.
139. Schreiner, *Paul*, 729.
140. Schreiner, *Paul*, 684.

appropriated Beasley-Murray's work throughout his own. He approvingly cites Beasley-Murray numerous times in references to exegetical and interpretative issues related to specific texts, which are closely tied to theological conclusions. He also approvingly cites some of Beasley-Murray's theological, historical, and hermeneutical claims.

This chapter has also demonstrated that Schreiner approaches the topic in the same way that Beasley-Murray does—as a New Testament scholar who focuses on exegesis. Schreiner focuses on many of the same biblical texts that Beasley-Murray focused on, and is concerned with many of the same exegetical and interpretive issues with which Beasley-Murray was concerned. The fact that Beasley-Murray had already thoroughly exegeted the same set of texts that are in Schreiner's purview provides some explanation as to why Schreiner interacts with Beasley-Murray to the extent that he does. In fact, Schreiner explicitly confirms that his appropriation of Beasley-Murray is owing to their common approach as New Testament scholars. When asked why he has appropriated the work of Beasley-Murray more than Timothy George or Tom Nettles have, and why his conclusions are more similar to Beasley-Murray's than George's or Nettles's are, Schreiner states, "I think the answer is simple. I am in biblical studies and Nettles and George are historians. I think it is natural therefore."[141]

It is not clear to what extent Beasley-Murray is responsible for Schreiner's view of baptism. At a minimum, Schreiner has found in Beasley-Murray support and confirmation of his own conclusions. What is clear is that Schreiner believes that appropriating Beasley-Murray often and approvingly gives additional weight and credibility to his argument. Indeed, the argument he makes has the backing of Beasley-Murray's exegesis and expertise related to baptism. As people read and interact with Schreiner's work on baptism, they are to a significant extent also reading and interacting with Beasley-Murray.

---

141. Thomas Schreiner, personal email, November 22, 2014.

PART 3

George Beasley-Murray
and BUGB Baptists

7

Baptist Union of Great Britain Contextual Factors

THE PREVIOUS SECTION DEMONSTRATED that George Beasley-Murray's work on baptism has influenced the arguments of three Southern Baptist scholars. This section will assess the extent to which Beasley-Murray's work has also influenced the arguments of three BUGB scholars. The present chapter will examine some of the contextual factors related to the baptismal debate among BUGB Baptists. The three subsequent chapters will analyze the role of Beasley-Murray's work in the work of the three specific English Baptist scholars.

THREE FACTORS

This chapter will present three specific contextual factors that should be taken into account when considering the debate about the meaning of baptism among BUGB Baptists. The three factors are the Oxford Movement, the BUGB Baptists' involvement in the ecumenical movement, and the charismatic renewal movement. A fourth factor, and perhaps the most significant—the sacramental resurgence—has already been discussed in chapter 1 and is therefore not examined in this chapter.

As with the Southern Baptist context discussed in chapter 3, there are likely other factors that could be considered in this chapter. However,

I have chosen to limit the focus to four factors—the three in this chapter and the sacramental resurgence in chapter 1—for the same reasons that the number of Southern Baptist contextual factors are limited. First, I consider these three to be highly significant factors. Second, I have attempted to distinguish factors that provide broad context from factors that are particularly prominent in the work of an individual scholar. Third, examining four contextual factors is sufficient to accomplish the purposes of this chapter.

The aims of this chapter are the same as those of the chapter on Southern Baptist contextual factors. The first purpose is to demonstrate that, though Beasley-Murray has significantly shaped the baptismal debate, there are factors other than Beasley-Murray that have affected the debate as well. The second purpose is to demonstrate that Beasley-Murray has helped shaped the debate in various contexts.

THE OXFORD MOVEMENT

The Oxford Movement, also known as the Tractarian Movement and Puseyism, was a nineteenth century movement within the Church of England intended to bring renewal and clarity in the midst of social and ecclesiastical changes. Brown and Nockles claim that the movement "transformed" the Church of England,[1] but as Owen Chadwick points out, the movement has been of "decisive importance to the religion of the English" even beyond the Church of England.[2] According to its leaders, the Oxford Movement began in 1833 with the Church of England facing political and religious threats.[3]

The changes that the church was facing were numerous. One had to do with the development of distinct streams within the Church of England.[4] There were also concerns about the rate of growth of the Church.[5] In addition to those internal developments, there was fear that the government might become hostile to the Church.[6] Turner points out

1. Brown and Nockles, *Oxford Movement*, 1.
2. Chadwick, *Mind of the Oxford Movement*, 11.
3. Ollard, *Short History of the Oxford Movement*, 20; Brown and Nockles, *Oxford Movement*, 1.
4. Church provides an overview of those developments in *Oxford Movement*, 14–16.
5. Chadwick, *Spirit of the Oxford Movement*, 202.
6. Church, *Oxford Movement*, 25.

that many in Parliament had a religious agenda, so that what was at stake, from the point of view of some at least, was "true religion in the established church."[7]

The confluence of these factors created the context for the Oxford Movement. As Church states, "To men interested in religion, the ground seemed confused and treacherous. There was room, and there was a call, for new effort."[8] He argues even more directly that the movement was a revolt against the "profound discontent at the state of religion in England."[9] Three men associated with Oxford—Keble, Froud, and Newman—decided the best way to address the changes was to write about their concerns "as each man felt" and that "each man should write and speak for himself, though working in concert and sympathy with others towards the supreme end."[10]

Between 1833 and 1841 they published ninety tracts,[11] with much attention given to matters related to the doctrine of the church. Edward Pusey, a leader of the Oxford Movement, who became so closely associated with it that it was at times referred to as "Puseyism," provided in list form a summary of what was generally meant by "Puseyism":[12]

1. High thoughts of the two sacraments.

2. High estimate of episcopacy as God's ordinance.

3. High estimate of the visible church and the body wherein we are made and continue to be members of Christ.

4. Regard for ordinances, as directing our devotions and disciplining us, such as daily public prayers, fasts and feasts, etc.

5. Regard for the visible part of devotion, such as the decoration of the house of God, which acts insensibly on the mind.

6. Reverence for and deference to the ancient church, of which our own church is looked upon as the representative to us, and by whose views and doctrines we interpret our own church when her meaning is questioned or doubtful; in a word, reference to the ancient

7. Turner, *John Henry Newman*, 19.
8. Church, *Oxford Movement*, 21.
9. Church, *Oxford Movement*, 11.
10. Church, *Oxford Movement*, 79.
11. Brown and Nockles, *Oxford Movement*, 1.
12. Chadwick, *Mind of the Oxford Movement*, 51, citing Liddon, *Life of Pusey*, ii, 140.

church, instead of the Reformers, as the ultimate expounder of the meaning of our church.

It is noteworthy that the first item on his list is "High thoughts of the two sacraments." As Brown and Nockles point out, one of the religious problems the Tractarians saw was that to many in the church the sacraments were not nearly as important as "the religion of the heart."[13] Indeed, the Tractarians' sacramental view of baptism became one of its most distinctive features. Nettles even refers to the Oxford Movement as the "strong high church sacramentalist movement in the Anglican church in 19th c."[14]

Nettles's assessment is fair. The leaders of the Oxford Movement did argue for a sacramental view of baptism. In fact, Geoffrey Rowell states, "The new life of Baptism and its regenerating power is one of the key themes of the Tractarians."[15] While acknowledging that the Tractarians were criticized for teaching that the sacraments were the source of divine grace and salvation comes to people through the sacraments,[16] Pusey stood his ground and made his case. He believed that justification is imputed through baptism, though faith is necessary to retain that gift.[17] It is through baptism that a person is engrafted into Christ.[18] In Scripture, Pusey argued, regeneration is connected to baptism and is nowhere severed from it.[19] The new life could be subsequently "choked" or "well-nigh extinguished," but baptism remains nevertheless the beginning of life in Christ.[20]

Pusey's fellow Tractarian, John Henry Newman, agreed. Newman once preached a sermon titled, "Regenerating Baptism," in which he claimed, "The ordinary and intelligible reason for the Baptism of infants, is the securing to them remission of sins, and the gifts of the Holy Spirit—Regeneration."[21] He goes on to paraphrase John the Baptist this way: "Christ's baptism shall not be mere water, as mine is. What you see

13. Brown and Nockles, *Oxford Movement*, 1.
14. Nettles, *The Baptists*, 50.
15. Rowell, *Vision Glorious*, 16.
16. Pusey, *Tract Sixty-Seven*, 201.
17. Pusey, *Tract Sixty-Seven*, 204.
18. Pusey, *Tract Sixty-Seven*, 208.
19. Pusey, *Tract Sixty-Seven*, 208.
20. Pusey, *Tract Sixty-Seven*, 211.
21. Newman, *J. H. Newman's Parochial and Plain Sermons*, 273.

of it indeed is water, but that is but the subordinate element of it; for it is water endued with high and supernatural qualities... having a searching and efficacious influence upon the soul itself."[22] Given that he is talking about infants, the implication is that forgiveness, the Holy Spirit, and regeneration are secured through baptism even when the person baptized possesses no faith in Christ. Sheridan Gilley has pointed this out in his book, *Newman And His Age*.[23] He suggests that Newman was aware of objections to the claim that regeneration is possible apart from faith, but dealt with that by insisting that regeneration belonged to the realm of mystery.[24]

Many Baptists in England reacted negatively to the sacramentalism espoused by the leaders of the Oxford Movement. Michael Walker notes that the Baptist response to the Oxford Movement was marked by "a negative attitude of anxiety and distrust."[25] In his view, some Baptists feared that too much emphasis on the sacraments devalued the spiritual nature of religion.[26] According to Walker, "Through the eyes of the nineteenth-century Baptists . . . the precious ground gained by the Protestant Reformation was in danger of being lost to the advancing cause of Catholic Christianity," which included the Oxford Movement.[27]

John Briggs agrees with Walker that many Baptists were opposed to the sacramentalism of the Tractarians, and argues that the Oxford Movement contributed significantly to the context in which English Baptists thought about baptism. Discussing the debate in the early nineteenth century regarding the relationship of baptism to regeneration, Briggs states, "The context for the debate soon became that heightened sacramentalism within the established church which mid-Victorian Baptists perceived to be the fruit of the Oxford Movement, with its accompanying secessions to Rome."[28]

One example of the negative reaction to the sacramentalism of the Oxford Movement is found in an article in *Baptist Magazine* (May 1841), which articulates a view held by at least some Baptists:

---

22. Newman, *J. H. Newman's Parochial and Plain Sermons*, 280.
23. Gilley, *Newman And His Age*, 52.
24. Gilley, *Newman And His Age*, 52.
25. Walker, *Baptists at the Table*, 85.
26. Walker, *Baptists at the Table*, 114.
27. Walker, *Baptists at the Table*, 84.
28. Briggs, *English Baptists*, 46.

> Puseyism does not profess to adopt the religion of the New Testament exclusively, but that religion as interpreted, and developed, and brought out in its full beauty by councils, and fathers, and apostolic traditions. It recognises the episcopally ordained clergy as a chartered corporation claiming, in virtue of official descent from the apostles, a monopoly of spiritual gifts and the sole guidance of the consciences of the laity. It proclaims the efficacy of sacraments as the channels of grace, imparting regeneration and justification when administered by official hands, whatever be the mental or moral qualifications of the authorised administrator. It is a mode of religion which glories in the observance of forms, and in the pomp of ceremonies; which views holiness as consisting not only in the love of God and man, but especially exemplified in fasts, and penances, and veneration rendered to holy times and places, to sacred relics, and departed saints. It is, in fine, a system which would place the reason and conscience, the nation and the government, the spiritual guidance of all adults, and the education of all children, under the authority of a priestly rule.[29]

Among other things, the author is concerned with what might be considered a mechanical view of baptism. He is concerned that baptism is portrayed as efficacious and the means of regeneration regardless of the qualifications of the administrators. From a Baptist perspective, the concern is amplified when we remember that the Tractarians affirmed infant baptism, so that baptism was also considered efficacious even apart from the faith of the person baptized. Rowell claims that theirs was not a "mechanical" view because the realities imparted in baptism must at some point in the future be appropriated by the person baptized.[30] Nevertheless, it is understandable that some would interpret their view as a mechanical understanding of baptism, as they do indeed claim that something happens in baptism apart from faith.

Charles Spurgeon also had concerns about the sacramentalism of the Oxford Movement. According to Nettles, "The rise of Puseyism convinced Spurgeon that the real tendencies of Anglicanism were toward Rome."[31] Indeed, he referred to the Tractarian movement as "a Romanism of the most fascinating form" and "an infidelity of the most cunning

---

29. *Baptist Magazine*, May 1841, 223.
30. Rowell, *Vision Glorious*, 16.
31. Nettles, *The Baptists*, 48.

character."[32] He went on to say, "No longer can we say that Puseyism is Romanism disguised; it has removed the mask, and is now openly and avowedly what it has always been—ritualism, sacramentarianism, priestcraft, Antichrist."[33]

He was particularly critical of the emphasis on outward, physical means of grace, believing that it took away from the spiritual nature of true religion.[34] In an 1866 sermon, "A Testimony Against Puseyite Idolatry," he refers to Puseyites as "idolaters" who focus on "outward symbols."[35] In the context of discussing Anglicanism, he stated, "I do beseech you to remember that you must have a new heart and a right Spirit, and baptism cannot give you these."[36]

Several scholars have argued that the Oxford Movement resulted in Baptists continuing to associate a sacramental view of baptism with an *ex opere operato* view of baptism and therefore rejecting a sacramental view.[37] Anthony Cross and Nigel Wright, two of the scholars under consideration in this book, are among those. Cross claims, "Since the mid-nineteenth-century Baptist understanding of the term 'Sacrament' has been clouded by an antipathy towards the type of sacramentalism characterised by the Oxford Movement, whether in terms of the phrases 'baptismal regeneration' or the ancient formula *ex opere operato* with its connotation of magical efficacy."[38] Nigel Wright agrees. According to Wright, the word "sacrament" is often "associated with more catholic traditions and with the idea that they are effective *ex opere operato*. . . . So, baptism brings regeneration of itself."[39]

Cross has argued that over time the influence of the Oxford Movement has gradually decreased.[40] Nevertheless, both he and Wright are aware of its legacy. This background may partially explain why the BUGB Baptist scholars considered in this project emphasize, as we shall

32. Spurgeon, *Sword and the Trowel*, 322.
33. Spurgeon, *Sword and the Trowel*, 340.
34. Spurgeon, *Metropolitan Tabernacle Pulpit*, 1865, 553–64.
35. Spurgeon, *Metropolitan Tabernacle Pulpit*, 1866, 331.
36. Spurgeon, *Sermons of the Rev. C. H. Spurgeon*, 27.
37. David Wright, though focused on paedobaptists, suggests that the negative reaction to the sacramentalism of the Oxford Movement extended beyond the Church of England, *What Has Infant Baptist Done to Baptism?*, 86–88.
38. Cross, "Faith-Baptism," 24.
39. Wright, *Free Church*, 95.
40. Cross, "Baptists and Baptism," 105.

see, that the sacramental view of baptism they are arguing for is not *ex opere operato*, and that the outward form of baptism apart from faith and the work of the Spirit is not efficacious. When leaders in the Church of England had argued for a sacramental view in the past, many English Baptists identified such a view with an *ex opere operato* view. When English Baptist scholars argued for a sacramental view during the twentieth century sacramental resurgence, they too were criticized for promoting an *ex opere operato* view. It is understandable, then, that the British scholars considered in this project are careful to distinguish their sacramental views from an *ex opere operato* view.

THE ECUMENICAL MOVEMENT

A second contextual factor is the ecumenical movement. To some extent, the ecumenical spirit has been around for centuries,[41] but by the end of the nineteenth century, the principle of ecumenism had led to a move toward ecumenical activity.[42] This trend continued and saw significant developments in the twentieth century. Davies considers ecumenism to be the distinctive feature of the twentieth century for the church.[43] David Thompson notes that the twentieth century has been called "the ecumenical century."[44]

Cross has demonstrated that many Baptists have been leaders in the ecumenical movement.[45] He notes that "Baptists have always been at the very heart of ecumenical life in Britain."[46] Many of them have also been leaders within the Baptist Union, which indicates that they "cannot be assigned to a marginal position within the denomination nor accused of sitting lightly to Baptist principles."[47] Morris West has made the same observation. He writes, "It is one of the continued ironies of British church life that Baptists, who on the whole are judged by most of the media to be extremely slow and backward ecumenically, have supplied a number of the leading officers within the organized ecumenical movement, par-

---

41. Gros, McManus, and Riggs, *Introduction to Ecumenism*, 26; McNeill, "Ecumenical Idea," 30; Calvin, *Institutes*, 13–20; Luther, *Large Catechism*, 61.
42. Brandreth, "Approaches of the Churches."
43. Davies, *Worship and Theology in England*, 5.
44. Thompson, "Ecumenism," 50.
45. Cross, "Service to the Ecumenical Movement," 107–22.
46. Cross, "Service to the Ecumenical Movement," 107.
47. Cross, "Service to the Ecumenical Movement," 107.

ticularly in the British Council of Churches and the Free Church Federal Council."[48] As we will see throughout this section, and in a more focused way at the end of the section, Baptists' involvement in the ecumenical movement became a factor in Baptist thinking about baptism.

There have been distinct strands within the ecumenical movement, and those strands have often overlapped, both in time and in focus. A tidy, chronological presentation of the developments, then, is not feasible. Instead, this section provides a general overview of some of the major individual strands, with particular attention given to those developments that are relevant to the baptismal debate.

Early Ecumenical Participation

The late nineteenth century saw the birth of the Free Church Movement, which had significant Baptist involvement from the beginning.[49] One of those leaders was J. H. Shakespeare, General Secretary of the BUGB from 1898 to 1924.[50] Among other pursuits, Shakespeare advocated for the Free Churches moving toward union with the Church of England.[51] The conversations about reunion raised questions about the nature of baptism.[52] What Shepherd calls "the Romeward tendencies" of some within the Church of England was regarded with "horror" by some in the Free Church,[53] and in the end, there was no union.[54]

The Free Church Movement eventually led to the Federal Council of the Evangelical Free Churches of England. In 1918, the Baptist Union approved the Declaratory Statement of Common Faith and Practice for the projected Council.[55] The Statement included a section on the sacraments, which it calls "signs and seals of [Christ's] gospel." It also states, "They confirm the promises and gifts of salvation, and, when rightly used by believers with faith and prayer, are, through the operation of the Holy

---

48. West, *To Be a Pilgrim*, 128.
49. Cross, "Service to the Ecumenical Movement," 108.
50. Shepherd, *Making of a Modern Denomination*, 94.
51. Shepherd, *Making of a Modern Denomination*, 111.
52. Shepherd, *Making of a Modern Denomination*, 124.
53. Shepherd, *Making of a Modern Denomination*, 110.
54. Shepherd, *Making of a Modern Denomination*, 126.
55. Payne, *Baptist Union*, 275.

Spirit, true means of grace."[56] Though the statement does not go into detail about what it means by "means of grace," the wording does imply that those who agreed with the statement understood baptism to be more than a symbol. From the early twentieth century, then, there was a connection between Baptist ecumenism and a sacramental view of baptism.

The Formation of the Baptist World Alliance

One of the first major ecumenical developments in the twentieth century was the creation of the Baptist World Alliance. The first Baptist World Congress met in 1905 in London. The meeting was made possible in large part through the efforts of the Baptist Union of Great Britain, which has remained an active member in the BWA ever since.[57]

Though the BWA comprises only Baptist bodies, it has been open to cooperating with other Churches,[58] and has participated in formal dialogues that at times have addressed the theology of baptism. The report on the dialogue with Lutherans, for example, calls the issue of infant baptism the dialogue's "most crucial and controversial subject."[59] Though disagreements remained concerning the meaning of baptism, the participants concluded, "Our meetings showed that we have much to learn from each other. Our differences constitute a mutual challenge to search for greater clarity in our praxis, convictions and traditions."[60] After Vatican II, Baptists began to have bilateral conversations with the Roman Catholic Church. In the 1980s they had a series of official international conversations, which produced a joint document entitled, "Summons to Witness to Christ in Today's World." In the section titled "Areas needing continued exploration," they address baptism. Part of that section reads, "The heart of the problem to be addressed here seems to be the nature of faith and the nature of the sacraments (called 'ordinances' by most Baptists), which raise a number of questions Baptists and Catholics must deal with together."[61] The report on the dialogue with the Anglican Church states, "In any conversations between Anglicans and Baptists the ques-

---

56. Payne, *Baptist Union*, 276.
57. Briggs, "From 1905 to the End of the First World War," 20.
58. Harmon, *Ecumenism Means You, Too*, 33.
59. Baptist-Lutheran Joint Commission, *Baptists and Lutherans*, 14.
60. Baptist-Lutheran Joint Commission, *Baptists and Lutherans*, 21.
61. Gros, Meyer, Rusch, *Growth in Agreement II*, 384.

tion of baptism will present something of an impasse,"[62] and then goes on to discuss the differences in their theology, the role of confirmation, and the possibility of open-membership.

Edinburgh (1910) and Faith and Order

A second event that had monumental importance for the ecumenical movement was the World Missionary Conference in Edinburgh (1910), which is considered the beginning of the ecumenical movement.[63] One important feature of the Edinburgh Conference is that it did not deal with matters of faith and order. During the conference, Bishop Charles Brent recognized the wisdom of such a decision for the purposes of Edinburgh but also publicly declared that at some point, differences must be addressed with a view to removing them.[64] Brent took it upon himself to take a lead role in that program, which eventually led to the World Conference on Faith and Order.[65] Numerous British Baptists have been involved in Faith and Order since that time, including J. E. Roberts, W. T. Whitley, M. E. Aubrey, C. T. Le Quesne, Gilbert Laws, J. H. Rushbrooke, and Hugh Martin.[66]

The Faith and Order Conference, with 108 churches represented, met in Lausanne in 1927. According to Thompson, the reports on "The church," "The ministry," and "The sacraments" became central.[67] The churches' responses to the Lausanne reports were reviewed and published as *Convictions* in 1934. The official response from the Baptist Union of Great Britain to the report on the sacraments reads, "We prefer to speak of 'ordinances' rather than of 'sacraments,' but to these matters also we are willing to give careful thought. We could emphasize again our insistence on faith in the recipient as a condition of the effectiveness of the Sacraments."[68]

---

62. *Conversations Around the World, 2000-2005*, 44.
63. Thompson, "Ecumenism," 50.
64. Latourette, "Ecumencial Bearings," 360-61.
65. Tatlow, "World Conference on Faith and Order," 407-8.
66. Cross, "Service to the Ecumenical Movement," 112.
67. Thompson, "Ecumenism," 57.
68. Hodgson, *Convictions*, 63.

For the purposes of this book, the most relevant contribution of Faith and Order is the document it produced in 1982 called "Baptism, Eucharist, and Ministry." In the commentary, BEM states,

> The inability of churches mutually to recognise their various practices of baptism as sharing in the one baptism, and their actual dividedness in spite of mutual baptism recognition, have given dramatic visibility to the broken witness of the Church.... The need to recover baptismal unity is at the heart of the ecumenical task as it is central for the realization of genuine partnership within the Christian communities.[69]

In an attempt to recover that unity, BEM sets forth a number of propositions about baptism, including the following:[70]

- "Baptism is the sign of new life through Jesus Christ. It unites the one baptised with Christ and with his people."
- "The baptism which makes Christians partakers of the mystery of Christ's death and resurrection implies confession of sin and conversion of heart."
- "The Holy Spirit is at work in the lives of people before, in and after their baptism."
- "Through baptism, Christians are brought into union with Christ, with each other and with the church of every time and place."
- "Baptism initiates the reality of the new life given in the midst of the present world."
- "Baptism is both God's gift and our human response to that gift.... The necessity of faith for the reception of the salvation embodied and set forth in baptism is acknowledged by all churches."
- Baptism of believers is "the most clearly attested pattern of baptism in the New Testament documents."
- Confession of faith is necessary; for believers, at time of baptism; for infants, at a later time.
- "Any practice which might be interpreted as 're-baptism' must be avoided."

---

69. "Baptism, Eucharist and Ministry," 3.
70. "Baptism, Eucharist and Ministry," 204.

The document is decidedly sacramental. It affirms that God is at work in baptism, including infant baptism, to unite the baptized person to Christ. Though it affirms the necessity of faith for salvation, it also allows, in the case of infants, for that faith to be separated from baptism. The result is that baptism is considered efficacious even without faith being present at the time of baptism.

The official responses to BEM were mixed. Among those who had some concerns about BEM were the Baptists. For some Baptists, the suggestion that infant baptism and believer baptism are "equivalent alternatives" did not do justice to the biblical witness to the practice of believer baptism, and leads to "theological difficulties" by concluding that there is one baptism in two forms.[71] The Baptist Union of Great Britain expressed appreciation for the emphasis on the necessity of faith and agreed that the concept of equivalent alternatives provides the best hope for making progress toward mutual recognition.[72] They also, however, expressed serious reservations about the meaning of baptism presented in the document. Specifically, they took issue with the wording that baptism "is," "gives," "initiates," "unites," and "effects." This could be read to mean that the actual performance itself achieves things that should only be attributed to God. "The language is at best hyperbole and at worst objectionable."[73] They expressed their general unease with the document by writing,

> What understanding of visible unity is here intended? What measure and kind of basic agreement is here required? Part of the felt difficulty with the total presentation of both baptism and eucharist is a sense that these sacraments are being filled with an exclusive theological weight which is more properly attributed to the deeper realities of which they are the visible signs and to which they bear witness, and that it is upon these deeper and more pervasive realities that unity is properly founded. This in turn reflects a widespread unease that the model of visible unity assumed and the nature of consensus sought make inadequate allowances for a diversity which is arguably compatible with living in communion one with another.[74]

---

71. "Baptism, Eucharist and Ministry, 1982–1990," 46.
72. Thurian, *Churches Respond to BEM*, 70, 71.
73. Thurian, *Churches Respond to BEM*, 70.
74. Thurian, *Churches Respond to BEM*, 77.

Because of the language used in BEM, it opens itself up to this type of criticism. More instrumental language emphasizing that God works through baptism may have led to more consensus. Nevertheless, BEM gave various traditions a common document to consider and provided the opportunity for increased debate about the meaning of baptism.

The Formation of the World Council of Churches

In 1936, both Faith and Order and Life and Work agreed to form a committee to consider a closer relationship. The committee met in London in 1937 and proposed a World Council of Churches. It was approved at the respective world conferences that same year.[75] The first assembly of the World Council of Churches was in Amsterdam in 1948. 147 Churches in 44 countries were represented by 351 delegates.[76] From early on, BUGB Baptists have held leadership roles in the WCC, including PW Evans, Ernest Brown, Ernest Payne, and Victor Hayward.[77] George Beasley-Murray was part of the Faith and Order Commission in 1960 and the Faith and Order Consultation in 1979.[78]

Local Ecumenical Partnerships

Local Ecumenical Partnerships, which began in the 1960s, are partnerships between churches from different denominations. They practice both infant baptism and believer baptism and are served by ministers in one or the other denomination.[79] Partnerships handle the baptismal issue in different ways. Some allow (re)baptism, but the person who desires it is officially moved to the Baptist roll.[80] Others will not practice (re)baptism. Still some offer the renewal of baptismal vows through immersion.[81] Baptists have been among the leaders in these partnerships. Cross states, "It should also not be overlooked that the General Superintendents represent the BU in the Regional Sponsoring Bodies which oversee all LEPs,

---

75. Visser't Hooft, *Genesis and Formation*, 40.
76. Visser't Hooft, "Genesis of the World Council of Churches," 709.
77. Cross, "Service to the Ecumenical Movement," 113.
78. Cross, "Service to the Ecumenical Movement," 114.
79. Cross, *Baptism and the Baptists*, 290.
80. Cross, *Baptism and the Baptists*, 296.
81. Cross, *Baptism and the Baptists*, 297.

though some are now overseen by the local Churches Together, and there are a great many Baptists, particularly at local and regional levels, who have been and are involved in formal LEPs and informal fellowship and mission with other denominations."[82]

Ecumenical Involvement and Baptism

John H. Y. Briggs noted that ecumenical involvement, specifically missionary partnerships, played a role in Christians from different traditions not wanting to remain separated.[83] Participation in the ecumenical movement, then, led Baptists to consider their differences with other traditions for the purpose of cooperating more closely and potentially even entering into more formal union. For Baptists associated with the Baptist Union of Great Britain the issue of baptism, perhaps more than any other doctrine, became a focus of Baptist thinking.[84]

Alec Gilmore has pointed out that baptismal reform was necessary to move closer to union with other churches, but such reform required ecumenical dialogue, since each separated tradition only has a partial understanding of the truth.[85] Beasley-Murray agreed. He claimed that on the part of Baptists, they must be willing to lay aside their "confessional pride" and be willing to listen to and learn from others who have valid insights into the meaning of baptism. On the part of paedobaptists, they must be willing to listen to and learn from Baptists.[86] Beasley-Murray makes a direct connection between the ecumenical movement and a sacramental understanding of baptism. In his view, the move toward a sacramental understanding of baptism in Europe is due "partly to a fresh examination of the Scriptures on baptism and partly to participation in the ecumenical discussion," which has included a "willingness to evaluate afresh all confessional teaching."[87]

Anthony Cross agrees. He considers the ecumenical movement to be "the major influence on the development of the Baptist theology

---

82. Cross, "Service to the Ecumenical Movement," 117.
83. Briggs, *Pulpit and People*, 16.
84. Briggs, *Pulpit and People*, 151.
85. Gilmore, *Pattern of the Church*, 157–58.
86. Beasley-Murray, *Baptism Today*, 112.
87. Beasley-Murray, *Baptism Today*, 15.

of baptism."[88] He claims, "The most significant and far-reaching factor affecting Baptist baptismal theology has been *the ecumenical context in which it has taken place* and the gradual lessening of the influence of the Oxford Movement." (italics mine).[89] In his book, *Baptism and the Baptists: Theology and Practice in Twentieth-Century Britain*, Cross weaves ecumenical developments into his overview of baptismal theology in the twentieth century. For example, he devotes 55 pages to ecumenical developments from 1900 to 1937 before he takes up the theology of baptism during that period.

Cross asserts that the ecumenical movement in the early twentieth century meant that many principles held so dear for generations, or so it seemed, came under the theological microscope, and established practices were increasingly challenged from within and from without.[90] He suggests that such ecumenical dialogue has affected many Baptists' thinking about the subjects of baptism, which is connected to the meaning of baptism. He claims that the debate has shifted from an either-or argument about believer baptism or infant baptism, to a discussion of the broader idea of Christian initiation.[91]

Southern Baptists and Ecumenism

One of the purposes of this chapter is to demonstrate that the Southern Baptist and BUGB contexts are different. A brief summary of Southern Baptists' involvement in the ecumenical movement is therefore needed. The Southern Baptist Convention has generally not joined these ecumenical movements. In addition to ecclesiological factors, such as the freedom of local churches,[92] there are a number of reasons why the SBC has not participated. Stanley Grenz has offered two reasons: 1) the SBC did not have a history of trans-denominational controversy and cooperation; 2) the SBC had already succeeded as a single denomination.[93] H. Leon McBeth adds four additional reasons: 1) Historically the SBC had been a regional denomination (though that

---

88. Cross, "Pneumatological Key," 152.
89. Cross, "Baptists and Baptism," 105.
90. Cross, "Pneumatological Key," 151.
91. Cross, *Baptism and the Baptists*, 320.
92. Cavert, *Church Cooperation*, 17.
93. Grenz, "Baptist and Evangelical," 65–66.

has now changed); 2) the SBC lacked the time to focus on ecumenism due to the attention given to its many programs; 3) the SBC was uneasy about joining with those who have a different doctrine of the church; 4) there were theological differences, especially concerning separation of church and state.[94]

One exception to the SBC's independence is its membership in the BWA. In 2004, however, the SBC voted to withdraw its membership from the BWA, alleging the BWA had moved toward theological liberalism, such as implicit support of homosexuality, and denial of the inerrancy or even infallibility of Scripture.[95] The SBC had recently worked through serious internal debates about these issues and it is understandable that it would not want to cooperate with a body that it felt supported views it had just worked to rid itself of.

Suggesting the self-sufficiency of the SBC, Paige Patterson cautioned against interpreting the SBC's action as "abdicating our position in the world," noting that the International Mission Board "will continue its ministry in far more nations than are touched in any way by the BWA." He also pointed out that LifeWay Christian Resources provides material to Baptists around the world, while all six SBC seminaries are involved in mission work with countries overseas.[96] In response to the move by the SBC, the BWA created a new category for individual membership to accommodate those Southern Baptists who wished to remain involved and contribute to the work of the BWA. Timothy George, whose baptismal theology was considered in chapter 4, is one of those who holds an individual membership.[97]

THE CHARISMATIC MOVEMENT

A third contextual factor is the charismatic renewal movement, which developed out of the Pentecostal movement. Stanley Burgess and Gary McGee argue that the Pentecostal movement can be traced to five theological developments.[98] The first is the Wesleyan notion that sanctification is a distinct second work of grace that follows justification. The

---

94. McBeth, "Baptist and Evangelical," 73–75.
95. Miller, "SBC Severs Ties."
96. Miller, "SBC Severs Ties."
97. Harmon, personal email, July 22, 2010.
98. Burgess and McGee, *Dictionary*, 2.

second is the Charles Finney "higher-life" teaching that subsequent to conversion the Spirit empowers believers for witness. The third is emergence of premillenialism. The fourth is the emphasis of the faith healing movement on miracles leading to physical wellbeing. The fifth is the restorationist emphasis on the vitality and miracles of the New Testament church.

With this background, the Pentecostal movement was born in the early 1900s out of a number of separate revivals.[99] Shortly after, as word about the revivals spread, there were Pentecostal revivals in several parts of the world, including England.[100] In the early 1900s A. A. Boddy organized the Sunderland Conventions, which Donald Gee contends "must occupy the supreme place in importance" in the early Pentecostal movement in Britain.[101] A number of future leaders in Pentecostal denominations were at the conventions.[102]

The charismatic movement, with roots in the Pentecostal movement, developed from a "desire for spiritual renewal in the historic and affluent mainline churches," which included an interest in spiritual gifts.[103] "The charismatic renewal, therefore, represents a transdenominational movement of Christians (both independent and denominational) who emphasise a 'life in the Spirit' and the importance of exercising extraordinary gifts of the Spirit."[104]

According to P. D. Hocken, the charismatic renewal in Europe "had its precursors in those Pentecostal pioneers who never left their churches of origin, including Alexander Boddy and Cecil Polhill in England."[105] In the 1960s it became a "conscious movement," primarily due to news from America of the charismatic "outbreak" among Episcopalians and Philip Hughes's description of his visit to California.[106] In Britain the movement

---

99. For a history of the Azusa Street revival that began in 1906 in Los Angeles, see Synan, *Holiness-Pentecostal Tradition*.

100. Robeck and Yong, *Cambridge Companion*, 75; Burgess and McGee, *Dictionary*, 3.

101. Gee, *Wind and Flame*, 37.

102. Kay, *Pentecostals In Britain*, 13.

103. Burgess and McGee, *Dictionary*, 3.

104. Burgess and McGee, *Dictionary*, 4.

105. Burgess and McGee, *Dictionary*, 144; see also, Robeck, and Yong, *Cambridge Companion*, 93–95; Synan, *Holiness-Pentecostal Tradition*, 131.

106. Burgess and McGee, *Dictionary*, 145.

grew steadily in the 1960s for a variety of reasons.[107] In 1964 Michael Harper established Fountain Trust as a service agency for the movement, which included a bimonthly magazine, *Renewal*.[108] Britain also had access to relevant American literature, such as David Wilkerson's *Cross and the Switchblade*. Another factor was the tours by charismatics such as Jean Stone and Dennis Bennett. Nigel Wright argues that the charismatic renewal movement made inroads into the mainstream church in England in the mid-1960s.[109] In his view, the movement has merged with the rest of the church and has become less "an entity in itself and more a seasoning and a dimension in the totality of the Church's life."[110]

One factor in the charismatic movement's continued impact is the influence of John Wimber. According to John Gunstone, "The influence of the Vineyard Christian Fellowship on hundreds and perhaps thousands of ordinary English Christians is immeasurable."[111] Nigel Wright agrees: "It is beyond dispute that Wimber's influence in Great Britain has been considerable. . . . In the early phases of the ministry, from 1981 onward, he was imparting decisively new influences into the contemporary scene."[112]

Theologically the charismatic movement emphasized the work of the Spirit. Indeed, Tom Smail points out that at times "center stage is held not by the incarnate, crucified, and risen Lord, but by the Spirit and the dramatic manifestations of His triumphant power."[113] The focus on the Spirit has the potential to intersect with the theology of baptism, which is the focus of this study. Those who hold to a sacramental view of baptism often argue that the Spirit is given in baptism, which is, or at least should be according to the biblical norm, the time of conversion. Paul Fiddes has made this connection between the charismatic movement and Baptists' thinking about baptism. He claims that for Baptists, the charismatic emphasis on baptism in the Spirit should not be thought of apart from baptism in water.[114] In Fiddes's view Baptists should respond by

---

107. Burgess and McGee, *Dictionary*, 145.
108. Burgess and McGee, *Dictionary*, 145.
109. Wright, "Pilgrimage in Renewal," 24; Wright, *Radical Kingdom*, 12, 47.
110. Wright, "Pilgrimage in Renewal," 31.
111. Gunstone, *Signs and Wonders*, 64.
112. Wright, "Theology and Methodology," 71.
113. Smail, Walker, Wright, *Love of Power*, 20.
114. Fiddes, *Charismatic Renewal*, 30.

emphasizing that a person receives the Holy Spirit in baptism.[115] Citing Beasley-Murray's *Baptism in the New Testament* for support, he claims, "According to the New Testament writers, 'baptism in the Spirit' belongs normatively within the event of water-baptism."[116] This situation, Fiddes argues, calls for further theological reflection on related matters, such as the connections between faith, conversion, church-membership and baptism.[117]

In some respects, however, that connection between the charismatic emphasis on the Spirit and Baptists' thinking about baptism has been minimized because, according to David Pawson, the charismatic renewal movement downplayed the Pentecostal emphasis on baptism in the Spirit. It preferred to focus on the gifts of the Spirit.[118] The influential Vineyard movement, for example, moved away from the controversial phrase, "baptism of the Spirit," to the "more functional and flexible notion of 'anointing.'"[119] This shift may partially explain Nigel Wright's observation that the charismatic movement sidestepped issues related to baptism.[120] It is noteworthy that when Wright critiques the theology of John Wimber, he does not mention baptism or the giving of the Spirit.[121]

Nevertheless, there is some evidence that the charismatic movement had some impact on Baptists' thinking about baptism.[122] Anthony Cross contends that there is no evidence that as a movement the charismatic renewal has contributed "in any significant way to the conduct of baptismal services, *except in the laying on of hands* which is widely practiced in charismatic circles."[123] Some of the scholars under consideration in this project have direct connections to the movement as well.

---

115. Fiddes, *Charismatic Renewal*, 30.

116. Fiddes, *Charismatic Renewal*, 31. He cites Beasley-Murray, *Baptism in the New Testament*, 275–79.

117. Fiddes, *Charismatic Renewal*, 31–37.

118. Pawson, *Jesus Baptises*, 161–62.

119. Wright, "Theology and Methodology," 72.

120. Wright, *New Baptists, New Agenda*, 47.

121. Wright, "Theology and Methodology."

122. Hocken claims that "after the Anglicans, the Baptists were the most affected in the early years, with the main leadership coming from David Pawson, Douglas McBain, Barney Coombs, Harold Owen, Edmund Heddle, and Jim Graham." Burgess and McGee, *Dictionary*, 145.

123. Cross, *Baptism and the Baptists*, 447. For a discussion of the practice among British Baptist, see Beasley-Murray, *Faith and Festivity*, 106–16. Emphasis added.

Nigel Wright's initial contact with the charismatic renewal was through reading David Wilkerson's *The Cross and the Switchblade*, which raised the issue of baptism in the Spirit and speaking in tongues. Wright recalls that he was "repelled (theologically ignorant though I was at this stage) by the theological language in which it was packaged—a state of affairs that has endured."[124] Though Wright does not explain how the charismatic movement has affected his theology of baptism, this statement does suggest that in the charismatic movement he was confronted with what he considered to be a theologically deficient view of Spirit-baptism and responded by reflecting theologically on the issue. John Colwell, another scholar under consideration in this book, was also part of the charismatic renewal movement. His experience with the movement had a profound influence on his understanding of baptism, which will be discussed in the chapter that focuses on him.

CONCLUSION

In this chapter we have considered three contextual factors related to baptism that are especially relevant to BUGB Baptists. A fourth factor, the sacramental resurgence, was considered in chapter 1. One of those factors, the charismatic renewal movement, led some Baptists to think theologically about Spirit-baptism and to reflect on the nature of the sacraments.[125] Two of the other factors helped pave the way for the sacramental arguments that will be examined in subsequent chapters. First, participation in the ecumenical movement led English Baptists to reevaluate their baptismal theology, which, according to Beasley-Murray, moved some in a more sacramental direction. Second, the sacramental resurgence generated significant debate about the meaning of baptism. By the time the English scholars under consideration in this project were writing on baptism, other prominent scholars within their tradition had been arguing for a sacramental understanding of baptism for decades.

The remaining contextual factor—the Oxford Movement—actually pushed some British Baptists in a decidedly anti-sacramental direction. Though, as mentioned earlier, the influence of the Oxford Movement has lessened, it has still had a role in shaping the debate, seen particularly in

---

124. Wright, "Pilgrimage in Renewal," 24.

125. This effect of the charismatic movement will be explored further in the chapter on John Colwell.

Wright's, Colwell's, and Cross's repeated insistence that their sacramental view is not the *ex opere operato* view that was often associated with the Oxford Movement.

While acknowledging that these four factors provide much of the contexts for the baptismal debate among BUGB Baptists, it is the contention of this project that the work of George Beasley-Murray has continued to influence the debate to a significant extent and that his impact has not been limited to a particular context. We have seen that the arguments of three Southern Baptist scholars, though in a greatly different context, have been shaped by Beasley-Murray. We will now turn our attention to three BUGB Baptist scholars to examine their interaction with Beasley-Murray.

8

Nigel Wright

THIS CHAPTER WILL EXAMINE the role of George Beasley-Murray's work in the baptism-related writings of Nigel Wright. After a brief biographical sketch, we will examine Wright's understanding of the meaning of baptism. We will see that his view of baptism has much in common with Beasley-Murray's. The last section will analyze Wright's appropriation of Beasley-Murray's work. Though Wright makes few references to Beasley-Murray, we will see that the extent and significance of his appropriation of Beasley-Murray cannot be measured by number of references alone. He has in fact appropriated Beasley-Murray's work in significant ways and to a significant extent.

A BIOGRAPHICAL SKETCH OF NIGEL WRIGHT

Nigel Wright was born in 1949 in Manchester.[1] His early years did not include "the practice of any religious faith."[2] He had some connection to the local Baptist church, but did not attend regularly. In Wright's words, "Conversion came without particular drama, but as a definite shift, at the age of fifteen. . . . Baptism and church membership were soon to

---

1. Biographical information can be found in Smail, Walker and Wright, *Charismatic Renewal,* 22–30; Garrett, *Baptist Theology,* 686–87; Nicholls, *Lights to the World,* 191; Randall, *School of the Prophets,* 8; Randall, "Part of a Movement."

2. Smail, Walker, and Wright, *Charismatic Renewal,* 23.

follow."[3] During that period the charismatic renewal was making inroads into the mainstream church, and Wright writes, "No sooner was I converted, therefore, than I came up against the charismatic movement."[4] The charismatic movement would prove to have a significant influence on Wright's life and ministry, and he would likewise have a significant influence on the movement.

In 1970 Wright received a BA from the University of Leeds. From 1970 to 1973 he studied at Spurgeon's College. While at Spurgeon's, Wright took a number of classes taught by George Beasley-Murray, including one on selected New Testament texts and another on textual criticism.[5] Wright was ordained by Beasley-Murray in 1973 and became pastor of a local church. During his time at that church, two events took place that helped shape Wright's ministry. First, in 1980, Wright spent a sabbatical with a Mennonite community in Pennsylvania. During that sabbatical, a keen interest in Anabaptism took root.[6] Wright's appreciation of the Anabaptist tradition became a major theme in his writing and teaching.[7]

The second event that had a lasting impact on Wright's career was the 1982 visit of John Wimber, a leader of the charismatic movement. Wright recalls that at a church meeting during Wimber's visit, "the Spirit of God had fallen upon a large proportion of the congregation," leading to trembling, speaking in tongues, and prophesying.[8] In the aftermath, Wright, along with the church, learned about some of the temptations related to the charismatic movement, such as "thinking that if we tremble the Spirit is bound to come." They also learned to "channel the spiritual energy we have been given into growth."[9] All of this led Wright to feel called to be a theological teacher. He states, "It became clear to me that wherever there is abundant spiritual energy allied to a less than adequate theology, trouble will ensue."[10]

In 1987 Wright returned to academic studies and received an MTh from the University of Glasgow, under the supervision of systematic

---

3. Smail, Walker, and Wright, *Charismatic Renewal*, 23.
4. Smail, Walker, and Wright, *Charismatic Renewal*, 24.
5. Wright, personal email, June 20, 2015.
6. Smail, Walker, and Wright, *Charismatic Renewal*, 26.
7. See Randall, "Part of a Movement," 9–12.
8. Smail, Walker, and Wright, *Charismatic Renewal*, 27.
9. Smail, Walker, and Wright, *Charismatic Renewal*, 29.
10. Smail, Walker, and Wright, *Charismatic Renewal*, 29–30.

theologian George Newlands.[11] Following his time at Glasgow, Wright joined the faculty of Spurgeon's College, where he was Tutor of Doctrine for eight years. During that time he also earned a PhD from King's College, London, where he was supervised by systematic theologian Colin Gunton.[12]

In 1995 Wright left his position at Spurgeon's to become a pastor of a local church. Five years later he returned to Spurgeon's as Principal of the College, a position he held until 2014. During his time as Principal, Spurgeon's graduated approximately 100 students each year, giving Wright the potential for significant influence within the Baptist Union.[13] While Principal, Wright also served a term as President of the Baptist Union of Great Britain. For years, Wright had been involved in the Union. In the 1990s he was influential in the restructuring of the BUGB.[14] He also worked with Mainstream, a movement that began in 1978 to address needs within Baptist life.[15] Wright regularly wrote for the publication *Mainstream Newsletter* and contributed to a book published by Mainstream titled *A Perspective on Baptist Identity*.[16] He was also a frequent contributor to *Baptist Times*, including his weekly "postcard" during his tenure as President of the Union.[17] In addition to those publications, Wright has written numerous articles, essays and books.[18] Ian Randall states, "Nigel Wright has contributed enormously to English Baptist life since the 1970s"[19] and has had "a significant impact" on the BUGB.[20]

---

11. Wright, personal email, June 20, 2015.
12. Wright, *Disavowing Constantine*, xi.
13. Pieter Lalleman, personal email, July 10, 2015.
14. Randall, "Part of a Movement," 14–15.
15. Mainstream has since been renamed Fresh Streams. Information can be found on its website www.freshstreams.net.
16. Randall, "Part of a Movement," 6–7.
17. Randall, "Part of a Movement," 16.
18. The EBSCOhost database includes forty works by Wright. Andy Goodliff has listed forty-four works by Wright.
19. Randall, "Part of a Movement," 19.
20. Randall, "Part of a Movement," 16.

NIGEL WRIGHT'S VIEW OF BAPTISM

The Symbolism of Baptism

Throughout his writings, Wright makes much of the symbolism of baptism, referring to it as "a highly symbolic act."[21] For him, the symbolism is multifaceted and pictures a range of realities. In his pamphlet, *Why Be a Baptist?*, he argues for believer baptism and also addresses the meaning of baptism. He refers to baptism as "the sign commanded by Jesus."[22] In another pamphlet he states that baptism "symbolises the death of the old life and rising to a new life" and is a "symbol of Christian discipleship."[23] It also symbolizes being immersed in the Holy Spirit.[24]

In his book, *Free Church, Free State*, Wright goes into greater detail concerning the symbolism of baptism. "Baptism is a form of drama," he writes, "a way of acting out what it means internally. With other Christian practices it may be seen as a 'visible,' as distinct from a spoken, word, in that the very drama of baptism communicates."[25] He goes on to discuss the following "images" which are expressed through baptism. First, baptism symbolizes being born. From John 3 he argues that baptism is "the sign of new life and new birth into the life of God in such as a way as to renew and transform us."[26] Second, baptism symbolizes being washed. From Titus 3:5 and 1 Pet 3:21 he argues, "Baptism is a public demonstration of the way in which on confession of repentance towards God and faith in Christ past and present sins are washed away and a new way of living begins."[27] Third, baptism symbolizes being buried and raised. Based on Rom 6 he claims, "Baptism signifies death to the old ways of living and those parts of ourselves that cling to them. This is part of its power. Joyfully this burial is accompanied by a resurrection signified by coming up out of the water."[28] Fourth, baptism symbolizes being immersed in the Holy Spirit. Baptism in water "signified a baptism into the realm of the

---

21. Wright, *The Church*, 24.
22. Wright, *Why Be A Baptist?*
23. Wright, *Believers' Baptism?*
24. Wright, *Believers' Baptism?*
25. Wright, *Free Church*, 73.
26. Wright, *Free Church*, 74.
27. Wright, *Free Church*, 74.
28. Wright, *Free Church*, 75.

Holy Spirit with all that means for our regeneration, sanctification and empowerment."[29]

Baptism as an Expression of Faith

In addition to being a symbol, Wright understands baptism to be an expression of faith in Christ. It is therefore an integral part of becoming a Christian and a marker of the beginning of a new life in Christ. He makes this point in *Believers' Baptism?* when he states, "By means of baptism, a person declares their desire to turn from a life without God to one which is lived for God through Jesus Christ."[30] He continues, "Baptism marks a new start. It is intended to take place near to a person's first commitment to Christ and as part of the process by which they pass from the world of unbelief to the life of faith."[31] Baptism is also like being buried and raised, he argues, and therefore "marks the end of one life and the beginning of a new one."[32]

In *Free Church, Free State* Wright points out that the practice of believer baptism follows from the nature of the church as "a community of the voluntarily committed, of confessing disciples."[33] He goes on to make the connection to baptism, stating, "in the community of disciples, commitment is the product of new birth and costly choice symbolised in the present age, as it was in the New Testament, by believers baptism."[34] Again, baptism is the expression of a commitment on the part of the one baptized. He later makes the same point in a different way. Because baptism is the "initiation rite," it is therefore "the definitive rite of entry into the kingdom of God and the church."[35] Putting it yet another way he writes, "Baptism becomes the point at which we make our personal confession of faith and take our stand for Christ, not being ashamed to own him as Lord."[36]

---

29. Wright, *Free Church*, 75.
30. Wright, *Believers' Baptism?*
31. Wright, *Believers' Baptism?*
32. Wright, *Believers' Baptism?*
33. Wright, *Free Church*, 70.
34. Wright, *Free Church*, 70.
35. Wright, *Free Church*, 72.
36. Wright, *Free Church*, 76.

For Wright, his belief that baptism is an expression of faith by the person baptized distinguishes his view from the Roman Catholic view and prevents it from being interpreted as an *ex opere operato* understanding of baptism. He describes the Roman Catholic connection between baptism and salvation, stating, "it is through the grace of baptism that eternal salvation is mediated by the Church and further sustained and completed by that same Church through other sacraments which it controls."[37] Wright seeks to distance himself from such an understanding of baptism. He acknowledges that his use of the term "sacrament" will not be well received by some due to the fact that it is often "associated with more catholic traditions and with the idea that they are effective *ex opere operato*. . . . So, baptism brings regeneration of itself."[38] Wright clarifies that he does not intend to imply such an understanding of baptism with his use of the term "sacrament."[39] Indeed, he affirms the reformation principle that "faith must be present to give efficacy to any administration of the sacraments."[40]

Baptism as a Means of Grace

While Wright emphasizes that baptism is a human expression of faith, he is equally emphatic that it is more. He cautions against an *ex opere operato* understanding of baptism and at the same time cautions against a merely symbolic understanding of the rite. "If the idea of *ex opere operato* is mistaken," he writes, "so is the common reaction which strips the sacraments of any spiritual power at all and leaves them as 'mere symbols' to be observed as a matter of sheer obedience rather than as a means of grace."[41] He explains,

> In the desire to avoid any sense of a magical rite which we control and to preserve the priority of faith, there is an instinct to reduce baptism to an act of bare witness with little expectation that anything would happen in the baptismal act which has not already happened in the regeneration of the heart. It becomes therefore an outward sign of an inward grace and nothing more.

---

37. Wright, *Free Church*, xx.
38. Wright, *Free Church*, 95.
39. Wright, *Free Church*, 95.
40. Wright, *Free Church*, 95.
41. Wright, *Free Church*, 95.

But the New Testament does suggest more. It shows that baptism was eventful.[42]

In *The Church* he claims that though baptism is "a highly symbolic act," it is not only a symbol. "When entered into in faith and with the right attitude of heart . . . there is great spiritual benefit in store for the believer."[43] The claims that baptism is a means of grace, is eventful, and is spiritually beneficial imply that God, and not only the person baptized, is active in baptism.

In fact, Wright makes that argument explicitly, and includes the church as an active participant as well. Understanding Acts 2:38 as a pattern for baptism, Wright concludes that there are three agents at work: the person being baptized, the church, and God.[44] He states that the person believes, the church baptizes, and God, though graciously at work throughout the entire process of conversion, "grants the gift of the Holy Spirit" in baptism.[45] In *Free Church, Free State* he expounds on that pattern by stating that, for our part, we respond to the message about Jesus with repentance and faith and by requesting baptism. The fact that we have to request it reminds us of our dependence and the fact that our salvation must come to us "from outside, through Christ who is our Saviour."[46] The church then administers baptism.[47] God then "grants the gift of the Holy Spirit as the divine response to our request."[48]

Behind Wright's belief that God is active in baptism is the conviction that, "A fundamental aspect of the way God works in the world is to do so mediately, incarnationally, using the earthly as the vehicle for the heavenly."[49] This conviction leads to "the principle of sacramentality, the freedom of God to take earthly means and make them means of grace for the salvation of human beings."[50] Wright believes this principle applies to the rite of baptism, a belief he reiterates a number of times. In *Free Church, Free State* he claims, "by means of what baptism signifies we

---

42. Wright, *Free Church*, 95.
43. Wright, *The Church*, 24.
44. Wright, *Believers' Baptism?*
45. Wright, *Believers' Baptism?*
46. Wright, *Free Church*, 77.
47. Wright, *Free Church*, 78.
48. Wright, *Free Church*, 78.
49. Wright, *Free Church*, 96.
50. Wright, *Free Church*, 97.

enter into God's promises as they are proclaimed over us and applied to us by the Spirit in the baptismal act."[51] He goes on to raise the question, "Does baptism achieve anything?" Wright answers, "yes." He writes, "It is a means of grace to the individual but also to the whole church which experiences renewal each time a baptism takes place. It is also a highly effective witness to the world. In all these ways baptism is not just a sign: it is an effective sign."[52] Later, when discussing both baptism and the Lord's Supper he states, "Baptism and communion are effective signs of God's kingdom and are placed as the two primary sacraments within the web of a wider pattern of practices which identify, shape and sustain the church and serve the transmission of the faith to new generations of believers."[53] He states his case again by arguing that baptism and communion are "dynamic means of grace which, when they are received in faith and used as instruments of the free and gracious spirit of God, become moments of spiritual encounter working in us the very things they dramatise and symbolise."[54]

In *Believers' Baptism?* Wright includes divine activity as one of the reasons why a person should be baptized. The first reason he provides is because Jesus has commanded it. The second reason is because to do so is to follow Jesus' example. The third reason is because it is the best way to confess Christ publicly. The fourth reason is because it is a means of grace. He writes, "Baptism is a powerful symbol. It is given extra depth because it is a means of grace, that is to say, the Holy Spirit uses it to convey spiritual blessing and benefit through it. The realities that baptism symbolizes, such as new life, cleansing, death to sin and immersion in the Spirit are deepened and renewed in the lives of believers through baptism. Baptism is never therefore a mere symbol, it is a spiritually powerful act." The fifth reason is because baptism is good for the church.[55]

In addition to affirming a general principle of sacramentality, Wright also believes that there is explicit biblical evidence that God is at work in baptism.[56] The examples he provides not only give support to his sacramental view, but also give clarity and specificity to his view. In the

---

51. Wright, *Free Church*, 76.
52. Wright, *Free Church*, 89.
53. Wright, *Free Church*, 94.
54. Wright, *Free Church*, 96.
55. Wright, *Believers' Baptism?*
56. Wright, *Free Church*, 95.

baptisms of Jesus, the people on the day of Pentecost, and the disciples of John in Acts 19, baptism was associated with the giving of the Holy Spirit.[57] Rom 6, according to Wright, implies that our death with Christ "took place through the act of baptism itself."[58] About 1 Pet 3:21 he states, "Peter can even claim that baptism 'now saves you,' and then goes on to clarify that this is not in the same way that it might remove dirt from the body but through its role as an appeal to God for a clear conscience. Even so, this is language that no Baptist would invent: most would be worried that it might be taken to imply baptismal regeneration."[59]

According to Wright, one thing God does in baptism is give his Spirit to the person baptized. Wright clarifies that the gift of the Spirit in baptism does not imply that the Spirit is not at work before that point "since we cannot sincerely come to this point without the influence of the Spirit within us."[60] Indeed, as Paul Fiddes states, "Any response we make is itself a product of the Holy Spirit already at work upon and within us since none can come to the Father unless they be drawn."[61]

Wright appears to sense some tension between the claim that the Spirit is at work in us before baptism and the claim that the Spirit is given to us in baptism. He resolves that tension by asserting, "But there are different aspects to the Spirit's work: first we are awakened to our need of God and convicted concerning our sins, then we are regenerated and enabled to repent and believe as the Spirit draws us out of ourselves and into relationship with God's self, then we are empowered by the Spirit to live as members of the messianic community."[62] He concludes, "Baptism captures all these elements in its symbolism and leads to their being embedded within us."[63] While it is unclear exactly what he means by the Spirit's work being "embedded within us," he appears to suggest that the giving of the Spirit in baptism involves the third work of the Spirit in his

---

57. Wright, *Free Church*, 97.

58. Wright, *Free Church*, 97. Not all scholars agree with Wright's interpretation of Rom 6. In *Romans*, 311, Dunn argues that Paul's reference to baptism is metaphorical. In *Romans*, 34–45, Lloyd-Jones contends that Paul is referring to baptism by the Holy Spirit.

59. Wright, *Free Church*, 97.

60. Wright, *Free Church*, 78.

61. As quoted in Wright, *Free Church*, 77.

62. Wright, *Free Church*, 78.

63. Wright, *Free Church*, 78.

list, namely, the baptized person being empowered by the Spirit to live a life of discipleship.

The claim that the Spirit is both at work before baptism and given in baptism fits with Wright's understanding of conversion as a process. In his view, baptism is not the only point at which God is at work in the person's life. It is, however, a "focal point," which expresses and deepens "that which is already under way and that which goes on happening even after baptism."[64] He makes a similar claim in *The Church*, writing, "[B]aptism is not seen as an optional extra but as part of the *process* of becoming a Christian."[65] Other scholars have made similar arguments for understanding baptism as part of a larger process. Paul Fiddes, for example, contends that a common Baptist "journey" may be from infant blessing through Christian nurture in childhood to believer baptism, laying on of hands for gifts of the Spirit, and then increasing use of those gifts in ministry in the world.[66]

Wright believes, then, that baptism is an expression of the faith of the person baptized and part of the process of a person being united to Christ in his death and resurrection and being given the Holy Spirit. For Wright, this has significant implications concerning the proper subjects of baptism. He contends that a proper understanding of the meaning of baptism provides a helpful and necessary argument for believer baptism. Addressing the issue of infant baptism, Wright notes that there is no unambiguous mandate for infant baptism in the New Testament. He then states, "But this ought not to surprise us. In the New Testament we are introduced to the first generation of Christians who would not yet have encountered with full force the question of how to nurture the faith of the second generation or beyond. A space is left here for later questions which must be filled with theological rather than directly biblical wisdom."[67]

The implications of this approach can be seen by contrasting Wright's position with that of his PhD supervisor, Colin Gunton. Gunton believed that baptism involves an "interrelation of divine acts and human response."[68] Such a statement would seem to imply that faith expressed by the one baptized is a necessary part of baptism, which would lead

---

64. Wright, *Free Church*, 98.
65. Wright, *The Church*, 23.
66. Fiddes, *Tracks and Traces*, 141.
67. Wright, *Free Church*, 81.
68. Gunton, *Christian Faith*, 145.

to the practice of believer baptism. Indeed, he claims that in baptism "justification is appropriated."[69] However, Gunton downplays the relevance of this theology to the debate concerning the subjects of baptism.

Instead, he argues that the strongest case for believer baptism is the "almost universal New Testament practice" of believer baptism.[70] For him, however, that case is not convincing. His conclusion is determined by other factors, primarily that "it would be a strange church that did not include within its membership the whole families of participants in its life."[71] Gunton and Wright agree, then, that the New Testament pattern alone does not settle the issue. The difference is that Wright, along with Beasley-Murray, allows the New Testament meaning of baptism to be the decisive factor, while Gunton considers his understanding of the nature of the church to be the decisive factor.

The Normal Pattern

Based on Acts 2:37–42, Wright states that the normal pattern is "conviction of sin, followed by repentance (and presumably faith), followed by baptism in the name of Jesus Christ (or Father, Son and Spirit), resulting in the gift of the Holy Spirit, leading to incorporation into the community of disciples, and then steadfast participation in the church, its disciplines and mission."[72] However, while maintaining that this is the normal pattern, he also claims that it is not the only possible pattern. He compares the process of conversion to physical human birth in that there is a normal way that children are born (head first), though some depart from that norm and are born another way (the other way around, or Caesarean section).[73]

According to Wright, the Bible sets out a pattern for "the normal Christian birth."[74] While not every conversion follows the pattern exactly, and God's Spirit "does not always stay within the pattern," that does not give us the freedom to depart from the patterns laid down for our

69. Gunton, *Christian Faith*, 145.
70. Gunton, *Christian Faith*, 146.
71. Gunton, *Christian Faith*, 146.
72. Wright, *Free Church*, 81. Wright cites Pawson's *The Normal Christian Birth* (1989), who himself identified four elements in the conversion process: repentance, belief, water baptism, and reception of the Holy Spirit.
73. Wright, *Free Church*, 77.
74. Wright, *Free Church*, 77.

instruction.⁷⁵ In other words, "although *God* is not bound even to the sacraments divinely appointed, *we are* since we are not God."⁷⁶ He later makes the point again. In response to the question, "Is baptism necessary for salvation," Wright answers in the negative. He states, "We are justified by grace through faith, so trust in Christ is the moment when salvation comes to the individual."⁷⁷ However, baptism is necessary for discipleship, since it is commanded by Jesus, and for the church in that it is "one of its 'norming norms' that safeguards its identity and mission."⁷⁸

WRIGHT'S APPROPRIATION OF THE WORK OF BEASLEY-MURRAY

When considering the factors that have shaped Nigel Wright's argument related to baptism, one notable feature of his work on baptism is how infrequently he refers to other sources, particularly non-biblical sources. Wright's works surveyed for this project contain only twenty references to other scholars. Eleven scholars are cited once each, two scholars—as well as the document *Baptism, Eucharist, and Ministry*—are cited twice each, and one scholar, George Beasley-Murray, is cited directly three times. The significance of Beasley-Murray's work in Wright's work, however, cannot be determined by the number of references alone. A closer examination of those references, along with a closer look at a reference to Anthony Cross, lead to the conclusion that Wright has appropriated Beasley-Murray's work in significant ways.

In terms of his understanding of the meaning of baptism, Wright has much in common with Beasley-Murray. In fact, Garrett, though he does not mention Beasley-Murray specifically, points out that Wright does not "differentiate his views from those of the British baptismal-sacramental school."⁷⁹ Like Beasley-Murray, Wright understands baptism to be an expression of faith in response to the gospel and the point at which a person is united to Christ and receives all the benefits that go with that union. Wright's appropriation of Beasley-Murray in crafting his argument is seen most clearly at three points.

---

75. Wright, *Free Church*, 79.
76. Wright, *Free Church*, 80.
77. Wright, *Free Church*, 86.
78. Wright, *Free Church*, 86.
79. Garrett, *Baptist Theology*, 689.

One of those points is Wright's reference to baptism as a place of rendezvous or a "trysting-place."[80] His use of the term "trysting-place" is significant for a number of reasons. First, he borrows the term itself from Beasley-Murray. He cites Beasley-Murray's claim in *Baptism, Today and Tomorrow*, "Baptism was given as a *trysting place* of the sinner with his Savior. He who has met Him there will not despise it, but will seek to conduct others to it for the same kind of meeting" (italics mine).[81] This indicates that Beasley-Murray's terminology regarding baptism has been picked up and incorporated into another scholar's work. Not only has Wright used Beasley-Murray's term, however, he also uses it in the way that Beasley-Murray does, indicating that he shares the theology Beasley-Murray was communicating with the term. Wright cites approvingly the entire above quote, not only the term itself. He agrees that baptism is a place in which the sinner meets the Savior.

Another reason this term is significant is that it safeguards against an *ex opere operato* understanding of baptism. By making clear that baptism is a place where a sinner meets the Savior, the term also implies that baptism itself is not the Savior. In the same endnote related to his use of the term "trysting-place," Wright also cites Beasley-Murray's statement in *Baptism in the New Testament*, "But in the last resort it is only a place: the Lord himself is its glory, as He is its grace."[82] Beasley-Murray, then, has provided an image that captures a certain understanding of baptism, an image that Wright agrees with and uses in his own work on baptism.

A second point at which Wright's appropriation of Beasley-Murray is clear is in Wright's connection between the meaning of baptism and the subjects of baptism. When arguing for believer baptism, Wright refers to *Baptism in the New Testament* as "the standard and unsurpassed Baptist work" on the appropriateness of believer baptism as opposed to infant baptism.[83] He quotes approvingly Beasley-Murray's perspective concerning infant baptism: "It seems that a small amount of water is bestowed on a small infant with a very small result."[84] In addition to the quote, he refers to pages 306–86 in *Baptism in the New Testament*. That reference is significant in two ways. First, though only a single reference, it is a

---

80. Wright, *Free Church*, 98.
81. Beasley-Murray, *Baptism Today*, 41.
82. Beasley-Murray, *Baptism in the New Testament*, 305.
83. Wright, *Free Church*, 91.
84. Beasley-Murray, *Baptism in the New Testament*, 385.

reference to 80 pages. He is not appropriating a single point related to baptism, but an entire section of Beasley-Murray's book and a substantial portion of his overall argument.

Another reason that Wright's reference to *Baptism* is significant is that, though the section referred to is about the subjects of baptism, it contains much about the meaning of baptism. That is because, like Wright, Beasley-Murray believed that there was a necessary connection between the proper subjects of baptism and a proper understanding of baptism. In that section, Beasley-Murray addresses issues such as the relationship of the covenant to baptism, the function of faith in baptism, infant baptism as confession, infant baptism and union with Christ in his death and resurrection, infant baptism and the forgiveness of sins, and infant baptism and entrance into the church. Beasley-Murray concludes, "New Testament utterances concerning the nature and meaning of baptism have been made with believers in mind."[85] A large part of Beasley-Murray's argument for believer baptism, then, is the biblical meaning of baptism. As mentioned earlier in this chapter, Wright takes the same approach. In a single endnote, then, Wright refers to 80 pages of Beasley-Murray's baptismal theology that represents a distinct approach to a major issue related to baptism.

The third point at which Wright appropriates Beasley-Murray is in Wright's claim that "virtually every saving gift that the New Testament attributes to faith it also ascribes to baptism."[86] This is an important feature of Wright's baptismal theology as it allows for a sacramental understanding of baptism while still holding firmly to salvation by grace through faith. Wright attributes this insight to Anthony Cross and references Cross's lecture "Faith-Baptism: The Key to an Evangelical Baptismal Sacramentalism."[87] In that lecture, however, Cross attributes the insight to Beasley-Murray, specifically *Baptism Today and Tomorrow*, "Baptism in the New Testament," and "Authority and Justification."[88] While the citation is actually a reference to Cross, then, the insight being appropriated is traceable to Beasley-Murray.

---

85. Beasley-Murray, *Baptism in the New Testament*, 359.
86. Wright, *Free Church*, 98.
87. Cross, "Faith-Baptism."
88. Cross, "Faith-Baptism," 35.

CONCLUSION

The goal of this chapter has been to demonstrate that Beasley-Murray's work has helped shaped Nigel Wright's argument concerning the meaning of baptism. Though Wright only references Beasley-Murray three times, that is more than he references anyone else. More significantly, Wright has incorporated some of Beasley-Murray's terminology, his connection between the theology and the subjects of baptism, and his insight that in the New Testament various realities related to salvation are associated with both faith and baptism. Through Wright, then, Beasley-Murray's argument continues to be an important part of the baptismal debate.

9

John Colwell

THIS CHAPTER WILL EXAMINE the role of George Beasley-Murray's work in the baptism-related writings of John Colwell. After a brief biographical sketch, we will examine Colwell's understanding of the meaning of baptism. We will then consider a number of factors that have shaped Colwell's theology of baptism. The last section will analyze Colwell's appropriation of Beasley-Murray's work and will show that Beasley-Murray has helped shape Colwell's argument in both direct and indirect ways.

A BIOGRAPHICAL SKETCH OF JOHN COLWELL

Following a brief period working in a Justices' Clerk's office, John Colwell trained for ministry at Spurgeon's College.[1] He was a student at Spurgeon's during the final three years of Beasley-Murray's tenure as Principal and studied New Testament under Beasley-Murray.[2] Colwell was called to the pastorate at Maldon Baptist Church, Essex in 1974. Sponsored by Spurgeon's College, he returned to study at King's College, London in 1979 to complete his PhD under the supervision of Colin Gunton. In 1982 Colwell became pastor of Catford Hill Baptist Church, which merged with Allerford Chapel in 1985 to form King's Church, Catford.

---

1. Unless otherwise noted, biographical information is taken from "Staff—John E. Colwell"; and Randall, *School of the Prophets*.

2. Colwell, "Catholicity and Confessionalism," 1.

In 1994 Colwell returned to Spurgeon's College, initially to establish a Master's course in Applied Theology and, after a year, to become Tutor in Christian Doctrine and Ethics. He also served for three years as Dean of Studies. In 2009 Colwell returned to pastoral ministry at Budleigh Salterton Baptist Church from where he retired in June 2014.

In addition to his professional accomplishments, two other pieces of biographical information should be noted at the beginning of this chapter. First, for a time Colwell was involved in the charismatic movement. His involvement with the charismatic movement began when he was seventeen but was renewed during his first year as a pastor in Maldon. He became more heavily involved when he moved back to London to continue his studies.[3] Since that time, Colwell has distanced himself from the charismatic movement theologically and has critiqued certain aspects of it.[4]

The second piece of biographical information that should be noted at this point is that Colwell has struggled with bipolar disorder for much of his adult life. He has written about his experience with mental illness in his book, *Why Have You Forsaken Me?* In Colwell's view, such biographical facts are important to establish before exploring his theology. He believes that one's personal story affects one's theology, and therefore the two should be considered together. He states, "All theology, of course, has a context: objective detachment is a foolish delusion that is neither desirable nor achievable; there is no theological reflection without a person reflecting, and that person has a story that has shaped them."[5] Some of the ways in which Colwell's experiences have impacted his theology will be addressed later in this chapter. First we will examine his theology of baptism.

JOHN COLWELL'S VIEW OF BAPTISM

Colwell and the Baptist Tradition

Anthony Cross considers Colwell to be one of the Baptists' "leading scholars" who has critiqued modern Baptist theologies of baptism.[6] Colwell

---

3. Colwell, *Why Have You Forsaken Me?*, 18.
4. Colwell, *Why Have You Forsaken Me?*, 18–22.
5. Colwell, *Why Have You Forsaken Me?*, xi.
6. Cross, "Evangelical Sacrament," 198.

believes that many modern Baptists have downplayed the significance of baptism in a way that is inconsistent with New Testament teaching on the subject. According to Colwell, "We find ourselves today enmeshed in the extraordinary contradiction of churches known distinctively for their theology and practice of baptism being among the congregations where baptism is granted the least significance."[7] He provides two major factors that he thinks have contributed to this situation.

One factor is theological. He notes that there has been "longstanding theological controversy and confusion" among Baptists concerning baptism, and Baptists have never been able to agree on the meaning of baptism.[8] While there remains some disagreement, Colwell also claims that many Baptists have concluded that baptism is a mere symbol. In fact, Colwell believes that most contemporary Baptists consider baptism to be a testimony to a conversion that has already taken place, making baptism a merely symbolic act.[9] In *Recovering the Evangelical Sacrament*, he claims that for most contemporary Baptists, baptism is "a witness to a conversion that has already occurred" it is an ethical act of human response rather than itself a spiritually transforming event.[10] Colwell disagrees on biblical grounds. He argues that with the exception of Cornelius, "nowhere in the New Testament is baptism reduced to a subsequent witness to a previous conversion experience."[11]

The other reason that Baptists are "strangely muted" about baptism, according to Colwell, is an "ecumenical sensitivity" which has actually led to many Baptist churches not insisting on baptism at all.[12] He points out that many Baptist churches in England practice open-membership and accept believers on profession of faith. Baptism is simply not a requirement for membership, and Christians from the Salvation Army or Society of Friends could be members.[13]

Colwell argues that one effect of taking away the sacramental significance of baptism is that Baptists have developed other pseudo-sacraments

---

7. Colwell, "Catholicity and Confessionalism," 139.
8. Colwell, *Promise*, 110.
9. Colwell, *Promise*, 111.
10. Colwell, "Foreword," xii.
11. Colwell, "Foreword," xii–xiii.
12. Colwell, *Promise*, 109.
13. Colwell, *Promise*, 109. Some scholars and pastors who favor open-membership agree with Colwell that having unbaptized church members is problematic. For John Piper's response, see Piper, "Response to Grudem."

to accomplish what baptism is meant to accomplish. In *Living the Christian Story*, he states,

> Whenever there has been a belittling of the sacramental dynamic of the Church's life, other symbols, events and experiences—themselves neither divinely ordained nor pregnant with a divine promise—have assumed a pseudo-sacramental significance. The proclamation of the gospel, instead of being accompanied by baptism, is accompanied by "altar calls" and "decision cards." . . . Having been given specific signs as means of specific promises, having been given specific means of indwelling the gospel story, such pseudo-sacramental inventions are simply perverse.[14]

He makes the same point in *Recovering the Evangelical Sacrament*, writing,

> From Matthew through to Revelation you will find no decision cards, no appeals to come to the front, no programmatic presentation of the gospel with the expectation of some standardised form of felt experience. What you will find instead, from beginning to end, is baptism, whether baptism itself or the imagery arising from baptism.[15]

By making such an argument, Colwell acknowledges that he is breaking with Baptist tradition.[16] Nevertheless, he maintains that baptism is more than a symbol of a past event. It is, rather, a sacrament in which God is active.

Sacramentality and the Doctrine of God

While Colwell believes that theology should take Scripture as its "starting point," he argues that questions related to the nature of the sacraments are "primarily and foundationally questions of the nature of God."[17] This serves as the premise upon which Colwell develops his argument for a sacramental understanding of baptism.

Colwell's most thorough argument along these lines is found in his book, *Promise and Presence: An Exploration of Sacramental Theology*. The first chapter is titled "Sacramentality and the Doctrine of God." Much of the chapter is devoted to refuting what Colwell considers to

14. Colwell, *Living*, 154.
15. Colwell, "Foreword," xii.
16. Colwell, *Promise*, xi.
17. Colwell, *Promise*, 2.

be Augustine's and Barth's depersonalizing of the Spirit. In response to Augustine's argument that the statement "God is love" implies a lover, a beloved, and love itself, Colwell claims Augustine depersonalizes the Spirit by identifying the Spirit with love. He believes that Barth has made the same mistake.[18] Colwell, on the other hand, insists not only that the Spirit is a person, but that he is the mediator between the Father and the Son.[19] He does not make an extended argument for that claim, but cites the arguments of John Owen and Richard Sibbes. Colwell states, "It is not sufficient, then, to refer to the Spirit as the (impersonal) love uniting Father and Son; he is rather the (personal) mediator of that love."[20] His claim that the Spirit is neither the source nor goal of divine love, but is instead the mediator of that love, is not given any direct biblical support. He cites Richard Sibbes in support of his position. According to Sibbes, "All the communion that Christ as man had with God was by the Holy Ghost."[21] Colwell also provides examples of the Spirit being involved in the work of the Father and the Son—such as the baptism of Jesus, the ministry of Jesus, and the resurrection of Jesus. However, he seems to go beyond the biblical evidence in claiming that "[t]here is no action within the narrative that is not an action mediated by the Spirit."[22]

Colwell is right to point out that the Spirit is active in the work of the Father and the Son. However, his claim that the Spirit is the mediator of that relationship has some theological weaknesses. One is the fact that the Son is said to be the unique son of the Father (monogenhV in John 1:18, 3:16) with no reference to the Spirit. Nowhere does the Bible suggest that the begottenness[23] of the Son is owing to a work of the Spirit. This implies that the Father and Son have an immediate relationship. A second weakness of Colwell's position is that it suggests that the Spirit is not loved by the Father or the Son. If the Spirit is indeed a personal being, then he must be an object of divine love and not merely the mediator of it. Other scholars argue along these lines. Gerald Bray, for example,

---

18. Colwell, *Promise*, 21; Augustine, *The Trinity*; Barth, *Church Dogmatics*.

19. Colwell, *Promise*, 37; Owen, *Discourse Concerning the Holy Spirit*; Sibbes, "Description of Christ."

20. Colwell, *Promise*, 39.

21. Sibbes, "Description of Christ," 17.

22. Colwell, *Promise*, 37.

23. This is the word that has often been used in reference to the Son's eternal relationship to the Father. See, for example, Gregory of Nazianus's discussion in Hardy, *Christology of the Later Fathers*, 165.

argues that the Father loves the Son and loves the Spirit, and the Son loves both Father and the Spirit.[24] Wayne Grudem also considers the Spirit to be a subject and object of divine love.[25] Still others have focused on the personality and deity of the Spirit, addressing his relationships to the Father and the Son with no reference to the Spirit being the mediator of the relationship between the Father and the Son.[26]

Nevertheless, for Colwell, the idea of God's love being mediated lays the theological groundwork for the principle of sacramentality: "In every respect and in every instance the relatedness of the Father to the Son and the relatedness of the Son to the Father as narrated in the gospel story is a mediated relatedness; it is never unmediated."[27] He infers from that conclusion, "And neither then is it sufficient to speak of God as the one who loves in freedom, he is rather the one who mediates his love in freedom."[28] In other words, in Colwell's view, God's love is always mediated, even within Himself.

Sacramentality and the Doctrine of Creation

Having argued that God's love is always mediated, Colwell goes on to argue that God's relationship to creation is also always mediated. He claims that not only does the Spirit mediate the relationship of the Father and the Son, but he also mediates "creation's relatedness to the Son before the Father."[29] He states, "There is, therefore, no unmediated presence or action of God within or toward creation; the relatedness of God to creation is mediated in the Son and through the Spirit."[30] Again, he finds support in the work of Richard Sibbes. According to Sibbes, "God the Father, the first person in the Trinity, and God the Son, the second, they work not immediately, but by the Holy Ghost, the third person. Therefore,

---

24. Bray, *God Is Love*, 117.

25. Grudem, *Systematic Theology*, 199.

26. Hardy, *Christology of the Later Fathers*; St. Basil, *On the Holy Spirit*; Ware, *Father, Son, & Holy Spirit*; Anselm, "Procession of the Spirit"; Ferguson, *Holy Spirit*.

27. Colwell, *Promise*, 38–39.

28. Colwell, *Promise*, 40.

29. Colwell, *Promise*, 47.

30. Colwell, *Promise*, 48.

whatsoever is wrought upon the creature, it comes from the Holy Ghost immediately."[31]

Other scholars agree that the work of God the Father toward creation is mediated but attribute the mediation to God the Son, not God the Spirit. Curtis Vaughn, for example, claims that "through him" in Col 1:16 indicates that Jesus, not the Spirit, is the "mediating Agent" of creation.[32] Kostenberger claims that "dia" in John 1:3 "conveys secondary agency on the part of the Son" in regards to creation.[33] According to D. A. Carson, that the pre-existent Christ was "God's Agent in the creation of all that exists," is a "common theme in the New Testament."[34] Richard Melick, on the other hand, is one who associates mediation in creation most directly with the Spirit. In his view, the Father is the architect who decided to bring creation into existence; the Son brought the detailed plans into existence; the Spirit does the actual work of applying the plans in a hands-on relationship to creation.[35]

Whether the act of creation was mediated by the Son or the Spirit, Colwell's point appears to be that the Father's relationship to creation and the Son's relationship to creation are both mediated. He does not provide any direct biblical support for his claim. He does, however, provide numerous biblical examples of God working through "physical, material means." The Incarnation is perhaps the clearest and most important example. When God revealed Himself most clearly, it was not unmediated, but was mediated through the flesh of a carpenter.[36] Colwell concludes, "Having established a material universe God tends not to bypass it."[37]

The Principle of Sacramentality

In light of his understanding of the doctrine of God and the doctrine of creation, Colwell concludes that God cannot be encountered in any unmediated way in this present age.[38] The concept of mediation is central to

---

31. Sibbes, "Description of Christ," 17.
32. Gaebelein, *Ephesians through Philemon*, 182.
33. Kostenberger, *John*, 29.
34. Carson, *Gospel According to John*, 118.
35. Melick, *Philippians, Colossians, Philemon*, 217.
36. Colwell, *Promise*, 56.
37. Colwell, *Promise*, 56.
38. Colwell, *Promise*, 3.

Colwell's understanding of the sacraments. He affirms that God is present with us and acts in our lives. He denies, however, that God's presence and actions are ever unmediated. In fact, he claims, "There is little Scriptural evidence of any unmediated immediacy."[39] This claim sheds light on his statement that he considers his book, *Promise and Presence*, to be "an exploration of sacramentality."[40] It is not about any single rite, but, rather, is about a larger principle concerning God's relatedness to His creation that is expressed in particular ways. Colwell claims, "God as narrated in the gospel story is one who promises to mediate his presence to us."[41] This leads him to "a general theology of sacramentality"[42] and an argument for an "underlying sacramental dynamic."[43]

The Principle of Sacramentality and Pansacramentalism

The argument for a general principle of sacramentality and the claim that all of God's actions are mediated raise the issue of pansacramentalism—whether everything in creation is able to mediate God's presence and activity. G. C. Berkouwer addresses this question in his discussion of Van der Leeuw.[44] Like Colwell, Van der Leeuw understands the sacraments in the context of creation. He does not limit the sacramental to certain Christian rites but claims that it is a "widespread phenomenon in reality." He argues for a "general sacramentality" that results from humanity's inability to "directly" arrive at the essence of reality apart from signs. This leads Van der Leeuw to affirm the truth of pansacramentalism, which he does not think becomes a problem until it is coupled with pantheism.

Tillich also addresses the tension between affirming a principle of sacramentality and affirming the uniqueness of specific sacraments. He acknowledges that some might conclude sacramental qualities could be attributed to everything. He argues that though that could theoretically be the case, and in fact sacramentality is "possible in everything and in every place," the reality is that we do not see the holy in every reality.

---

39. Colwell, *Promise*, 118.
40. Colwell, *Promise*, xi.
41. Colwell, *Promise*, 3.
42. Colwell, *Promise*, 3.
43. Colwell, *Promise*, 4.
44. Berkouwer, *Sacraments*, 18–24.

Rather, "the holy appears only in special places, in special contexts."[45] At the same time, the specific elements of the sacraments represent all of nature, and thus point to "the universality of the sacramental principle."[46]

Carl Braaten is also aware of the tension and has expressed his concern about pansacramentalism. He writes, "If everything in general is a sacrament of God's presence in the world, then what is the point of sacraments in particular? If we can encounter God equally everywhere through anything, then what is the meaning of the specific sacraments which the Christian community believes to be 'means of grace'"?[47] Braaten suggests that instead of providing a metaphysical basis for the sacraments resulting from a philosophy of nature as sacramental, our understanding of the sacraments should be traced back to a verbal institution by Jesus.[48]

Colwell does not follow the methodology of Braaten. Nevertheless, he denies that his view leads to pansacramentalism, for two reasons. First, Colwell maintains that while God uses creation to mediate his presence and activity, God remains distinct from creation.[49] He agrees with Begbie that a panscramental view would undermine God's distinction from creation.[50] For Colwell, it is primarily this distinction that precludes a principle of sacramentality from leading to a pansacramental view of creation.[51]

Another important factor for Colwell is the very definition of a sacrament. While it is true that the principle of sacramentality means that God can use any aspect of creation to mediate his presence and activity, it does not follow that God does in fact use all of creation in the same way. The principle of sacramentality does not mean that all things are sacramental but that "any single particular may be sacramental."[52] As Colwell puts it, "That God once encountered Moses through a burning bush (Exod 3.2ff.) does not imply that all bushes are sacramental."[53] In Colwell's view, a sacrament is not merely something that God could use, or even something that He has used, but something that He promises

---

45. Tillich, *Protestant Era*, 110–11
46. Tillich, *Protestant Era*, 111.
47. Braaten, *Principles of Lutheran Theology*, 89.
48. Braaten, *Principles of Lutheran Theology*, 88.
49. Colwell, *Promise*, 54.
50. Colwell, *Promise*, 54.
51. Colwell, *Promise*, 54.
52. Colwell, *Promise*, 56.
53. Colwell, *Promise*, 56.

to use to mediate His presence. Although God mediates his presence through a variety of physical means—such as the burning bush—he does not promise to continually use those means to mediate his presence, and therefore we should not think of those particulars in sacramental terms.[54] Here is an important distinction for Colwell: "a sacramental sign is constituted as such through a promise of God."[55]

Baptism and the Promise of the Spirit

According to Colwell, one of the divine promises associated with baptism is the promise that the baptized person will receive the Holy Spirit. He points to Acts 2 as evidence of the promise that God will act in baptism, specifically that He will give His Spirit.[56] In reference to Acts 2, he claims that people were baptized "not merely as an outward sign of their new found faith but, again, under a promise of God that this baptism in water will issue in a baptism of the Spirit."[57] Colwell understands this event to indicate that God has promised to give His Spirit "in response to baptism."[58] Consequently, people may go to the waters of baptism expecting that promise to be fulfilled.[59]

Colwell is aware that not all scholars agree with his understanding of the connection between water-baptism and Spirit-baptism. In *Living the Christian Story*, he brings up and disagrees with Barth's distinction between water-baptism and Spirit-baptism, and Barth's claim that water-baptism is merely a human act.[60] In fact, Colwell develops his argument in that chapter in large part by refuting Barth's distinction. To make his case that water-baptism and Spirit-baptism are held together in the New Testament, Colwell refers to two primary passages. One is John 3:3–6. Colwell states that the best reading of those verses is "that to be born of water and to be born of the Spirit are inextricably linked, that the significance of the former is the reality of the latter."[61] Though he also acknowl-

---

54. Colwell, *Promise*, 57.
55. Colwell, *Promise*, 57.
56. Colwell, *Promise*, 111.
57. Colwell, *Rhythm of Doctrine*, 96.
58. Colwell, "Baptism," 220.
59. Colwell, *Promise*, 113.
60. Colwell, *Living*, 149.
61. Colwell, *Promise*, 113.

edges that this passage is "perhaps the most contested" passage about baptism, he also considers it to be the strongest New Testament witness to the meaning of baptism.[62] He also refers to Acts 2. Responding to the position that water-baptism is a witness to a previous Spirit-baptism, Colwell states, "It would seem quite impossible (to this writer at least) to reconcile this view of baptism . . . with the recorded words of Peter on the day of Pentecost."[63] Peter did not counsel the crowds to postpone baptism until they had received the Spirit.[64]

Baptism and Union With Christ

In Colwell's view, the giving of the Spirit and union with Christ should be held together. In baptism, then, not only does a person receive the Holy Spirit, he is also united to Christ. Colwell argues that the Spirit mediates our union with Christ, and baptism is the means of that mediation.[65] Baptism is therefore the means by which we are united to Christ in his death and resurrection. In Colwell's words, "And in this sense, therefore, the narrative of Jesus' baptism is the narrative of our baptism: just as he comes to baptism (as he also comes to the Cross) identifying with repentant sinners, so we come to his Cross through baptism, identifying ourselves as those with whom he identifies and for whom he dies."[66] In fact, Colwell claims that there is no account in the New Testament of a person being united to Christ apart from baptism.[67] He puts it another, more personal, way, stating, "In response to the question posed by the song, Were you there when they crucified my Lord?, the answer is 'Yes: (for me) on 2 December 1962 when I was baptised into his death and, subsequently, whenever I share in the bread and wine of Communion.'"[68] Colwell concludes that baptism in New Testament was "the climatic and crucial moment" of conversion.[69]

---

62. Colwell, *Promise*, 112.
63. Colwell, *Promise*, 119.
64. Colwell, *Promise*, 120.
65. Colwell, *Promise*, 121.
66. Colwell, *Promise*, 121.
67. Colwell, *Promise*, 125.
68. Colwell, *Promise*, 121.
69. Colwell, "Foreword," xii.

Baptism and a New Way of Life

For Colwell, union with Christ—and therefore baptism—necessarily involves a new orientation toward God and a new way of life. He points out that in 1 Pet 3:21 baptism is associated with the resurrection of Jesus and therefore signifies an entire new way of life.[70] He therefore states that "baptism is a matter of the orientation of the totality of life to God."[71] Indeed, he argues that the focus of baptism is not on dealing with past sins, but rather on a present and future participation in the resurrected life of Christ.[72] While not denying it completely, he downplays forgiveness of sins as a result of baptism and emphasizes instead a new "God-consciousness" that "issues in a life that is integrated with the gospel"—a concept he does not define.[73] He concludes that baptism is ethical in its focus. It involves a new orientation of our lives which is integrated with the life of Christ.[74]

Baptism as Both a Human Act and a Divine Act

While Colwell affirms that God is active in baptism, he also affirms that the person baptized is active in baptism. Baptism, then, is both a human act and a divine act. As we have seen, the divine activity consists of God giving the Holy Spirit and uniting the baptized person to Christ. The human activity consists of expressing repentance, appealing to God for salvation, and pledging one's life to God. Colwell especially highlights these human acts in his discussion of 1 Pet 3:21, which he considers to be a definition of baptism.[75] Concerning 1 Pet 3:21, Colwell claims that baptism is an enacted prayer, an appeal to God, which makes it possible for the baptized person to pledge his life to God.[76] In another essay, he simply refers to baptism as a "form of prayer."[77]

---

70. Colwell, "Baptism," 216.
71. Colwell, "Baptism," 216.
72. Colwell, "Baptism," 218.
73. Colwell, "Baptism," 219.
74. Colwell, "Baptism," 219.
75. Colwell, "Baptism," 210.
76. Colwell, *Promise*, 115. Colwell extrapolates this principle to all the sacraments (except marriage) and considers them to be human prayers in expectation of a divine event.
77. Colwell, *Living*, 153.

Understanding baptism as a prayer has implications for the proper subjects of baptism. As Colwell notes, as an enacted prayer, baptism must include the prayer of the one baptized,[78] which would seem to eliminate infants as proper subjects of baptism. However, Colwell argues that infant baptism is not completely invalid, but is instead "irregular."[79] This conclusion is in line with Beasley-Murray's final position on the issue.[80] In fact, Colwell says of Beasley-Murray, "His move to accept the validity of infant baptism (for all its irregularity) I found especially thought provoking and encouraging."[81]

Colwell indicates that he is sympathetic to, though not in full agreement with, Calvin's argument that reserving baptism for believers excludes infants from the church's "sacramental life, from the very means through which God's grace is mediated to us,"[82] though he offers no biblical support for the implication that God's grace is mediated to non-believing infants through the sacramental life of the church. He does claim that it is "perilous to belittle the unformed (and uninformed) faith of an infant,"[83] and raises the question of whether baptism might be a means through which faith is formed, including in infants.[84] Colwell comes across, at least in this portion of his writing, as considering the possibility of the validity of infant baptism more so than establishing a dogmatic position.

Like Beasley-Murray, Colwell also argues that while baptists are correct on the proper subjects of baptism, non-sacramental baptists are guilty of the same basic theological error made by paedobaptists. He suggests that both paedobaptists and non-sacramental baptists tend to separate the human activity and the divine activity that the New Testament indicates should both be present in baptism. For the paedobaptist, faith and prayer for salvation occur after baptism. For the non-sacramental baptist, faith and prayer for salvation occur before baptism.[85]

---

78. Colwell, *Promise*, 133.
79. Colwell, *Promise*, 134.
80. Beasley-Murray, "Problem of Infant Baptism," 13–14.
81. In response to a questionnaire, October 19, 2015.
82. Colwell, *Promise*, 129.
83. Colwell, *Promise*, 129.
84. Colwell, *Promise*, 130.
85. Colwell, *Promise*, 133.

In Colwell's view, though baptism is both a human act and a divine act, there is a priority given to the divine act in that the human act is dependent upon the divine. This priority shows up in his discussion of 1 Pet 3:21. He understands this verse to teach that baptism is a "prayerful promise." It is a promise to live a life consistent with God's life, but it is also a prayer because the promise is dependent upon the prior promise of God to be our God.[86] He makes a similar point in *Living the Christian Story*, writing, "The Christian can identify with Christ in baptism only because Christ has first, in his baptism, identified fully with sinful and repenting humanity. The Christian can be brought into coherence with the humanity of Christ through baptism only inasmuch as baptism, as a form of prayer, is enacted in light of the Father's promise to bring the Christian into this coherence through the Spirit."[87] Consequently, there is an expectation that God will keep His promises in the sacramental act. He writes, "if the sacraments are prayers in the light of prior divine promises then such prayers are offered in the confident expectation that those promises will be fulfilled."[88]

Two Clarifications

Colwell clarifies his view of baptism in two primary ways. The first has to do with the cause of salvation. Colwell is clear in his affirmation that baptism is a means of being united with Christ and therefore a means of conversion. He says explicitly, "I am not baptised in order to demonstrate to others that I have been converted (whether in the near or distant past). I am baptised as the means of that conversion."[89] However, he repeatedly distinguishes between being saved through baptism and being saved by baptism. Colwell consistently maintains that we are saved by God, through baptism.[90] We go wrong, Colwell argues, when we confuse instrumentality and agency.[91] Colwell is emphatic that "God is the efficient cause of grace with a sacrament." The Spirit and the Son are "agents" of

---

86. Colwell, "Baptism," 224.
87. Colwell, *Living*, 155.
88. Colwell, "Sacramental Nature," 237.
89. Colwell, "Foreword," xiii.
90. Colwell, "Baptism," 221.
91. Colwell, *Promise*, 60.

God's presence and action; all else is "instrumental."[92] Put another way, "We are saved *by* God *through* faith and *through* the sacraments,"[93] though here he offers no justification for adding "through the sacraments" to the biblical statement that we are saved by grace through faith (Eph 2:8).[94] While he has made a strong case for holding faith and the sacraments together, the reference to the sacraments in the above statement seems to suggest that the sacraments are not so much an expression of faith, but a means of salvation in addition to faith. Where the Bible places the emphasis on faith itself, Colwell adds the emphasis on the sacraments.

Writing about 1 Pet 3:21, Colwell claims that the focus of 1 Pet 3:21 is on the instrumental causality, and in three different senses—we are saved through baptism, through our orientation to God, and through the resurrection of Jesus.[95] He explains this verse by stating,

> This is not to imply that baptism is, in itself, the efficient cause of this new identity that reaches its fulfillment in final salvation. The text in question does not focus on the efficient cause of salvation. The only efficient cause (or "first") of salvation is the merciful and gracious love of God . . . the focus here is on instrumental causality—and that in three quite distinct senses, for to say that we are saved through baptism is not quite the same as saying that we are saved through our orientation to God, nor is it quite the same as saying that we are saved through the resurrection of Jesus Christ.[96]

He continues,

> We are now saved through baptism—we are not saved by baptism; baptism, like the waters of the flood, is the means God uses to bring us to the salvation that we now have through the resurrection of Jesus Christ. Baptism, like the waters of the flood, is the means God has chosen to bring us through judgment to a new beginning, it is grounded in his promise, but its efficacy is located in that promise rather than in itself.[97]

---

92. Colwell, *Promise*, 60.

93. Colwell, *Promise*, 130.

94. I am not aware of any commentator on Eph 2:8 who brings baptism into the discussion of that verse. See Wood, "Ephesians"; MacArthur, *Ephesians*; Chapell, *Ephesians*; Stott, *Message of Ephesians;* Theilman, *Ephesians;* Bruce, *Epistles to the Colossians.*

95. Colwell, "Baptism," 217.

96. Colwell, "Baptism," 217.

97. Colwell, "Baptism," 221.

The second way in which Colwell clarifies his position is to affirm that while God promises to use the sacrament of baptism, God is not bound by that sacrament. He remains free to give His Spirit and save people apart from baptism. He states repeatedly that baptism is not God's "prison." He argues that though God has promised to give His Spirit "in response to baptism," He can also give His Spirit at other times, since He is "never the prisoner of his own promise."[98] In *Promise and Presence* he claims that God "is not capricious, but neither is he subject to necessity; a sacrament may be the means of his presence, but it is never his prison."[99] Later he writes, "God is never confined or imprisoned in a sacramental sign; he remains free to mediate his presence and action elsewhere."[100] Colwell points out that God mediated His presence to Israel in the Temple, but He was not limited to the Temple.[101]

While maintaining that in the New Testament people were given the Spirit through baptism, Colwell concedes that there may be extraordinary reasons for God giving his Spirit through some other means.[102] We might note that given the current and historical situation in which both paedobaptists and many baptists have separated baptism from conversion, either the majority of professed Christians do not possess the Spirit, or the giving of the Spirit through some other means is not altogether extraordinary but is quite ordinary. Indeed, Colwell admits that "anomalies now abound."[103] Addressing the fact that some professed Christians have never been baptized, he affirms that unbaptized people can be saved, since "we are saved by the mercy of God *and nothing else.*"[104] He does not think, however, that unbaptized groups should be considered "Church," since they cannot be part of the visible church without the sacraments.[105] Such groups should be called "connections," but not "Church."[106]

---

98. Colwell, "Baptism," 220.
99. Colwell, *Promise*, 29.
100. Colwell, *Promise*, 59.
101. Colwell, *Promise*, 59.
102. Colwell, *Promise*, 124.
103. Colwell, *Promise*, 125.
104. Colwell, *Promise*, 125.
105. Colwell, *Promise*, 125.
106. Colwell, *Promise*, 126.

INFLUENCES ON COLWELL'S BAPTISMAL THEOLOGY

In his preface to *Promise and Presence,* Colwell acknowledges his gratitude to certain "mentors, conversation partners, colleagues, and editors" who have helped shape his theology of baptism.[107] One person who has been a significant influence on Colwell's thinking is Colin Gunton, who supervized Colwell's PhD. In Colwell's words, "Virtually every academic thought I have had has, in some respects, been a response to him and to his theological perception."[108] Colwell notes that the first section of *Promise and Presence*—which deals with the principle of sacramentality—is "dependent upon his insights."[109] Gunton's influence comes not so much from his writing on baptism but from his thoughts on the doctrine of God and the doctrine of creation, thoughts that are foundational to Colwell's understanding of the principle of sacramentality.

In *Promise and Presence,* Colwell engages Gunton's *The Triune Creator* and quotes it extensively at times. In that work, though Gunton does not address the sacraments, he does argue for "a satisfactory conception of mediation,"[110] by which he means that God creates, sustains and saves mediately, primarily through the Son and the Spirit. Colwell cites Gunton's argument that the Spirit relates the world to the Father,[111] as well as his claim that the material world is good and God relates to creation through material means.[112] These two ideas are axiomatic in Colwell's understanding of the sacraments, including baptism. Gunton, then, provides Colwell with a theological framework in which he develops his understanding of baptism.

Another significant conversation partner is Thomas Aquinas. Around 1998–1999, Colwell took a sabbatical during which he read *Summa Theologica.*[113] In 2015, Colwell stated, "Looking back all these years later I realise that it was a quite formative experience."[114] According to Colwell, Aquinas provides a "thoroughly systematic treatment of the sacraments," which develops the way in which the sacraments convey

---

107. Colwell, *Promise,* x.
108. Colwell, *Promise,* x.
109. Colwell, *Promise,* x.
110. Gunton, *Triune Creator,* 183.
111. Gunton, *Triune Creator,* 48.
112. Gunton, *Triune Creator,* 116.
113. Colwell, personal email, September 9, 2015.
114. Colwell, personal email, September 9, 2015.

grace.[115] Especially noteworthy is Aquinas's denial that the sacraments are the efficient cause of grace. God alone is the "efficient" or "first" cause of grace.[116] That distinction is central to Colwell's argument concerning the meaning of baptism, and affirming that Aquinas maintained this distinction is a theme that runs throughout Colwell's book.[117]

Colwell also frequently interacts with John Calvin. He especially highlights Calvin's distinction between the efficient cause and the instrumental cause of a sacrament, as well as the distinction between the immediate and the mediate.[118] He affirms Calvin's association of the sacraments with the promises of God,[119] which for Colwell, is an essential aspect of the very definition of a sacrament. Colwell is in agreement with Calvin that, not only are the sacraments a sign of "God's gracious promise to us," but they are also "a sign through which God, by His Spirit, accomplishes that which is signified."[120] Colwell states, "The point to note here is that Calvin, like Thomas, defines a sacrament primarily with respect to the dynamic of God's action."[121]

Karl Barth also serves as a conversation partner for Colwell, albeit a partner with whom Colwell has significant disagreement. According to Colwell,[122] in his *The Teaching of the Church Regarding Baptism*,[123] Barth argued for a more sacramental view of baptism. However, by 1967, "Barth had come to abandon any form of sacramental understanding of water-baptism."[124] Colwell is especially critical of Barth's distinction between divine action and human action.[125] His critique of Barth is in line with Gunton's critique of Barth, which again points to Gunton's influence on Colwell's thinking.[126]

---

115. Colwell, *Promise*, 7.
116. Aquinas, *Summa Theologica* III 62 1.
117. Colwell, *Promise*, 7.
118. Colwell, *Promise*, 9–10.
119. Colwell, *Promise*, 10, citing Calvin, *Institutes*, IV xiv 1.
120. Colwell, *Promise*, 10
121. Colwell, *Promise*, 10
122. Colwell, *Living*, 149–50.
123. Barth, *Teaching of the Church*.
124. Colwell, *Living*, 150.
125. Colwell, *Living*, 150.
126. Gunton, *Brief Theology of Revelation*, 16, 61.

BAPTISM, MANIC DEPRESSION, AND THE CHARISMATIC MOVEMENT[127]

As mentioned earlier, Colwell's involvement with the charismatic movement began when he was seventeen and was renewed and increased later in life.[128] He has since distanced himself theologically from the charismatic movement, which is seen in his writings as early as 1999.[129] The distancing was due largely to the movement's emphasis on an immediate experience of God's Spirit, an emphasis that is not limited to the charismatic movement. Colwell states that claims to immediacy are "assumed in any popular evangelical work that speaks of being born again as an unmediated felt experience; they're assumed (arguably) in IV/4 of Barth's *Church Dogmatics* and his discussion of Spirit-baptism; they're assumed in more popular works on Spirit-baptism and charismatic gifts; they were similarly assumed in standard Puritan accounts of conversion experience (e.g. as depicted in Bunyan's *Pilgrim's Progress* or *Grace Abounding*)."[130] He continues, "It's not that I repudiate such felt experiences (as I hope I make clear) but rather that I recognise that they are not universal and ought not to be taken as the basis of assurance."[131]

Colwell's concern about an emphasis on the immediate presence of the Spirit is not only theological but also experiential. By his own assessment, he had a negative and painful experience with the charismatic movement. He writes,

> I write not just as a student of theology but as a Christian pastor deeply disturbed by the spiritual and emotional damage wrought by the rival claims to immediacy (in the sense of the unmediated) and agency of which this book is a sustained rebuttal. In the second place, I write in conscious reflection on a personal pilgrimage marred at various points through the beguiling temptation to those rival claims, but marked more formatively (I trust) by an unpresuming confidence in the promise

---

127. Manic depression is sometimes referred to as "bipolar disorder." Colwell, however, uses the term "manic depression"(*Why?*, 11). That is the term, therefore, used here.

128. Colwell, *Why?*, 18.

129. Colwell, "Baptism."

130. Colwell, personal email, September 9, 2015.

131. Colwell, personal email, September 9, 2015.

of a mediated presence that lies at the root of a truly sacramental theology and spirituality.[132]

Colwell's negative and painful experience related to the idea of an unmediated presence is explained in large part by his ongoing struggle with manic depression, which has caused him to rely less on subjective feelings and more on external, objective helps. Due to not always recognizing when he is manic, even in the course of routine activities he relies on external help—such as an indication from his wife or a colleague—to help him function in the desired way.[133] This dependence on external means rather than subjective feelings carries over into spiritual realities. For Colwell, it can be a challenge to distinguish between clinical mania and authentic ecstatic spiritual experiences.[134] While affirming that the Spirit sometimes does strange things, and not dismissing felt experiences, Colwell became distrustful of his own felt experience[135] and finds assurance instead in God's promises and the sacraments. He explains,

> the sacraments of the Church took on a deeper significance as promises and seals of that which I could not feel or experience. Whether or not I felt like a child of God, I was baptised. Whether or not I still felt called by God, I was ordained. . . . I may lack any sense of feeling, I may struggle to believe at all, I may be convinced only of my wretchedness, I may feel abandoned by God, but the promise of his sacramental presence, not bound by my feelings or lack of feelings, remains.[136]

Tom Smail has made a similar point about his own experience. He states,

> When I taught in St John's College, Nottingham, I worshipped most days in the charismatic exuberance of the college chapel, but I was glad every Sunday to be part of a local parish of distinctly catholic churchmanship, where I was not under any pressure to shine with joy or glow with gifts, but was constantly reminded in the sacrament that, however I might be feeling or faring, what Christ had done on Calvary was done for ever and was available for me.[137]

---

132. Colwell, *Promise*, x.
133. Colwell, *Why?*, 22.
134. Colwell, *Why?*, 18.
135. Colwell, *Why?*, 19.
136. Colwell, *Why?*, 40.
137. Tom Smail, "In Spirit and in Truth," 112.

In *Promise and Presence* Colwell states, "I write as one who has wrestled with recurring depression for most of my adult life; I write as one for whom felt-experience is frequently elusive; I write as one for whom spiritual and emotional darkness have become common companions; I write as one for whom promise and mediated presence have therefore become increasingly precious."[138]

Three things should be said in response to Colwell's concern that felt-experience may be overemphasized. First, the Acts 2 narrative does in fact involve felt religious experience, as the cutting to the heart suggests in v. 37. As Bock points out, "The verb refers to a sharp pain or a stab, often associated with emotion."[139]

Second, such felt experiences can be, and should be, interpreted in light of God's promise that He will forgive and accept a person united to Christ through faith. In other words, for people on both sides of this issue, conversion can be associated with a promise of God. For Colwell, it is the promise to give the Spirit in baptism, assuming the presence of faith on the part of the one baptized.[140] For others, it is the promise to give the Spirit to faith apart from baptism. MacArthur, for example, affirms that forgiveness and the Spirit are promised to those who respond to the gospel in faith, but argues that the promise is associated with "repentance not baptism."[141]

Third, it is legitimate for Colwell to recognize that God has used these rites in his own life in a particular way—and it may even be helpful for other people to think about that particular function of the rites in their own lives. However, he goes too far in concluding his own experience with the rites is normative and should be decisive in our theology of the rites. Berkhof provides a more balanced approach, acknowledging that personal experience has a legitimate role to play in theology, while maintaining that "Scripture never refers to religious consciousness as a source and norm of the truth. Moreover, the religious consciousness is determined to a great extent by the environment in which man lives,

---

138. Colwell, *Promise*, x.

139. Bock, *Acts*, 140. MacArthur associates the term with "grief and remorse" in *Acts 1–12*, 71

140. Polhill, *Acts*, 116, agrees, "Here [in Acts 2:38–39] the Spirit seems to be promised immediately following or as a concomitant of baptism."

141. MacArthur, *Acts 1–12*, 74–75.

reveals significant variations, and therefore cannot be regarded as a dependable source."[142]

COLWELL'S APPROPRIATION OF THE WORK OF BEASLEY-MURRAY

Colwell was a student at Spurgeon's during the final three years of Beasley-Murray's tenure as Principal and studied New Testament under Beasley-Murray.[143] He writes about Beasley-Murray's influence on him in a number of places. In his *George Beasley-Murray Memorial Lecture* titled, "Catholicity and Confessionalism: responding to George Beasley-Murray on unity and distinctiveness," Colwell states, "Firstly, and most obviously, as one of his former pupils I owe a significant debt to his teaching, his influence, and his example."[144] Specifically, he mentions certain "habits of reading and expounding Scripture," "the clarity of his teaching and his tireless effort," and "his infectious passion for the gospel and for those distinctives that identified him as thoroughly Baptist."[145]

In *Promise and Presence* Colwell acknowledges Beasley-Murray's influence particularly in the area of baptismal theology. He expresses his gratitude to Beasley-Murray, "not just for his magisterial and definitive writing on the subject, but for his insistence to his students that there was a great deal more to baptism than mere witness—would that he had been better heeded by more of us."[146] When asked whether the work of George Beasley-Murray had shaped his own understanding of the meaning of baptism, Colwell answered,

> I couldn't really say that [Beasley-Murray's] views had significantly "shaped" my thinking about baptism. It would be more accurate to say that his emphases and example provoked my thinking about baptism. As a student (in the early 1970s) I had assumed a typically non-sacramental view of baptism (an outer witness to an inner work). George's stress on baptism's importance prompted me to think (and read) more deeply.[147]

142. Berkhof, *Systematic Theology*, 67
143. Colwell, "Catholicity and Confessionalism," 1.
144. Colwell, "Catholicity and Confessionalism," 1.
145. Colwell, "Catholicity and Confessionalism," 1.
146. Colwell, *Promise*, xi.
147. Colwell, in response to a questionnaire, October 19, 2015.

Despite Beasley-Murray's influence on Colwell personally, and Colwell's acknowledgement of the significance of *Baptism in the New Testament*,[148] Colwell does not often explicitly appropriate the work of Beasley-Murray in his own writing on baptism. In Colwell's works considered for this book, there are eight references to Beasley-Murray that are directly related to the meaning of baptism. Several of the citations are related to specific exegetical issues. Referring to his use of Beasley-Murray's exegesis, Colwell states, "Not being primarily a NT scholar, I have tended to take for granted the accuracy of [Beasley-Murray's] textual work and persuasiveness."[149]

Four of Colwell's references to Beasley-Murray are in his essay, "Baptism, Conscience and the Resurrection: A Reappraisal of 1 Pet 3:21." Twice Colwell cites Beasley-Murray's exegesis related to the phrase "through the water." Colwell believes the phrase is a parallel to the phrase "through the resurrection of Jesus Christ."[150] Colwell's primary reference is to Peter Davids's *The First Epistle of Peter*, though he also cites Beasley-Murray's *Baptism in the New Testament*, Grudem's *The First Epistle of Peter*, Marshall's *1 Peter*, and Achtmeier's *First Peter*. The purpose of citing Beasley-Murray at this point is to add support to Colwell's exegetical conclusion.

Colwell also references Beasley-Murray's claim that the phrase "through the water" should be understood in a locative, rather than an instrumental, sense.[151] Despite his tendency to "take for granted the accuracy of [Beasley-Murray's] textual work," on this particular point Colwell disagrees. He argues instead that 1 Pet 3:21 indicates that "baptism, like the waters of the flood, is the means God has chosen to bring us through judgment to a new beginning."[152] He cites Beasley-Murray, then, as a representation of an opposing view.

He again cites Beasley-Murray in connection with the claim that "baptism is ethical in focus."[153] According to Beasley-Murray, "the baptismal pattern of doctrine and conduct appears to be at the root of most of

---

148. Colwell, *Promise*, 110.
149. In response to a questionnaire, October 19, 2015.
150. Colwell, "Baptism," 217.
151. Colwell, "Baptism," 221.
152. Colwell, "Baptism," 221.
153. Colwell, "Baptism," 219.

1 Peter."¹⁵⁴ In this case, Colwell appears to appropriate an exegetical claim in support of an argument that is more theological in nature. Colwell relies on Beasley-Murray's expertise related to the book of 1 Peter in order to develop a theology of baptism.

The fourth reference to Beasley-Murray in this essay comes in Colwell's discussion of the word that can be translated as either "pledge" or "appeal."¹⁵⁵ In support of his claim that we should be cautious in our translation of a word that appears only once in the New Testament, he notes that Beasley-Murray, while appearing to favor an interpretation of "pledge," did not rule out the possibility of interpreting the word as "prayer."¹⁵⁶ In *Promise and Presence*, Colwell again cites Beasley-Murray's position on this verse. There, he notes that Beasley-Murray admits the possibility that it could be translated as "pledge" or "appeal," while others "simply assume the word refers to an 'appeal.'"¹⁵⁷ Colwell concludes that while the term could be translated either way, baptism can only be understood as a "pledge" if it is first understood as an "appeal," as that would protect the priority of divine action in relation to human action. This conclusion maintains proper caution in regards to the translation of the term while still putting forth a position that is theologically consistent with the rest of Scripture.

The remaining references to Beasley-Murray are found in Colwell's chapter on baptism in his book, *Promise and Presence*. In that chapter, he mentions the efforts of some British Baptists to argue for a sacramental view of baptism and lists several "contributions of particular note," including *Baptism in the New Testament*.¹⁵⁸ Though the inclusion of Beasley-Murray's book in this list does not necessarily indicate that it had an impact on Colwell's own work, it does indicate that Colwell considers it to be a significant work in the baptismal debate.

In his discussion of John 3, he mentions that one interpretation of Jesus' assertion that a person must be born of water is that a person must be born physically. He notes that Beasley-Murray refers to ideas related to that interpretation and dismisses them in his commentary on John.¹⁵⁹

154. Beasley-Murray, *Baptism in the New Testament*, 228.
155. Colwell, "Baptism," 222
156. Beasley-Murray, *Baptism Today*, 31–32, 96.
157. Colwell, *Promise*, 115.
158. Colwell, *Promise*, 110.
159. Colwell, *Promise*, 113.

This is another instance of appropriating and agreeing with Beasley-Murray's exegetical work.

The final reference to Beasley-Murray in the chapter on baptism concerns the relationship between faith, baptism, and salvation. Colwell refers to the insight that in the New Testament the same blessings are attributed to both faith and baptism, and he attributes that insight to Anthony Cross. He states, "I am grateful to Anthony R. Cross for painstakingly demonstrating that nothing is affirmed within the New Testament of baptism that is not also affirmed of faith and that nothing is affirmed within the New Testament of faith which is not also affirmed of baptism."[160] However, though he attributes the insight to Cross, he cites Beasley-Murray's *Baptism in the New Testament*. In the footnote he refers to "Anthony R. Cross' summary of Beasley-Murray's various expositions" of this insight. Colwell seems to have either received Beasley-Murray's insight through Anthony Cross—as did Nigel Wright—or has found Cross's presentation of the insight to be more helpful. In either case, he has appropriated a significant insight that originated with Beasley-Murray.

CONCLUSION

When considered in light of all the citations in Colwell's works on baptism, his references to Beasley-Murray are few. Nevertheless, Beasley-Murray's impact on Colwell's argument is evident in a number of ways. First, Colwell claims that Beasley-Murray has influenced him indirectly. Beasley-Murray challenged Colwell to reconsider his non-sacramental view and to think more deeply about the meaning of baptism. In that sense, then, Beasley-Murray stands in the background of Colwell's entire argument.

Second, if we take Colwell at his word, the exegetical work of Beasley-Murray is assumed throughout Colwell's work. At times, Beasley-Murray's work rises to the surface as Colwell cites specific exegetical points. This relationship between Beasley-Murray's work and Colwell's argument is explained by the differing expertise of the two scholars. Colwell, as a systematic theologian, relies on the exegetical work of New Testament scholars, but formulates his own argument theologically.

Third, as noted earlier, Colwell appropriates Beasley-Murray's insight that in the New Testament the same blessings are attributed to both

---

160. Colwell, *Promise*, 129–30.

faith and baptism. Though it is a single reference, it is a reference to a significant insight that incorporates a good deal of biblical material and is an important piece of Colwell's argument.

10

Anthony Cross

THIS CHAPTER WILL EXAMINE the role of George Beasley-Murray's work in the baptism-related writings of Anthony Cross. After a brief biographical sketch, the next section will focus on Cross's explicit acknowledgement of Beasley-Murray's influence on his own thinking about baptism. We will then examine Cross's view of baptism. Consideration of his integration of other scholars, including Beasley-Murray, will be included throughout the section on his own view of baptism.

This structure is a departure from the pattern of previous chapters. In previous chapters, we have first examined the baptismal theology of the scholar under consideration, and then, having established his view, we have considered his appropriation of Beasley-Murray and other scholars in a subsequent section. The different structure in this chapter is due to the way in which Cross develops his argument. He frequently advances his argument by appropriating the arguments of other people. For example, in his chapter, "The Spirit, the Sacraments, and the Material World," Cross advances the argument by examining the views of Calvin and Barth in a section titled "On the Sacraments and Spirit in Calvin and Barth: A Case Study."[1] At other points, as will be discussed below, he uses James D. G. Dunn as an extended conversation partner and develops his own argument by interacting extensively with Dunn. As for his interaction with Beasley-Murray, Cross often incorporates Beasley-Murray's arguments without any commentary or critique. At key points

---

1. Cross, *Recovering*, 158.

in his argument, he includes summaries of Beasley-Murray's arguments, long quotations of Beasley-Murray, or a series of references within a single section. Cross's own argument is, then, so intertwined with the arguments of others that separating them out can be problematic. This chapter, therefore, will consider them together. It will end with a consideration of why Cross appropriates Beasley-Murray the way that he does.

A BIOGRAPHICAL SKETCH OF ANTHONY CROSS

Anthony Cross's first pastorate was at Zion Baptist Church in Cambridge. George Beasley-Murray had previously served as pastor of that church and supplied Cross with materials and talked with him during Cross's tenure there.[2] Cross went on to pastor Calne Baptist Church in Witlshire, where Beasley-Murray preached at the first anniversary of Cross's induction.[3] Cross received his PhD from the University of Keele in 1997,[4] with George Beasley-Murray serving as one of two external examiners.[5] He then served as Research Fellow at the Centre for Advanced Theological Research, University of Roehampton (1998–2001); Research Fellow, Centre for Baptist History and Heritage, Regent's Park College (2003–2009); and Director of the Centre for Baptist History and Heritage, Regent's Park College (2009–2012).[6] At the time of writing, he serves as Emeritus Director of the Centre for Baptist History and Heritage and as a Research Fellow, Regent's Park College.[7]

Much of Cross's writing has focused on the theology of baptism. He contends that "Baptists—and, I want to add, believer-baptist Evangelicals—have so stressed the subjects of baptism that they fail to say anything about baptism itself."[8] Cross argues that more attention should be given to the meaning of baptism due to baptism's significance in the New Testament. He states,

> Those who would question whether baptism deserves the attention it is now receiving should stop and consider that it was

2. Cross, personal email, April 23, 2016.
3. Cross, personal email, April 23, 2016.
4. Goodliff, "British Baptist Theologians No. 6."
5. Cross, personal email, April 23, 2016.
6. Goodliff, "British Baptist Theologians No. 6."
7. Cross, Faculty Profile.
8. Cross, *Recovering*, 252

ordained by the risen Christ (Mt. 28.19) in such a clear way that Christians over 2,000 years have given it and the Lord's supper a special place in the life and worship of the Christian community; that on the day of Pentecost the apostle Peter includes it, along with repentance, as one aspect of the response required from the respondents to the gospel (Acts 2.38); the apostle Paul states that all believers were baptised in the one Spirit (1 Cor. 12.13); and Peter states we are saved by baptism (1 Pet. 3.21).[9]

Much of Cross's career has been an attempt to help Christians, particularly Baptists, think more biblically about baptism. His aim, in his own words, is "to build a cumulative and coherent case for the reintroduction of conversion-baptism/faith-baptism/mission-baptism into contemporary theology and practice."[10]

Cross has published a number of works related to the theology of baptism, and many will be considered in this study. Several of them have been compiled and published together in a single volume, *Recovering the Evangelical Sacrament*. Cross notes that this book is the product of over 20 years of researching the theology and practice of baptism. Much of the material previously appeared in other publications, and some has been "revised, refined, updated, sometimes I have taken issue with previous views, and in other instances material has been moved to different parts of the argument."[11] In the "Foreword," John Colwell offers this assessment of *Recovering the Evangelical Sacrament*,

> It is now fifty years since the publication of George Beasley-Murray's magisterial *Baptism in the New Testament*. There have been many notable, perceptive, and challenging contributions to the baptismal debate since then, but the comprehensiveness, critical scholarly care, and uncompromising challenge of this present volume has few rivals.[12]

---

9. Cross, *Recovering*, 313.

10. Cross, *Recovering*, 39.

11. Cross, *Recovering*, xiv. This is why many, though not all, references in this chapter are to a single source.

12. Colwell, *Recovering*, xiii.

ANTHONY CROSS AND GEORGE BEASLEY-MURRAY

As will be demonstrated in the next section, the significance of Beasley-Murray's work in Cross's argument is evident throughout Cross's writings. It is also, however, explicitly acknowledged by Cross in a number of places. Cross states, "It was as a result of reading Beasley-Murray that I started to move away from the traditional, symbolic view of baptism, and toward an understanding of baptism as a means of grace, and an essential part of NT conversion, i.e., faith-baptism."[13] In *Recovering the Evangelical Sacrament*, Cross acknowledges Beasley-Murray as one of several people who "have taught, challenged, and encouraged" him.[14] He states that his work, *Should We Take Peter at His Word (Acts 2:38)?*, was written "In memory of the Rev. Dr George R. Beasley-Murray, who, more than any other Baptist scholar, has led the way to the recovery of a biblically-based, Baptist baptismal sacramentalism. In love and with gratitude."[15] In the introduction to *Baptist Sacramentalism*, Cross and Philip Thompson claim the exchange between L. A. Read and Beasley-Murray after the publication of *Christian Baptism* provides "the scriptural basis for a sacramental reading of various New Testament passages related to baptism."[16] They also state, "Further, we believe it is impossible to read Beasley-Murray's sacramentalist interpretation of baptism, *Baptism in the New Testament*, and not be impressed by the integrity of the author in seeking to understand New Testament baptism."[17] When Cross argued for what he calls "faith-baptism" in his Dr. G. R. Beasley-Murray Memorial Lecture, he stated that his intent was to "allow Beasley-Murray to speak for himself."[18] His lecture was essentially a summary of Beasley-Murray's view.

In addition to Cross's own acknowledgment of Beasley-Murray's influence, Andy Goodliff has also noted the impact of Beasley-Murray's work on Cross:

> Anthony R. Cross has been thinking and writing about baptism for well over twenty years. His doctoral studies were published as *Baptism and the Baptists* (Paternoster, 2000) and he has now followed that with *Recovering the Evangelical Sacrament*, the

---

13. Cross, personal email, April 23, 2016.
14. Cross, *Recovering*, xv.
15. Cross, *Should We Take?*
16. Cross and Thompson, "Introduction," 3
17. Cross and Thompson, "Introduction," 3–4.
18. Cross, "Faith-Baptism," 19.

product of his work done since then. Cross is an evangelical about baptism and, what he argues, as a proper evangelical understanding of baptism, which he says is the New Testament understanding of baptism, which is conversion-baptism. The book is a collection of essays and articles (some published) in the last ten years, which offer a sustained argument for conversion-baptism. In this Cross is a disciple of George Beasley-Murray, who argued to his own generation for a rich theological and biblical understanding of baptism.[19]

He points out that in *Recovering the Evangelical Sacrament*, "Beasley-Murray is the most cited name in the numerous (and often long) footnotes."[20]

ANTHONY CROSS'S VIEW OF BAPTISM AND HIS APPROPRIATION OF GEORGE BEASLEY-MURRAY

Baptism as a Sacrament

Cross argues that baptism is more than a human act with a merely symbolic significance. He claims that God is active in baptism. He notes that for many Baptists, baptism is primarily "our act for God, our response to a salvation already given by God and received in faith." It is, then, "the expression of spiritual realities already appropriated."[21] To refute that claim, Cross immediately refers to Beasley-Murray, who denied that the confessional dimension of baptism was the primary meaning of baptism. What is primary, according to Beasley-Murray—and Cross—is "God's work in Christ on our behalf."[22]

Against the symbolic view of baptism, then, Cross argues for a sacramental understanding of baptism. In *Recovering the Evangelical Sacrament,* he defines the term "sacrament." After noting that there is no agreed definition, he asserts that the best definition is "a visible sign of a sacred thing, or a visible form of an invisible grace."[23] He relies heavily on Beasley-Murray to explain the meaning of "sacrament." He asserts that Beasley-Murray allows the New Testament teaching on baptism to "give

19. Andy Goodliff, "Book Review."
20. Andy Goodliff, "Book Review."
21. Cross, "Evangelical Sacrament," 201.
22. Cross, "Evangelical Sacrament," 201.
23. Cross, *Recovering*, 188.

meaning to it as a sacrament."²⁴ He goes on to point out that Beasley-Murray approved of two definitions of the term "sacrament"—"sacramentum" and "means of grace."²⁵ Cross clarifies that Beasley-Murray meant more by "means of grace" than is usually meant, since in Beasley-Murray's view "the whole height and depth of grace is bound up with the experience of baptism."²⁶ Cross also quotes Beasley-Murray's claim that a sacrament is "the Word of God in action" which "must be responded to in the act of participating."²⁷ He includes a quote from *Worship and the Sacraments* in which Beasley-Murray rejects a mechanical understanding of baptism and insists that baptism is effective because of the nature of God, the promises of God, the work of Christ, the work of the Spirit, and the faith of the believer.²⁸

Cross refers to, and agrees with, Beasley-Murray's claim that baptism and the Lord's Supper are "pre-eminent among the means of grace," but are not the only means of grace.²⁹ They are pre-eminent because they were ordained by Christ. There are other means of grace, however, because God is free to use any part of his creation to relate to His people.³⁰ Cross agrees with Pinnock that "Created reality [is] richly imbued with sacramental possibilities."³¹ He argues that while God is not limited in how he gives grace, he often does so through material means. The most significant example is the incarnation. He points out that our salvation was achieved by the physical death and resurrection of Jesus.³²

Cross acknowledges that some Baptists are uncomfortable with the term "sacrament," against the backdrop of the Oxford Movement, as was shown in chapter 7.³³ Nevertheless, he states, "it is the teaching of the New Testament which determines our theology not our historically con-

---

24. Cross, *Recovering*, 189.

25. Cross, *Recovering*, 189.

26. Cross, *Recovering*, 189, quoting Beasley-Murray, "The Spirit Is There," 8.

27. Cross, *Recovering*, 189, quoting Beasley-Murray, "Baptism and the Sacramental View," 11.

28. Cross, *Recovering*, 190, quoting Beasley-Murray, *Worship and the Sacraments*, 9.

29. Cross, *Recovering*, 190, quoting Beasley-Murray, *Worship and the Sacraments*, 9.

30. Cross, *Recovering*, 192.

31. Cross, *Recovering*, 189, quoting, Pinnock, *Flame of Love*, 120

32. Cross, *Should We Take?*, 19

33. Cross, "Faith-Baptism," 24.

ditioned aversion to a particular post-biblical theological development summarised in one particular understanding of the phrase 'baptismal regeneration.' Baptists should not reject a term simply because of some of the excesses ascribed to it."[34] Though Cross does not mention Thomas Schreiner, his argument at this point offers a rebuttal to Schreiner's reluctance to use the term "sacrament." As was discussed in the chapter on Schreiner, he understands a "sacramental" view of baptism to be one in which saving grace is automatically conferred through baptism.[35] He associates a sacramental view with an *ex opere operato* view, in which baptism "saves by virtue of the action itself being performed."[36] Again, Cross is aware of that concern related to the term "sacrament" but maintains that a term should not be rejected simply because it has been abused.[37]

Citing Fowler's *More Than a Symbol* for support, Cross maintains that a sacramental understanding of baptism is not an innovation for Baptists but a recovery of earlier Baptist thought.[38] Even more importantly for Cross, he believes that "a sacramental theology of baptism can be found in the New Testament."[39]

Faith-Baptism

Cross refers to his view of baptism as "faith-baptism."[40] By that, he means that in the New Testament baptism is an expression of faith in response to the gospel.[41] Quoting Beasley-Murray, Cross argues, "in the New Testament faith and baptism are viewed as inseparable whenever the subject of Christian initiation is under discussion, so that if one is referred to, the other is presupposed, even if not mentioned."[42] He quotes approvingly James Denney's conclusion that "baptism and faith are but the outside and inside of the same thing."[43]

34. Cross, *Should We Take?*, 16–17; Cross, *Recovering*, 189.
35. Schreiner, "Baptism in the Epistles," 69.
36. Schreiner, "Baptism in the Epistles," 70.
37. Cross, *Recovering*, 189.
38. Cross, *Should We Take?*, 3.
39. Cross, *Should We Take?*, 11.
40. Cross, *Should We Take?*, 12.
41. Cross, *Recovering*, 91.
42. Cross, "'One Baptism,'" 174, quoting Beasley-Murray, *Baptism in the New Testament*, 272.
43. Cross, *Recovering*, 56, quoting Denney, *Death of Christ*, 101.

Like Beasley-Murray, Cross believes that both paedobaptists and credobaptists have made the same fundamental mistake of separating faith from baptism.[44] Cross mentions Charles Spurgeon as one example of a Baptist who made this mistake.[45] He also interacts with Nettles on this point. Cross devotes a lengthy paragraph to an explanation of Nettles's view. After a series of quotations from Nettles's essay, "Baptist View: Baptism as a Symbol of Christ Saving Work," Cross concludes, "According to Nettles Paul distinguishes between faith and baptism."[46]

Cross considers such a separation to be unbiblical, and to wrongly drive a wedge between spirit and matter.[47] He points out that in the New Testament, "Baptism was also intimately connected to the forgiveness of sins and the reception of the Spirit (Acts 2.38), union with Christ in his death and resurrection (Rom. 6.3–9), incorporation into the body of Christ, the church (1 Cor. 12.13), and regeneration (Tit. 3.5)."[48] He recognizes that this appears to attribute to baptism what should only be attributed to faith. He addresses that concern by asserting that in the New Testament, faith is always implicit in any reference to baptism,[49] and claims, "We can better understand New Testament baptism when we recognize that it is faith-baptism."[50]

To make his case, he relies heavily on the work of Beasley-Murray. Cross states, "If there is any doubt that New Testament baptism is faith-baptism, then the work of George Beasley-Murray should dispel it once for all."[51] He quotes Beasley-Murray's observation that "the New Testament writers associate the full range of salvation on the one hand with baptism and on the other hand with faith."[52] He provides a detailed chart, which is "a summary of the work in various places of G. R. Beasley-Murray," which shows that in the New Testament each of the following is at times associated with faith, and at times associated with baptism: forgiveness, justification, union with Christ, being crucified with Christ,

44. Cross, *Should We Take?*, 8.
45. Cross, *Should We Take?*, 1.
46. Cross, *Recovering*, 64–65.
47. Cross, "Evangelical Sacrament," 203.
48. Cross, "Evangelical Sacrament," 202.
49. Cross, *Recovering*, 56.
50. Cross, "Evangelical Sacrament," 202.
51. Cross, "Evangelical Sacrament," 206.
52. Cross, "Evangelical Sacrament," 206; quoting, Beasley-Murray, "Authority and Justification," 65.

death and resurrection, sonship, Holy Spirit, entry into the church, regeneration and life, the kingdom and eternal life, and salvation.[53] Cross concludes, "It is clear, therefore, that God's gift to faith and baptism is one, namely, salvation in Christ."[54] There is an "intimate and inseparable connection of faith and baptism *in the New Testament*" (italics his).[55]

It has been pointed out in previous chapters that other scholars have made use of Beasley-Murray's observation that in the New Testament the same blessings are associated with both faith and baptism. As is the case with those other scholars, this observation is a fundamental premise in Cross's argument. However, this is not the only way in which Cross appropriates Beasley-Murray in his argument that New Testament baptism is faith-baptism. Cross also asserts that studies of Acts have demonstrated the "legitimacy of sacramental interpretations."[56] As evidence, he cites Beasley-Murray's *Baptism in the New Testament*, pp. 93–125. Though a single citation, it is a reference to 32 pages of Beasley-Murray's argument.

At another point, Cross states, "As we have shown, a major key to interpreting baptism sacramentally is highlighted in the many writings of George Beasley-Murray and his demonstration that baptism in the New Testament is to be understood as nothing less than faith-baptism. While it is not necessary to repeat all that Beasley-Murray says, it is worth noting what he says on two key baptismal passages—Gal 3.26–27 and 1 Pet 3.21."[57] Cross then makes 12 references to Beasley-Murray, including three lengthy quotes, by which Cross argues that New Testament baptism is faith-baptism.[58]

Conversion-Baptism

Understanding baptism as faith-baptism leads Cross to a related conclusion, namely, that baptism is also conversion-baptism, a term he attributes to Beasley-Murray.[59] In fact, Cross refers approvingly to Beasley-Murray's

---

53. Cross, "Evangelical Sacrament," 207; Cross, *Recovering*, 59.
54. Cross, *Recovering*, 60.
55. Cross, *Recovering*, 60.
56. Cross, *Recovering*, 163.
57. Cross, *Recovering*, 176.
58. Cross, *Recovering*, 177–78.
59. Cross, *Should We Take?*, 9.

claim that in the New Testament "baptism was conversion."[60] In his chapter, "Baptism: Becoming a Christian,"[61] Cross draws extensively from Beasley-Murray to argue that baptism in the New Testament is conversion-baptism. He writes, "Beasley-Murray then demonstrates from other baptismal passages the means God uses to impart his saving grace."[62] He provides Beasley-Murray's list of the blessings that God bestows on believers, in which he shows that each blessing is associated with both faith and baptism. He then states Beasley-Murray's conclusion:

> Beasley-Murray sees the only possible conclusion from this as, "If God gives his gracious gifts to faith and baptism, he gives them in association, i. e., he gives them to faith in baptism, or (which amounts to the same) to baptism in faith." He acknowledges how different this is from our way of thinking about baptism, but is driven to the position that "baptism, for Paul, was the climax of conversion. Because the experiences of conversion and baptism were viewed as a unity, he could ascribe to baptism a content that we normally reserve for conversion and which, in fact, can be predicated only of a radical turning to God in Christ. But that was precisely what constituted the heart of apostolic baptism."[63]

In his lecture, "Faith-Baptism: The Key to an Evangelical Baptismal Sacramentalism," Cross again argues that baptism and conversion should be held together. He quotes Beasley-Murray's Holdsworth-Grigg Memorial Lecture at Whitley College in Melbourne:

> The descriptions of baptism in the New Testament, and the indications of the apostolic teaching on its meaning, make it plain that the early church viewed baptism as the completion of conversion to God. The baptism of John the Baptist is described by Mark as a "repentance baptism" (Mark 1:4), and scholars are agreed that in this context repentance means "turning to God"; i.e. what we mean by conversion. This way of viewing baptism became normative in the Christian church, whatever else was attached to the significance of the rite.[64]

60. Cross, *Recovering*, 42.

61. Though the book was co-authored with Haymes and Gouldbourne, Cross wrote the chapters on baptism (Cross, personal email, April 23, 2016).

62. Haymes, Gouldbourne, and Cross, *On Being the Church*, 63.

63. Haymes, Gouldbourne, and Cross, *On Being the Church*, 63; quoting Beasley-Murray, *Baptism in the New Testament*, 28.

64. Cross, "Faith-Baptism."

Cross agrees with Beasley-Murray that in the New Testament it is "axiomatic that conversion and baptism are inseparable, if not indistinguishable. In the primitive apostolic Church baptism was 'conversion-baptism.'"[65] Cross contends that while the separation of conversion and baptism may at times have been made for "highly commendable, ecumenical reasons,"[66] "our desire to be thoroughly biblical might (and I believe should) lead us to restore baptism to its New Testament place in conversion and in the gospel we proclaim."[67]

Closely associated with conversion is a person's union with Christ. The concept of conversion-baptism, then, carries with it the idea that a person is united to Christ in baptism. According to Cross, the fact that baptism is in the name of the triune God implies that it is in baptism that a person is united to Christ. He notes that much exegetical work has been done concerning the baptism formula "in the name of the Father and of the Son and the Holy Spirit" in relation to the accounts in Acts of baptism being "in the name of Jesus Christ" or "in the name of the Lord Jesus."[68] He specifically cites Beasley-Murray's *Baptism in the New Testament*, pp. 77–92, 100. He goes on to quote Beasley-Murray's conclusion: "On this analogy baptism, in the name of the [Trinity], sets the baptised in a definite relation to God; the Father, Son and Holy Spirit become to the baptised what their name signifies. . . . From this point of view baptism in the name of the [Trinity] takes place for the sake of God, to make the baptised over to God."[69] Cross highlights our union with Christ even more explicitly in his defense of baptism by immersion, again drawing from Beasley-Murray. He devotes a paragraph to Beasley-Murray's argument in favor of baptism by immersion, citing *Baptism Today and Tomorrow*. Summarizing approximately four pages, Cross states, "The act of immersion beneath the water and then rising out of it is peculiarly appropriate to an action which derives its meaning from our identification with Christ who died, was buried and rose again for humanity's salvation."[70]

---

65. Cross, "'One Baptism,'" 174; quoting Beasley-Murray, *Baptism Today*, 37–38.

66. Cross, "Evangelical Sacrament," 214.

67. Cross, "Evangelical Sacrament," 215.

68. Haymes, Gouldbourne, and Cross, *On Being the Church*, 63; quoting Beasley-Murray, *Baptism in the New Testament*, 57.

69. Haymes, Gouldbourne, and Cross, *On Being the Church*, 63; quoting Beasley-Murray, *Baptism in the New Testament*, 57.

70. Cross, *Recovering*, 282.

One practical implication of baptism being conversion-baptism is that the biblical norm is immediate baptism upon belief in the gospel. Cross cites Beasley-Murray's observation in "The Sacraments" that in the New Testament "every recorded baptism takes place immediately upon profession of faith."[71] At another point he refers to Beasley-Murray's observation that in the conversion stories in Acts, there was not sufficient time between the profession of faith and baptism for extended instruction. Teaching came after baptism, not before.[72] Cross writes, "Many will object that baptism needs to be postponed so that a candidate's fitness for baptism can be ascertained. But we must recall Beasley-Murray's comments that in doing so we in fact alter New Testament baptism."[73] At this point, Cross has appropriated and integrated Beasley-Murray's argument as his own.

Baptism and the Gift of the Holy Spirit

Cross believes that the biblical norm is for the Holy Spirit to be given in baptism. In *On Being the Church*, Cross argues that in the New Testament water-baptism and Spirit-baptism are coterminous.[74] In support of that claim he references *Baptism in New Testament*, pp. 167–71, 275–79. Although not all scholars agree with that view, as will be discussed below, Cross claims that there is a now a general consensus among scholars about the relationship between water-baptism and Spirit-baptism, and he attributes that consensus to Beasley-Murray and others.[75] In reference to closely associating water-baptism with Spirit-baptism, Cross asserts that the association must be justified not only with exegetical arguments but also with theological reasons. He states, "Beasley-Murray provides such justification in his exegetically *and* theologically-based study."[76] Cross, therefore, leans on Beasley-Murray for both exegetical and theological insight.

Exegetically, Cross focuses much of his discussion on 1 Cor 12:13. About that verse he writes, "While the primary reference is clearly to

71. Cross, "'One Baptism,'" 186.
72. Cross, *Recovering*, 95.
73. Cross, *Should We Take?*, 24.
74. Haymes, Gouldbourne, and Cross, *On Being the Church*, 59.
75. Cross, "'One Baptism,'" 174.
76. Cross, *Recovering*, 144.

Spirit-baptism, there seems to be no strong reason to doubt that the Corinthians would have recalled their water-baptism, particularly if these elements were not just closely associated within the conversion-initiation process, as the New Testament texts clearly witness (most explicitly in Jn 3.5; Acts 2.38), but also in time, that is, immediate baptism."[77]

In his chapter, "Spirit- and Water-Baptism in 1 Cor 12:13," Cross identifies two positions on this verse—one is that it is a reference to water-baptism and Spirit-baptism, the other is that it is a reference to Spirit-baptism only. He examines the first position "through one of its main advocates, George R. Beasley-Murray."[78] Cross refers to the position that Paul is talking about water-baptism as the view "championed by Beasley-Murray."[79] In a section titled, "Water-Baptism as the Locus for the Reception of the Spirit," Cross takes over two pages to simply present Beasley-Murray's argument that water-baptism is the "supreme moment" of the impartation of the Spirit and of the work of the Spirit in the believer. Again, Cross not only draws from Beasley-Murray, but actually presents Beasley-Murray's argument as a way of making his own case.

Not all commentators agree with Cross's and Beasley-Murray's interpretation of this verse. Fee, for example, who cites *Baptism in the New Testament* as representative of the view that Paul is referring to the sacrament of baptism, contends that "baptized" by itself would imply baptism with water, but the phrase "baptized in the Spirit" refers only to Spirit-baptism. While he may have a point, his claim that in Paul water-baptism and Spirit-baptism are not tied together in a way that suggests the Spirit is given in baptism, while debatable in itself, certainly does not take into consideration the baptismal accounts in Acts and therefore weakens his overall argument.[80] Garland, in his commentary on this verse, concludes that it is not clear whether Paul has in mind Spirit-baptism or water-baptism, though he suggests the phrase "baptized into the name of Paul" earlier in the letter certainly recalled water-baptism.[81]

Cross also integrates Beasley-Murray in his discussion of the phrase "one baptism" in Eph 4:5. First, he uses Beasley-Murray to establish that the New Testament does not allow for a separation of water-baptism and

---

77. Cross, "'One Baptism,'" 191.
78. Cross, *Recovering*, 130.
79. Cross, *Recovering*, 142.
80. Fee, *First Epistle to the Corinthians*, 604.
81. Garland, *1 Corinthians*, 591.

Spirit-Baptism. He quotes *Baptism in the New Testament* (p. 278 and p. 275): "the New Testament writers . . . think of baptism in terms of grace and faith—always grace, always faith." He continues with Beasley-Murray's statement, "in the Acts and Epistles baptism is the supreme moment of the impartation of the Spirit and of the work of the Spirit in the believer."[82]

In addition to exegetical reasons, Cross believes there is a theological reason for associating water-baptism and Spirit-baptism. He cites a lengthy quotation from Beasley-Murray claiming that Christ and his gifts cannot be divided from the Spirit.[83] Cross maintains that if baptism is associated with one, it must be associated with the other as well. Nevertheless, Cross is in agreement with the others in this study who hold a sacramental view, that God is not bound by the sacraments and is free to bestow His Spirit however He chooses. To make his case, Cross again references Beasley-Murray.[84]

Baptismal Regeneration

Consistent with the view that in the New Testament baptism is the moment of conversion, which includes a person's union with Christ and reception of the Spirit, Cross argues that in the New Testament baptism is also the moment of regeneration. He begins his argument by demonstrating that theologians throughout the church's history have believed in baptismal regeneration.[85] He starts with Justin Martyr, who said of those who believe the gospel, "Then we lead them to a place where there is water, and they are regenerated in the same manner in which we ourselves were regenerated. In the name of God, the Father and Lord of all, and of our Savior, Jesus Christ, and of the Holy Spirit, then they receive the washing of water."[86] Cross also quotes Theophilus of Antioch (c. 180) Irenaeus (c. 202), Clement of Alexandria (c. 170), and Cyprian (c. 250), who claim that baptism is the occasion of forgiveness and new birth.[87]

---

82. Cross, "'One Baptism,'" 186.
83. Cross, *Recovering*, 150.
84. Cross, *Should We Take?*, 18–19.
85. Cross, *Recovering*, 198–99.
86. Justin Martyr, "First Apology 61," 38–39.
87. Cross, *Recovering*, 201; see Augustine, "Letter 98, section 2," 407.

Cross also claims that Calvin argued for baptismal regeneration.[88] Indeed, Calvin claims that "through baptism Christ makes us sharers in his death," and that "those who receive baptism with right faith truly feel the effective working of Christ's death" (Inst 4.15.5). However, Cross may press Calvin too far in service of Cross's argument for baptismal regeneration. As David Wright points out, for Calvin, infants were baptized because they were already regenerate.[89]

Cross claims that the reason baptismal regeneration has been present in theologians throughout the church's history is that it is present in the New Testament.[90] When he begins to discuss the New Testament evidence, he turns immediately to Beasley-Murray, stating, "That baptismal regeneration is to be found within the New Testament has been argued for by Beasley-Murray. His argument for it is a thorough-going and biblical-theological one."[91] Cross cites *Baptism in the New Testament*, where Beasley-Murray does in fact associate baptism with regeneration.

> Baptism witnesses to a rising from the dead (Rom. 6.1ff, Col 2.12), the reception of the Spirit (1 Cor. 12.13), life in Christ (Gal 3.27), which involves the believer in participation in the new creation (2 Cor. 5.17); the believer puts on the "new man" (Col. 3.9ff), which is the new nature bestowed through union with the Second Adam, thus again signifying the life of the new creation. What is all this but "regeneration" under different images? It is the reality without the word. The reality and the word come together in Tit. 3.5ff.[92]

Among the scholars under consideration in this book, Cross is not alone in associating baptism with regeneration. Cross references Schreiner's view that in Titus 3:5 "regeneration" and "washing" both refer to the same reality, namely, the believer's new life upon conversion.[93] Cross also notes the similarity between Schreiner's position and Beasley-Murray's position at this point.[94]

---

88. Cross, *Recovering*, 201.
89. Wright, *What Has Infant Baptism Done?* 100.
90. Cross, *Recovering*, 205.
91. Cross, *Recovering*, 205.
92. Beasley-Murray, *Baptism in the New Testament*, 278.
93. Cross, *Recovering*, 207; referencing Schreiner, "Baptism in the Epistles," 85.
94. Cross, *Recovering*, 207.

Some scholars, however, interpret Titus 3:5 differently, denying that it is a reference to baptism. John MacArthur, for example, understands "washing" as a reference to sins being washed away with no mention of baptism. He connects this verse to Eph 5:26, which refers to "the washing of water with the word." For him, it is the word of God, seemingly apart from baptism, that cleanses.[95]

Towner comments, "But here, as in Eph 5:26, [washing] falls into the metaphorical sphere, with the image of washing referring to a spiritual cleansing. Some have seen in this image a reference to the rite of water-baptism, but there is reason to see it rather as a reference to the work of the Spirit in terms of a 'washing' that, then, the outward rite of water-baptism might serve to symbolise."[96]

George Knight III also understands it metaphorically, noting that Paul could have used the word for baptism if that was what he meant but instead used a term that refers to an inner washing. He concludes, "They did not speak of baptism as saving them or as being the means of salvation but of a past action wrought by regeneration, which baptism symbolised and represented."[97]

Because there is no explicit mention of baptism in this verse, a person's theology of baptism will inform whether he understands this "washing" as a reference to baptism. Beasley-Murray, Schreiner, and Cross have developed a sacramental understanding of baptism from many other verses and are therefore more likely to interpret this verse sacramentally as well.

Cross is aware that baptismal regeneration is often associated with an *ex opere operato* view of baptism,[98] largely due to the legacy of the Oxford Movement.[99] Like the others in this study who hold a sacramental view, Cross safeguards against what is sometimes called a "magical" [that is, *ex opere operato*] understanding of baptism by insisting that faith is necessary for baptism.[100] He points to Gal 3:26–27 and Col 2:12, both of which associate faith with baptism.[101] He also cites Beasley-Murray, who

---

95. MacArthur, *Titus*, 154.
96. Towner, *Letters to Timothy and Titus*, 781.
97. Knight, *Pastoral Epistles*, 350.
98. Cross, *Recovering*, 207.
99. Cross, "Faith-Baptism," 24.
100. Cross, *Should We Take?*, 11.
101. Cross, *Should We Take?*, 12.

claimed that faith is "not simply an adjunct to baptism but is part of its structure."[102]

In another place he notes that Beasley-Murray safeguards against an *ex opere operato* view by asserting that in the New Testament both grace and faith are present in baptism.[103] In another essay Cross again quotes Beasley-Murray to emphasize the necessity of faith in biblical baptism. "The responsive element of baptism is underscored by the confessional context in which it appears to have been set from the beginning: the candidate confessed Jesus as Lord and faith in the gospel (Rom 10.9)."[104]

As discussed above, the necessity of faith is central to Cross's view of baptism, which he calls "faith-baptism." When we talk about baptism, then, we should also be talking about faith. That is certainly the case, according to Cross, for the New Testament writers. This allows Cross to emphatically maintain that people are saved by grace through faith,[105] while at the exact same time maintaining that people are regenerated in baptism. For Cross, baptism in the New Testament is nothing less than the meeting of divine grace and human faith. He states,

> If separated from the gracious work of God by his Spirit and faith in Christ, baptismal regeneration is, of course, to be rejected, but when understood as the believer's faithful, subjective response to the gracious, objective call of God in the gospel of Christ and the working of the Holy Spirit, then it is something we need to re-discover in our quest to be more biblical in our theology and practice of baptism.[106]

Baptism as a Trysting Place

Because Cross understands baptism as a meeting of divine grace and human faith, he refers to it as "a trysting place" between God and the person baptized, a term that Cross attributes to Beasley-Murray.[107] Though Lu-

---

102. Cross, *Should We Take?*, 11.

103. Cross, *Recovering*, 205; referencing Beasley-Murray, *Baptism in the New Testament*, 278.

104. Cross, *Recovering*, 251; quoting Beasley-Murray, *Baptism in the New Testament*, 285.

105. Cross, *Recovering*, 51.

106. Cross, *Recovering*, 213.

107. Cross, *Recovering*, 278.

ther used that term as well,[108] Cross claims "there is nothing to indicate that [Beasley-Murray] was indebted to Luther for it."[109] Cross not only borrows the term from Beasley-Murray but appropriates Beasley-Murray in order to explain the concept.

When arguing that baptism is a "trysting place" in *Should We Take Peter at His Word (Acts 2:38)?*, Cross incorporates Beasley-Murray's argument. Cross writes, "Baptism is, therefore, 'the trysting place' of the sinner with their Saviour in what Emil Brunner terms the divine-human encounter. Beasley-Murray notes that while in Paul's teaching of baptism as dying and rising with Christ in Rom 6.1–11 the emphasis is wholly on God's action, nevertheless a believer's responsiveness is indivisibly one with it." He continues, "[Beasley-Murray] concludes that from the human side 'faith is viewed as the operative power of baptism,' and adds that for the apostolic writers 'Baptism was never conceived of . . . apart from faith that turns to the Lord for salvation. Any interpretation of baptism that diminishes the crucial significance of faith is unfaithful to the apostolic gospel.'"[110] In *On Being the Church*, Cross follows the same pattern. He borrows Beasley-Murray's term and then refers to the same passages quoted above to allow him to explain its meaning.[111]

Baptism as Synecdoche

Cross believes that some references to baptism in the New Testament are synecdoche, meaning baptism, as part of the process of conversion, is used as a reference to the entire process. This view includes the belief that conversion is in fact a process. Cross notes that Beasley-Murray has argued for this view and claims that "an increasing number of scholars agree with Beasley-Murray that becoming a Christian is a process."[112]

Cross is among those who agree. He denies that conversion is punctiliar.[113] Though he thinks it is unnecessary to introduce a "time-element" into the process, conversion is nonetheless a process comprising multiple

---

108. Trigg, *Baptism in the Theology of Martin Luther*, 59.
109. Cross, *Recovering*, 184.
110. Cross, *Should We Take?*, 15; quoting Beasley-Murray, *Baptism in the New Testament*, 305, and Beasley-Murray, "Baptism," 27–29.
111. Haymes, Gouldbourne, and Cross, *On Being the Church*, 63–64.
112. Cross, *Recovering*, 136.
113. Cross, *Recovering*, 47.

events.[114] He claims that understanding salvation as a process is "key to understanding baptism in the New Testament."[115] Other elements include hearing the gospel, repentance, faith, entrance into the church and the reception of the Holy Spirit.[116] Seeing baptism as a part of the process of salvation, according to Cross, "frees us from trying to determine which is the normative order of becoming a Christian. There isn't one, because the Spirit comes to people differently and brings them into God's kingdom by a process which can be long and protracted or swift, even sudden. What matters is that people come to new life in Christ."[117]

The conversion narratives in the book of Acts are a primary reason that Cross believes conversion is a process. For Cross, if conversion is seen as a punctiliar event, then the accounts in Acts pose problems.

> Which is the normal order of conversion: repentance, water-baptism, forgiveness and reception of the Spirit (Acts 2:38, 41); believing, water-baptism, laying on of hands and reception of the Spirit (Acts 8:12–17); reception of the Spirit, speaking in tongues and water-baptism (Acts 16:31–33); or believing, water-baptism, laying on of hands, reception of the Spirit and speaking in tongues (Acts 19:1–6; see also 9:17–18; 22:16)? But when we recognise conversion as a process, that is conversion-initiation, such questions lose their relevance, as the sovereign activity of the Spirit of God is recognised along with the probable explanation that Luke was not concerned with providing a pattern of conversion-initiation.[118]

Understanding conversion as a process with multiple parts allows Cross to understand certain references to baptism—such as 1 Cor 12:13; Gal 3:27–28; and Matt 28:19—as synecdoche. However, he has not always understood those references in that way. Earlier in his writings, Cross understood some of those references as metonymy, a figure of speech in which one word or phrase is substituted for another with which it is closely associated.[119] He provides the examples of "Washington" being used to refer to the United States government or "sword" being used for

---

114. Cross, *Recovering*, 45.
115. Cross, *Should We Take?*, 8.
116. Cross, *Should We Take?*, 9.
117. Cross, *Should We Take?*, 14.
118. Cross, "'One Baptism,'" 177.
119. Cross, *Recovering*, 74.

the military.[120] "In this case," Cross writes, "the something is becoming a Christian, conversion, represented by baptism which is closely related to it."[121] Others, such as Calvin and Beza, have understood references to baptism in this way as well.[122]

More recently, Cross has refined his position and argued that those references to baptism are synecdoche.[123] He notes that the terms "metonymy" and "synecdoche" are often used synonymously, as meaning an attribute or a part of something is used to represent the whole.[124] For Cross, though, there is a distinction. Whereas metonymy uses a term that is associated with something else, synecdoche uses a part to refer to the whole. In his view, then, baptism is part of a process and often gets used in the New Testament as a reference to the whole. For example, when 1 Pet 3:21 says, "baptism now saves you," baptism refers to the overall process of salvation—faith, repentance, baptism.[125] He makes the same case in another place, claiming about 1 Pet 3:21, "In short, baptism here stands for everything implied in the gospel."[126] He also asserts that the "one baptism" in Eph 4:5 is a reference to "the whole conversion-initiation process."[127]

One instance in which Cross's interpretation of a reference to baptism relies upon the use of synecdoche is 1 Cor 12:13. To develop his argument, Cross engages with Dunn as a conversation partner. Cross uses Dunn as a representative of an opposing view, namely, that Paul uses "baptism" metaphorically in 1 Cor 12:13.[128] Dunn's thesis is that some uses of "baptized" or "baptized into" in the New Testament—such as its first use in Rom 6, Gal 3:26, and 1 Cor 12:13—are metaphorical and not a reference to literal water-baptism.[129] Dunn points out "the extent and prevalence of metaphor in the New Testament."[130] Most significantly, he points out that in both Rom 6:3 and Gal 3:27, the phrase "baptized into

---

120. Cross, *Recovering*, 74.
121. Cross, *Recovering*, 74.
122. Pelikan, *Christian Tradition*, 194.
123. Cross, *Recovering*, 76.
124. Cross, *Should We Take?*, 13.
125. Cross, "Evangelical Sacrament," 209.
126. Cross, "'One Baptism,'" 192.
127. Cross, *Recovering*, 102.
128. Cross, *Recovering*, 136–40.
129. Dunn, "Baptised as Metaphor," 294.
130. Dunn, "Baptised as Metaphor," 295.

Christ" is used in close proximity to other phrases that are—in his view—clearly metaphors.[131] Dunn claims that he does not wish to completely separate the rite from the metaphor, but to demonstrate that the metaphor is different from the literal act.[132] Nevertheless, Dunn claims that understanding references to baptism as metaphor does not necessarily diminish a sacramental understanding of baptism.[133] In fact, he points out that in Rom 6 we are buried with Christ "dia" baptism.[134]

Dunn makes a good case for understanding certain references to baptism, including 1 Cor 12:13, as metaphor. Dunn's view provides a way to develop a rich theology, even a sacramental theology, of baptism without reading water-baptism into every passage that uses the word, or some form of the word, "baptized."

Despite Hartman's claim that "Dunn is virtually alone in regarding 'baptize' as metaphor [in Gal 3:27],"[135] Dunn has offered an alternative interpretation of at least some references to baptism in the New Testament. Cross even acknowledges that, in reference to 1 Cor 12:13, "Dunn has put forward a strong exegetical argument that there is no reference here to water-baptism but only to Spirit-baptism."[136] He remains unconvinced, however, by Dunn's argument, largely due to the fact that Dunn's position allows for a separation between water-baptism and Spirit-baptism.[137]

Cross continues to maintain that the reference to baptism in 1 Cor 12:13 is synecdoche, and that "recognition that Spirit- and water-baptism are integral components of conversion-initiation means that it is a false dichotomy to separate the two."[138] He relies heavily on Beasley-Murray's argument to respond to Dunn.[139] This is due in part to the fact that Dunn himself critiques Beasley-Murray, and Cross is therefore allowing Beasley-Murray to answer Dunn. Cross advances his own argument, then, by putting representatives of various positions in conversation with each other.

131. Dunn, "Baptised as Metaphor," 298–99.
132. Dunn, "Baptised as Metaphor," 307.
133. Dunn, "Baptised as Metaphor," 298.
134. Dunn, "Baptised as Metaphor," 298.
135. Hartman, *Into the Name of the Lord Jesus*, 55.
136. Cross, "Being Open," 359.
137. Dunn, *Baptism in the Holy Spirit*, 4.
138. Cross, *Recovering*, 142.
139. Cross, *Recovering*, 142–43.

At this point, it is helpful to evaluate Cross's argument for understanding baptism as synecdoche instead of metaphor. His argument has two weaknesses. First, a number of commentators are in agreement that there is at least one example of "baptism" used as metaphor in the New Testament, which is found in Mark 10:38.[140] William Lane, for example, writes about that verse, "In popular Greek usage the vocabulary of baptism was used to speak of being overwhelmed by disaster or danger, and a similar metaphorical use of submersion is present in Scripture."[141] Dunn is also correct to point out that in Rom 6 and Gal 3:27, "baptized" is closely connected to other images that are certainly metaphors, such as "crucified," "slaves," and "put on Christ." It is possible that other references are synecdoche, but Cross's position could be strengthened by allowing for a variety of uses of the term "baptized."

The second weakness with understanding baptism as synecdoche is that it depends too much on understanding conversion as a process. This is especially problematic for Cross as he places so much emphasis on the occasion of baptism. Throughout most of his argument, conversion is not depicted as a process but as punctiliar. In fact, as already noted, Cross, in agreement with Beasley-Murray, claims that in the New Testament "baptism was conversion."[142] He also argues that "baptism and faith are but the outside and inside of the same thing."[143] That is quite different than the view that they are separate elements of a singular process. Cross's case could be helped if he consistently emphasized that the "process" of salvation includes multiple elements that occur at or near the same time. However, when he appeals to the various orders of the process of salvation in the book of Acts, he appears to suggest that this process does indeed involve a sequence of events. Cross's position could be strengthened by providing more clarity on this point.

Baptismal Reforms

Cross's book, *Recovering the Evangelical Sacrament*, ends with a chapter titled "The Reform of Baptism." In that chapter Cross states his goal for

---

140. France, *Gospel of Mark*, 416–17; Brooks, *Mark*, 168; MacArthur, *1 Corinthians*, 311–12.
141. Lane, *Gospel of Mark*, 380.
142. Cross, *Recovering*, 42.
143. Cross, *Recovering*, 56.

his writings on baptism. "What I am proposing in this book, then, is the recovery of New Testament baptism . . . it is a wholesale reform of credo- and paedobaptism to the faith-baptism, the conversion-initiation, mission-baptism of the earliest Christian communities."[144] In the opening sentence of this concluding chapter he refers to Beasley-Murray, thus using Beasley-Murray to frame his own call for reform. Cross writes, "Throughout his writings George Beasley-Murray refers to Baptist criticisms of other traditions whose baptismal theology does not accord with New Testament teaching, but he rightly notes that doing such a thing carries with it the requirement that Baptists themselves also test their beliefs and practices at the bar of Scripture."[145] He then includes a lengthy quote from "Baptism in the New Testament," in which Beasley-Murray argues that Baptists should be prepared to reform their baptismal theology and practices.[146] He also quotes Timothy George ("The Reformed Doctrine of Believers' Baptism") who made the same argument.[147] Later in the chapter Cross states, "Beasley-Murray and others remind us that any reform must be according to the word of God."[148] Significantly, though others have made the same point, and Cross mentions "others," the one person he names is Beasley-Murray.

Cross then proposes specific reforms that Baptists should make. A similar list appears in *On Being the Church*.[149] Due to the similarities in the two lists, the specific proposals will all be considered together here. In both places Cross appropriates Beasley-Murray's own proposals for reform. Cross's first suggestion is that we make sure that baptism is primarily about what God has done in Christ through the Spirit. Cross suggests a threefold act of immersion to highlight that the triune God is the most important participant in baptism.[150]

Second, baptism should not be seen in individualistic terms, but as a corporate act.[151] This is achieved by focusing not on the action of the individual, but on what God has done for his people, so that the

---

144. Cross, *Recovering*, 312.
145. Cross, *Recovering*, 308.
146. Cross, *Recovering*, 308.
147. Cross, *Recovering*, 309.
148. Cross, *Recovering*, 313.
149. Haymes, Gouldbourne, and Cross, *On Being the Church*, 94–100.
150. Cross, *Recovering*, 314.
151. Cross, *Recovering*, 314.

entire congregation can experience God's grace afresh.[152] Third, citing Beasley-Murray's *Baptism in the New Testament*, p. 393, Cross argues that baptism should be made integral to the gospel and should be included in our preaching and teaching.[153]

Fourth, baptism should be made integral to conversion.[154] Cross cites *Baptism in the New Testament* (393) in support of this suggestion. Responding to the argument that baptism should be postponed until the candidate's fitness for baptism can be determined, Cross again appeals to Beasley-Murray. "But we must recall Beasley-Murray's comments that in doing so we in fact alter New Testament baptism. He does not diminish the importance of instruction, which he sees as 'always necessary,' but notes that it 'need not wholly precede baptism' for 'much of it can more fittingly come after baptism,' adding, 'and in any case the instruction ought never to cease at baptism.'"[155]

Fifth, Cross, again appealing to Beasley-Murray, suggests that baptism should include a question and answer or a testimony before the congregation. This would help the baptized person see their baptism as "the instrument of the surrender to the Lord and the assurance of their acceptance by God in Christ."[156] Sixth, Cross suggests that Baptists need to develop a proper theology of children. He notes that the topic is receiving increased attention and cites four of Beasley-Murray's works on that subject as examples.[157]

Cross's final suggested reform is to make baptism integral to church membership, which is consistent with the New Testament understanding that baptism is "at once to Christ and the Body."[158] When making his case for this reform in *Recovering the Evangelical Sacrament*, Cross summarizes Beasley-Murray's argument in *Baptism in the New Testament*,

---

152. Cross, *Recovering*, 315.

153. Cross, *Recovering*, 315; Haymes, Gouldbourne, and Cross, *On Being the Church*, 96.

154. Cross, *Recovering*, 315–16; Haymes, Gouldbourne, and Cross, *On Being the Church*, 96.

155. Cross, *Recovering*, 315–16; quoting Beasley-Murray, *Baptism in the New Testament*, 394.

156. Cross, *Recovering*, 316–17; Haymes, Gouldbourne, and Cross, *On Being the Church*, 96; referencing Beasley-Murray, "Worship and the Sacraments," 7

157. Haymes, Gouldbourne, and Cross, *On Being the Church*, 99.

158. Cross, *Recovering*, 317; Haymes, Gouldbourne, and Cross, *On Being the Church*, 97.

pp. 394–95. The relationship of baptism to membership raises the question of how Baptists should relate to paedobaptists in terms of church membership. Cross relies heavily on Beasley-Murray when suggesting a way forward. He quotes Beasley-Murray's argument that not only is the New Testament silent on the practice of infant baptism, but that the New Testament practices and teaching regarding baptism are contrary to the thoughts and practices regarding infant baptism.[159] Cross later summarizes Beasley-Murray's argument for open-membership. While maintaining that faith-baptism alone is biblical, Beasley-Murray acknowledged that most Christians have not received baptism in that manner. Accepting into membership members of other churches recognizes the reality of that situation as well as God's freedom in his dealing with his people. Though Cross does not explicitly state that this is his position, he does describe Beasley-Murray's view positively and points out its strength.[160]

In *On Being the Church*, Cross and the other authors again summarize Beasley-Murray's argument for a qualified open-membership, that is, one that is "solely for members of other Churches transferring into a Baptist church."[161] The authors commend his approach, believing that it "has the strength of maintaining the church as the baptised community and conversion-baptism/conversion-initiation/faith-baptism as the norm, while recognizing the freedom of God in his dealings with people and the complex situation we live in which many believe their baptism as infants and later confirmation is legitimate Christian initiation."[162]

Regarding open-membership, Cross claims that Baptists can recognize others as being in the body of Christ "regardless of which mode of initiation they have had."[163] He also acknowledges that Beasley-Murray's suggestion might be the most realistic option and highly commends it.[164] However, he opts for another possible solution, which is baptismal reform, or a return to conversion-baptism by all the Churches.[165] For paedobaptists, this would mean ending the practice of infant baptism.

159. Cross, *Recovering*, 123.
160. Cross, *Recovering*, 319–21.
161. Beasley-Murray, *Baptism Today*, 86.
162. Haymes, Gouldbourne, and Cross, *On Being the Church*, 98–99. Paul Fiddes has also argued for this approach to open-membership in Fiddes, *Tracks and Traces*, 141–48.
163. Cross, "'One Baptism,'" 203.
164. Cross, "'One Baptism,'" 206.
165. Cross, "'One Baptism,'" 206.

For credobaptists, this would mean maintaining the connection between conversion and baptism and recognizing the efficacy of baptism.[166] He points out that Beasley-Murray himself sees this option as the ideal and worth working toward. He quotes from *Baptism Today and Tomorrow*, in which Beasley-Murray calls for a return to conversion-baptism for the sake of the church's witness to the world: "Its proclamation of the Gospel will be far more effective if its baptismal practice is reformed according to the New Testament pattern. In that setting baptism is the conclusion of Gospel proclamation. Any move to rehabilitate that relationship is to be welcomed."[167]

It was noted above that Cross begins his chapter, "The Reform of Baptism" by quoting Beasley-Murray. After appropriating Beasley-Murray's work throughout the chapter, Cross quotes him at length near the conclusion of the chapter, which is also the conclusion of the book. He ends *Should We Take Peter At His Word (Acts 2:38)?* and his chapter, "Baptism: Becoming a Christian," with the same quote. In "Baptism: Becoming a Christian," Cross concludes,

> It is fitting to conclude with Beasley-Murray's closing words, which are firmly based on the understanding of the triune God, in what is regarded as the most important book by a Baptist on baptism in the twentieth century, and certainly one of the most important books by any Baptist on the subject, *Baptism in the New Testament*:
>
> "All of us in all the Churches need to consider afresh our ways before God, with the Bible open before us and a prayer for the guidance of the Holy Spirit and a preparedness to listen to what the Spirit is saying to all the Churches. With such a prayer answered—and it would be unbelief to assume that it will not be—and obedience pledged to guidance vouchsafed, the inadequate insights of frail individuals and of our very fallible traditions would surely give place to a fuller understanding of the divine will made known, and the glory of God in Christ be furthered through the church by the Spirit."[168]

---

166. Cross, "'One Baptism,'" 207.
167. Cross, "'One Baptism,'" 208.
168. Haymes, Gouldbourne, and Cross, *On Being the Church*, 100; quoting Beasley-Murray, *Baptism in the New Testament*, 395.

CONCLUDING OBSERVATIONS

It does indeed seem fitting that Beasley-Murray's closing words have become Cross's closing words. In fact, as has been demonstrated, much of Beasley-Murray's argument has become Cross's argument. In addition to specific exegetical, hermeneutical, and historical insights that have been borrowed from Beasley-Murray to support particular points,[169] his overarching argument and key points of it have been directly and explicitly appropriated into Cross's own argument.

The primary reason for this seems to be related to Cross's methodology. Instead of merely citing other scholars in support of claims, Cross frequently advances his argument by interacting with other scholars. At times, this method involves using as conversation partners scholars with whom Cross disagrees. Such is the case with Dunn and Barth, for example, who both separate water-baptism from Spirit-baptism.[170] At other times this methodology involves presenting the arguments of scholars with whom Cross agrees. Of those scholars, Beasley-Murray is primary.

It is apparent that Cross believes Beasley-Murray has made a strong case and is the best possible representative of the position for which Cross is arguing. Consider again some of the statements mentioned above. "If there is any doubt that New Testament baptism is faith-baptism, then the work of George Beasley-Murray should dispel it once and for all."[171] The view that Paul is talking about Spirit-baptism in 1 Cor 12:13 is the view "championed by Beasley-Murray."[172] "A major key to interpreting baptism sacramentally is highlighted in the many writings of George Beasley-Murray."[173] Beasley-Murray's argument for baptismal regeneration is "a thorough-going and biblical-theological one."[174] This is but a sample of Cross's own statements in his published writings indicating that he considers Beasley-Murray to be a significant representative of the sacramental view of baptism. Cross has confirmed this observation, stating, "Beasley-Murray is, for me, simply the most important and significant Baptist ever to write on baptism. Personally, I would rank him as the

---

169. Cross, *Recovering*, 116, 117, 119, 129.

170. Cross's interaction with Dunn has been examined above. For his interaction with Barth, see *Recovering*, 158–69.

171. Cross, *Recovering*, 55.

172. Cross, *Recovering*, 142.

173. Cross, *Recovering*, 176.

174. Cross, *Recovering*, 205.

best. He is also one of the most important NT scholars ever to explore NT baptism, and his *Baptism in the New Testament* is for me still today an indispensable book on the subject—as are his other works."[175] Not only has Beasley-Murray shaped Cross's argument, then, but by appropriating Beasley-Murray to the extent and in the ways that Cross has, Beasley-Murray's voice continues to be heard and his argument continues to be made.

175. Anthony Cross, personal email, April 23, 2016.

Conclusion

As mentioned in the introduction, a number of scholars across the years have highlighted the significance of Beasley-Murray's work on baptism and they have quoted his work often. I have examined the work of six Baptist scholars to test the extent of Beasley-Murray's influence. This final chapter will lay out the major conclusions and provide some possible lines for further inquiry.

MAJOR CONCLUSIONS

1. *Identifying the factors that have influenced the baptismal debate.* While the focus of this book is on Beasley-Murray's influence, there is in fact a complex of factors, in various combinations, that provide the context for any individual who is writing about baptism. It has been necessary, then, to acknowledge and explore other factors that have shaped the debate. Some of those factors are more general in nature, and others are more specific to particular scholars. The more general factors were discussed primarily in chapter 3 (Southern Baptist contextual factors) and chapter 7 (BUGB Baptist contextual factors). For Southern Baptists, those factors include the Campbellite controversy, the lack of sacramentalism in Southern Baptist history, and the inerrancy debate. For BUGB Baptists, the factors include the sacramental resurgence, the Oxford Movement, ecumenical engagement, and the charismatic movement.

Individual factors have been addressed within the chapters on specific scholars. The role of a person's theological assumptions in the development of an argument is displayed in the work of Nettles. The significance of a person's own experience is highlighted in the work of Colwell. The importance of a person's methodology is evident in several chapters. Though each of the scholars under consideration in this work understands Scripture to be the ultimate authority for our beliefs and desires his position to be consistent with Scripture, some of them approach the subject of baptism in different ways and utilize different methodologies. For example, George Beasley-Murray and Tom Schreiner both take an exegetical approach, thoroughly exegeting the relevant texts and then drawing theological conclusions. Timothy George thinks about baptism through the lens of historical theology, particularly Reformation theology. John Colwell takes a theological approach. While he believes that theology should take Scripture as its "starting point," he argues that questions related to the nature of the sacraments are "primarily and foundationally questions of the nature of God."[1] This serves as the premise upon which Colwell develops his argument for a sacramental understanding of baptism.

2. *Four ways the work of Beasley-Murray has influenced the debate about the meaning of baptism.* Within that complex of factors discussed above, Beasley-Murray's work stands out for two reasons. First, the scholars under consideration in this book engage directly with Beasley-Murray's work. This is a contrast to the factors that provide general context and indirect influence. Second, whereas certain factors have influenced some scholars' arguments, but not others, Beasley-Murray's work is a common thread that runs throughout the arguments of these six scholars.

There are four main ways that Beasley-Murray has shaped the debate. First, his exegesis of baptismal texts has been appropriated by other scholars. This is seen most clearly in the chapter on Schreiner, who exegetes many baptismal passages and cites Beasley-Murray frequently, and the chapter on Colwell, who has acknowledged that Beasley-Murray's exegesis is assumed throughout his own work on baptism.

A second way that Beasley-Murray has shaped the debate is by his use of the term "trysting place" to describe baptism. Influencing the terminology of a debate can shape the debate itself. In this case, the term, which has significant theological implications, has been borrowed by Nigel Wright and Anthony Cross. The chapter on Cross includes a discussion of the term.

A third way that Beasley-Murray has influenced the debate is through his observation that in the New Testament salvation and its related blessings are associated with both faith and baptism. The insight is significant because it allows for a sacramental understanding of baptism

---

1. Colwell, *Promise*, 2.

while still holding firmly to salvation by grace through faith. Originally published in a document produced by the World Council of Churches, it is an important piece of the arguments of Wright, Colwell, and Cross, and it is arguably Beasley-Murray's single most significant contribution to the baptismal debate.

A fourth way that Beasley-Murray has influenced the debate is by serving as a representative of the sacramental position. Chapter 1 demonstrated that others before Beasley-Murray had argued for a sacramental view of baptism and that he had appropriated arguments from other scholars. Though not all of the ideas he put forth were original to him, then, he has, at least to some, come to be seen as a representative of the sacramental position. In the works of Nettles and George, this has led to them contrasting their own positions with those of Beasley-Murray in particular. Anthony Cross uses Beasley-Murray in a more positive way. As stated in the chapter on Cross, it is apparent that Cross believes Beasley-Murray has made a strong case and is the best possible representative of the position for which Cross is arguing. Consequently, though others hold a similar position, it is Beasley-Murray's argument that has been incorporated into Cross's argument more than any other's.

3. *Beasley-Murray has influenced the debate among both Southern Baptists and BUGB Baptists.* One of the goals of this study was to compare Beasley-Murray's influence among Southern Baptists with his influence among BUGB Baptists. Taken as a whole, the British Baptists in this study are more aligned with Beasley-Murray theologically, and have appropriated his work in more positive ways than the Southern Baptists.

With that said, the contrast is not as absolute as I had anticipated. In fact, one of the biggest surprises in this study was the fact that two of the Southern Baptists (George and Schreiner) hold to a sacramental view— though George's view is not as sacramental as Beasley-Murray's, and Schreiner does not prefer the language of "sacrament." Another surprise was that one of the Southern Baptists (Schreiner) appropriates Beasley-Murray more often than two of the BUGB Baptists (Wright and Colwell). That does not necessarily mean that Beasley-Murray had more influence on Schreiner's argument, but it is an indication that Beasley-Murray has affected the debate among both groups.

It should also be remembered that my contention is that Beasley-Murray has shaped the debate, not that he has won it. The fact that one Southern Baptist (Nettles) explicitly disagrees with Beasley-Murray's overall argument and another (George) explicitly disagrees with

Beasley-Murray at a key point actually supports this thesis. While their works have not been shaped by Beasley-Murray as much as others have, he has nevertheless affected the development of their arguments by prompting them to include a response to his position.

4. *Four reasons why Beasley-Murray has had such a significant impact on the debate.* One reason is simply the amount of work he produced on the topic of baptism. In addition to two books about baptism, he published multiple essays and articles, delivered a lecture on baptism, and taught on it in his classes. Chapter 2 of this book, which examines Beasley-Murray's baptismal theology, includes 25 sources from Beasley-Murray that are related to baptism. The size of his corpus alone commands attention.

In addition to the quantity of his work, another reason for his influence is the quality of his work. In the Introduction I pointed out that there has been much agreement that he has made a strong argument which should be taken seriously. This may explain why even the two scholars who have significant theological disagreements with Beasley-Murray (Nettles and George) do not simply dismiss his work but feel the need to respond to it.

A third reason for the extent of Beasley-Murray's influence is his methodology. His overall pattern is to engage in thorough exegesis of the relevant texts and then draw theological conclusions. This is significant for two reasons. One is that it gives weight to his argument because it is the result of biblical studies. He forces his readers to move beyond their own assumptions and their own traditions and to ask whether he is right about what the Bible says. However, he does not stop with exegesis. He also makes theological claims about the meaning of baptism. This is the other reason that his methodology is significant. His work is somewhat of a crossover between two fields—New Testament studies and theology—and he has contributed significantly to both. For those who want exegesis of baptismal texts, it can be found in Beasley-Murray's work. For those wanting theological discussion of baptism, it can also be found in Beasley-Murray.

A fourth likely reason for Beasley-Murray's influence is the various positions that he held during his career. As a Professor and Principal he had the potential to have much influence and the opportunity to introduce students to his view of baptism. It also gives him increased credibility, since his academic ability was recognized by multiple institutions. The fact that he taught at both Spurgeon's College and The Southern Baptist

Theological Seminary gave him a direct connection to both BUGB Baptists and Southern Baptists, allowing scholars in both traditions to have significant exposure to his baptismal theology.

FURTHER RESEARCH

1. *Have any contextual factors shaped the debate more directly than this project concludes?* Given that the focus of this book is on Beasley-Murray's influence on the arguments of six specific scholars, it was necessary to explore other influences on the debate, but not in a way that shifted the focus. It may be helpful, therefore, to begin a similar project by focusing on a particular contextual factor. Anthony Cross has done this by looking at the effect of the ecumenical movement on the debate among British Baptists, but there is more work to be done that takes into account Southern Baptists and other contextual factors. Doing so would complement the research in this book and provide additional insight into why the debate has developed as it has.

2. *Have the arguments of other Southern Baptists and BUGB Baptists been influenced by Beasley-Murray?* As discussed in the Introduction, for this project I chose scholars who have some connection to Beasley-Murray and have produced a significant body of work on baptism. The research could be continued by broadening the parameters. Scholars who have no discernable connection to Beasley-Murray could be considered, as well as those who have written anything at all, however little, about baptism.

3. *Has Beasley-Murray shaped the arguments of non-Baptists?* This project has focused on the debate about the meaning of baptism among Baptists. As another way of broadening the parameters, the work of non-Baptists could be considered. Given Beasley-Murray's ecumenical engagement, it would be insightful to consider how scholars in other traditions have interacted with him.

4. *Has Beasley-Murray's work had an effect on the beliefs and practice of non-scholars?* This project has focused on Beasley-Murray's influence on the arguments of scholars. Beasley-Murray himself believed that there can be a disconnect between what many scholars believe about baptism and what many in the church believe and practice.[2] Further research could test his assumption and seek to determine whether his influence

---

2. Beasley-Murray, *Baptism Today*, 14.

has moved beyond the scholarly debate to the actual teaching and practice of churches.

It was noted earlier that William Hull referred to *Baptism in the New Testament* as a "bombshell in the baptistery."[3] This book is essentially an attempt to get into the baptisteries of Southern Baptists and BUGB Baptists to determine whether the ripples of that bombshell are still being felt. Though there are other people and trends that have made waves as well, it seems safe to conclude that the work of Beasley-Murray has indeed, at least to this point, had a lasting effect.

---

3. Hull, "Baptism in the New Testament," 3.

Bibliography

Akin, Daniel, ed. *A Theology for the Church*. Nashville: B&H, 2007.
Ally, Robert. *Revolt Against the Faithful: A Biblical Case for Inspiration as Encounter*. Philadelphia: Lippincott, 1970.
Ammerman, Nancy Tatom. *Baptist Battles: Social Change and Religious Conflict in the Southern Baptist Convention*. New Brunswick: Rutgers University Press, 1990.
Anselm. "The Procession of the Spirit." In *Readings in the Doctrine of the Trinity*, edited by Gerald Bray. Birmingham: Beeson Divinity School, 2001.
Aquinas, Thomas. *Summa Theologica*. III 62 1. London: Burns Oats and Washbourne, 1920.
Augustine. "Faith and Creed." In *On Christian Belief*, edited by Boniface Ramsey, 151–74. Hyde Park: New City, 2005.
———. "Letter 98, section 2." In *The Nicene and Post-Nicene Fathers*. Vol. 1, *The Confessions and Letters of St. Augustine*, edited by P. Schaff, 407. Edinburgh: T. & T. Clark, 1994.
———. "On Baptism, Against the Donatists." In *The Nicene and Post-Nicene Fathers*. Vol. 4, edited by Philip Schaff, 411–514. Buffalo: Christian Literature, 1887.
———. *On the Catechizing of the Uninstructed*, 26.50. http://www.ccel.org/ccel/schaff/npnf103.iv.iii.xxvii.html.
———. *The Trinity*. Hyde Park: New City, 2007.
Baker, Robert. "Baptist Sacramentalism." In *Chapel Messages*, edited by H. C Brown, Jr. and Charles P. Johnson, 23–28. Grand Rapids: Baker, 1966.
———. *The Southern Baptist Convention and Its People, 1607–1972*. Nashville: Broadman, 1974.
"Baptism, Eucharist and Ministry." Faith and Order Paper no. 111. Geneva: WCC, 1982.
"Baptism, Eucharist and Ministry, 1982–1990: Report on the Process and Responses." Faith and Order Paper no 149. Geneva: WCC, 1990.
Baptist-Lutheran Joint Commission. *Baptists and Lutherans In Conversation*. Geneva: Baptist World Alliance and Lutheran World Federation, 1990.
Barth, Karl. *Church Dogmatics*. Vol. 1, translated and edited by G. W. Bromiley and T. F. Torrance. Edinburgh: T. & T. Clark, 1969.
———. *The Teaching of the Church Regarding Baptism*. London: SCM, 1963.
Basden, Paul, and David Dockery, eds. *The People of God: Essays on the Believers' Church*. Nashville: Broadman, 1991.
Beach, J. Mark. "Baptism in the New Testament." *Mid-American Journal of Theology* 11 (2000) 203–6.

Beasley-Murray, George. "2 Corinthians." In vol. 11 of *Broadman Bible Commentary*, edited by C. J. Allen. Nashville: Broadman, 1971.

———. "The Authority and Justification for Believers' Baptism." *Review and Expositor* 77 (1980) 63–70.

———. "Baptism." In *Dictionary of Paul and His Letters*, edited by Gerald F. Hawthorne, Ralph P. Martin, and Daniel G. Reid. The IVP Bible Dictionary Series. Downers Grove, IL: InterVarsity, 1993.

———. "Baptism and the Sacramental View." *Baptist Times*, February 11, 1960.

———. "Baptism in the Epistles of Paul." In *Christian Baptism*, edited by Alec Gilmore, 128–48. Chicago: Judson, 1959.

———. *Baptism in the New Testament*. London: Macmillan, 1963.

———. *Baptism Today and Tomorrow*. New York: St. Martin's, 1966.

———. "Baptists and the Baptism of Other Churches." In *The Truth That Makes Men Free*, edited by Josef Nordenhaug, 261–78. Nashville: Broadman, 1966.

———. *The Book of Revelation*. New Century Bible. London: Marshall, Morgan, and Scott, 1974.

———. "The Child and the Church." In *Children and Conversion*, edited by Clifford Ingle, 127–41. Nashville: Broadman, 1970.

———. *Christ Is Alive*. London: Lutterworth, 1947.

———. "The Church of Scotland and Baptism." *The Fraternal* 99 (1956) 7–10.

———. *A Commentary on Mark Thirteen*. New York: Macmillan, 1957.

———. "Ezekiel." *The New Bible Commentary*, edited by Francis Davidson. London: InterVarsity Fellowship, 1953.

———. "Faith in the New Testament: A Baptist Perspective." *American Baptist Quarterly* 1 (1982) 137–43.

———. *The General Epistles*. Edited by William Barclay and F. F. Bruce. Bible Guides 21. London: Lutterworth, 1965.

———. *The General Epistles: James, 1 Peter, Jude, 2 Peter*. London: Lutterworth, 1965.

———. *The Gospel of John*. Word Biblical Commentary. Waco: Word, 1987.

———. "The Holy Spirit." *Baptist Union Christian Training Program*. London: Baptist Union.

———. "The Holy Spirit, Baptism and the Body of Christ." *Review and Expositor* 63 (1966) 177–85.

———. "I Still Find Infant Baptism Difficult." *Baptist Quarterly* 22 (1967) 225–36.

———. *John*. Word Biblical Commentary. Nashville: Thomas Nelson, 1999.

———. "John 3:3–5, Baptism, Spirit, and Kingdom." *Expository Times* 97 (1986) 160–70.

———. *Matthew*. Bible Study Commentary. London: Scripture Union, 1984.

———. "Philippians." In *Peake's Commentary on the Bible*, edited by Matthew Black and H. H. Rowley. Nashville: Thomas Nelson, 1962.

———. *Preaching the Gospel From the Gospels*. Philadelphia: Judson, 1956.

———. "The Problem of Infant Baptism: An Exercise in Possibilities." In Faculty of Baptist Theological Seminary, *Festschrift Gunter Wagner*, 114. Bern: Peter Lang, 1994.

———. *The Resurrection of Jesus Christ*. London: Oliphants, 1964.

———. "The Sacraments." *The Fraternal* 70 (1948) 3–7.

———. "Second Chapter of Colossians." *Review and Expositor* 70 (1973) 469–79.

———. "The Spirit Is There—Declares Dr. G. R. Beasley-Murray." *Baptist Times*, December 10, 1959.

———. "Worship and the Sacraments." The Second Holdsworth-Grigg Memorial Lecture, Whitley College, 1970.

Beasley-Murray, Paul. "Believers' Baptism," Baptist Basics. Oxfordshire: The Baptist Union of Great Britain.

———. *Faith and Festivity: Guide for Today's Worship Leaders*. Eastbourne: MARC, 1991.

———. *Fearless for Truth: A Personal Portrait of the Life of George Beasley-Murray*. Carlisle: Paternoster, 2002.

———. "Obituary of George Raymond Beasley-Murray." Church Matters. https://www.paulbeasleymurray.com/family/gbm/.

———. *Radical Believers: The Baptist Way of Being the Church*. Brightwell: Baptist Union of Great Britain,1992.

Beattie, N. "Christian Baptism." *Baptist Times*, November 12, 1959.

Berkhof, Louis. *Systematic Theology*. Grand Rapids: Eerdmans, 1996.

Berkouwer, G. C. *The Sacraments*. Grand Rapids: Eerdmans, 1981.

Bird, Herbert. "Baptism in the New Testament." *Westminster Theological Journal* 36 (1974) 390–94.

Bock, Darrell. *Acts*. Grand Rapids: Baker, 2007.

Booth, Abraham. *An Apology for the Baptists*. London: Paternoster-Row, 1812.

Bosnall, H. Edgar. *John Clifford Will Speak: Extracts From Sermons and Lectures Delivered by Revd. John Clifford*. London: Westbourne Park Baptist Church, 1973.

Boyce, James P. *Abstract of Systematic Theology*. Philadelphia: American Baptist, 1899.

———. *A Brief Catechism of Bible Doctrine*. http://www.reformedreader.org/ccc/bcbd.htm.

Braaten, Carl E. *Principles of Lutheran Theology*. Philadelphia: Fortress, 1983.

Brandreth, H. R. T. "Approaches of the Churches Towards Each Other in the Nineteenth Century." In *A History of the Ecumenical Movement 1517–1948*, edited by Ruth Rouse and Stephen Neill, 263–308. Philadelphia: Westminster, 1967.

Bray, Gerald. *God Is Love: A Biblical and Systematic Theology*. Wheaton, IL: Crossway, 2012.

Brewer, Brian. "Signs of the Covenant: The Development of Sacramental Thought in Baptist Circles." *Perspectives in Religious Studies* 36 (Winter 2009) 406–20.

Briggs, J. H. Y. *The English Baptists of the Nineteenth Century*. Didcot: The Baptist Historical Society, 1994.

———, ed. *Pulpit and People: Studies in Eighteenth Century Life and Thought*. Milton Keynes: Paternoster, 2009.

Brooks, James. *Mark*. Nashville: Broadman, 1991.

Brooks, Oscar. *The Drama of Decision: Baptism in the New Testament*. Peabody: Hendrickson, 1987.

Brown, Stewart, and Peter Nockles, eds. *The Oxford Movement*. Cambridge: Cambridge, 2013.

Bruce, F. F. *Acts*. Grand Rapids: Eerdmans, 1988.

———. *Commentary on the Book of Acts*. Grand Rapids: Eerdmans, 1971.

———. *The Epistles to the Colossians, to Philemon, and to the Ephesians*. Grand Rapids: Eerdmans, 1984.

Bultmann, Rudolf. *The Gospel of John: A Commentary*. Translated by G. R. Beasley-Murray. Oxford: Blackwell, 1971.

———. *Theology of the New Testament*. New York: Charles Scribner's Sons, 1951.

Bunyan, John. "A Confession of My Faith, and a Reason of My Practice." In *The Whole Works of John Bunyan*, Vol. 2, edited by George Offor, 593–617. Glasgow: Blackie & Son 1862.

———. "Differences in Judgment About Water-Baptism, No Bar to Communion." In *The Whole Works of John Bunyan*, Vol. 2, edited by Georg Offor, 618–47. Glasgow: Blackie & Son 1862.

———. "Peaceable Principles and True." In *The Whole Works of John Bunyan* Vol. 2, edited by George Offor, 648–56. Glasgow: Blackie & Son 1862.

Burgess, Stanley, and Gary McGee, eds. *Dictionary of Pentecostal and Charismatic Movements*. Grand Rapids: Zondervan, 1988.

Bush, L. Russ, and Tom J. Nettles, *Baptists and the Bible*. Chicago: Moody, 1980.

Byrt, G. W. *John Clifford*. London: Kingsgate, 1947.

Calhoun, David. *Grace Abounding: The Life, Books, and Influence of John Bunyan*. Fearn: Christian Focus, 2005.

Calvin, John. *Commentary on the Gospel According to John*. Vol. 1. Translated by William Pringle. Grand Rapids: Eerdmans, 1949.

———. *Commentary Upon the Acts of the Apostles*. Vol. 1. Grand Rapids: Eerdmans, 1949.

———. *Institutes of the Christian Religion*. Vol. 1. Edited by John T. McNeil, translated by Ford Lewis Battles. Louisville: Westminster John Knox, 1960.

Campbell, Alexander. *Christian Baptism: With Its Antecedents and Consequents*. London: Forgotten Books, 2012.

Carr, Warren. *Baptism: Conscience and Clue for the Church*. New York: Holt, Rinehart and Winston, 1964.

Carroll, B. H. *Baptism: Its Law, Its Administrator, Its Subject, Its Form, Its Design*. Waco: Baptist Standard, 1893.

———. *Baptists and Their Doctrines*. Nashville: Broadman and Holman, 1995.

Carson, D. A. *The Gospel According to John*. Grand Rapids: Eerdmans, 1991.

Carter, S. F. Letter to *The Baptist Times*, January 28, 1960.

Carver, W. O. "Introduction." *What is the Church?*, edited by Duke McCall. Nashville: Broadman, 1958.

Castelein, John. "A Christian Churches/Churches of Christ Response." In *Understanding Four Views on Baptism*, edited by John Armstrong, 51–58. Grand Rapids: Zondervan, 2007.

Catechism of the Catholic Church. New York: Doubleday, 1995.

Cavert, Samuel. *Church Cooperation and Unity in America: A Historical Review: 1900–1970*. New York: Association, 1970.

Chadwick, Owen. *The Mind of the Oxford Movement*. Stanford: Stanford University Press, 1960.

———. *The Spirit of the Oxford Movement*. Cambridge: Cambridge University Press, 1990.

Chapell, Bryan. *Ephesians*. Phillipsburg: P&R, 2009.

Church, R. W. *The Oxford Movement: Twelve Years, 1833–1845*. Chicago: University of Chicago, 1970.

Churches Together in Britain and Ireland. https://ctbi.org.uk/wp-content/uploads/2014/10/Story-of-the-BCC-pdf_view.pdf.

Clark, Neville. *An Approach to the Theology of the Sacraments.* Chicago: Alec R. Allenson, 1956.

———. "Christian Initiation: A Baptist Point of View." *Studia liturgica*, 4 (1965) 156–65.

———. "The Theology of Baptism." In *Christian Baptism*, edited by Alec Gilmore, 325. Chicago: Judson, 1959.

Clark, Robert. "Christian Baptism." *Baptist Times*, August 13, 1959.

———. "Christian Baptism." *Baptist Times*, October 8, 1959.

———. Letter to *The Baptist Times*, October 8, 1959.

Clements, K. W., ed. *Baptists in the Twentieth Century.* London: Baptist Historical Society, 1983.

Cole, Graham. *He Who Gives Life: The Doctrine of the Holy Spirit.* Wheaton, IL: Crossway, 2007.

Colson, Charles, and Richard Neuhaus, eds., *Evangelicals and Catholics Together.* Dallas: Word, 1995.

Colwell, John. "Baptism, Conscience and the Resurrection: A Reappraisal of 1 Peter 3.21." In *Baptism, the New Testament and the Church: Historical and Contemporary Studies in Honour of R.E.O. White,* edited by Stanley Porter and Anthony Cross, 210–27. Sheffield: Sheffield Academic, 1999.

———. "Catholicity and Confessionalism: Responding to George Beasley-Murray on Unity and Distinctiveness." In *Truth That Never Dies: The Dr. G. R. Beasley-Murray Memorial Lectures 2002–2012,* edited by Nigel Wright, 131–51. Eugene, OR: Pickwick, 2014.

———. "Foreword." In *Recovering the Evangelical Sacrament,* edited by Anthony Cross, xi–xii. Eugene, OR: Pickwick, 2013.

———. *Living the Christian Story: The Distinctiveness of Christian Ethics.* Edinburgh: T. & T. Clark, 2001.

———. Personal email, September 9, 2015.

——— *Promise and Presence: An Exploration of Sacramental Theology.* Waynesboro, GA: Paternoster, 2005.

———. *The Rhythm of Doctrine: A Liturgical Sketch of Christian Faith and Faithfulness.* Bletchley: Paternoster, 2007.

———. "The Sacramental Nature of Ordination." In *Baptist Sacramentalism,* edited by Anthony Cross and Philip Thompson, 228–46. Eugene, OR: Wipf & Stock, 2003.

———. *Why Have You Forsaken Me?: A Personal Reflection on the Experience of Desolation.* Eugene, OR: Cascade Books, 2012.

Conner, W. T. *Christian Doctrine.* Nashville: Broadman, 1937.

Conversations Around the World, 2000–2005. London: The Anglican Communion Office, 2005. http://www.anglicancommunion.org/media/101713/conversations_around_the_world.pdf.

Covenant of 1780 of a group of Christians who met at the Meeting House in St. Peter-le-Bailey, in the City of Oxford. http://newroad.org.uk/wp-content/uploads/2017/06/NRBC-Covenant.pdf.

Crehan, Joseph. *Early Christian Baptism and the Creed.* London: Burns Oates & Washbourne, 1950.

Criswell, W. A. *Why I Preach That the Bible Is Literally True.* Nashville: Broadman, 1969.

Cross, Anthony. *Baptism and the Baptists: Theology and Practice in Twentieth-Century Britain.* Waynesboro: Paternoster, 2000.

———. "Baptismal Regeneration: Rehabilitating a Lost Dimension of New Testament Baptism." In *Baptist Sacramentalism 2*, edited by Anthony Cross and Philip E. Thompson, 149–74. Milton Keynes: Paternoster, 2008.

———. "Baptists and Baptism—A British Perspective." *Baptist History and Heritage* 35 (2000) 104–21.

———. "Being Open to God's Sacramental Work." In *Semper Reformandum: Studies in Honour of Clark H. Pinnock*, edited by Stanley Porter and Anthony Cross, 355–77. Carlisle: Paternoster, 2003.

———. "The Evangelical Sacrament: baptisma semper reformandum." *Evangelical Quarterly* 80 (2008) 195–217.

———. Faculty Profile. Faculty of Theology and Religion, University of Oxford. https://www.theology.ox.ac.uk/people/dr-anthony-r-cross.

———. "Faith-Baptism: The Key to an Evangelical Baptismal Sacramentalism." In *Truth That Never Dies: The Dr. G. R. Beasley-Murray Memorial Lectures 2002–2012*, edited by Nigel Wright, 19–42. Eugene, OR: Pickwick, 2014.

———. "The Myth of English Baptist Anti-Sacramentalism." In *Recycling the Past or Researching History?: Studies in Baptist Historiography and Myths*, edited by Philip E. Thompson and Anthony R. Cross, 128–62. Milton Keynes: Paternoster, 2005.

———. "'One Baptism' (Ephesians 4.5): A Challenge to the Church." In *Baptism, the New Testament and the Church: Historical and Contemporary Studies in Honour of R.E.O. White*, edited by Stanley Porter and Anthony Cross, 173–209. Sheffield: Sheffield Academic, 1999.

———. Personal email, April 23, 2016.

———. "The Pneumatological Key to H. Wheeler Robinson's Baptismal Sacramentalism." In *Baptist Sacramentalism*, by Anthony R. Cross and Philip E. Thompson, 151–76. Studies in Baptist History and Thought 5. Carlisle: Paternoster, 2003.

———. *Recovering the Evangelical Sacrament: Baptisma Semper Reformandum.* Eugene, OR: Pickwick, 2013.

———. "Service to the Ecumenical Movement: The Contribution of British Baptists." *Baptist Quarterly* 38 (1999) 107–22.

———. *Should We Take Peter at His Word (Acts 2:38)?.* Oxford: Centre for Baptist History and Heritage, 2010.

Cross, Anthony, and Philip Thompson. "Introduction: Baptist Sacramentalism." In *Baptist Sacramentalism*, edited by Anthony Cross and Philip Thompson, 1–7. Waynesboro: Paternoster, 2003.

———. eds. *Baptist Sacramentalism.* Waynesboro: Paternoster, 2003.

———, eds. *Baptist Sacramentalism 2.* Milton Keynes: Paternoster, 2008.

Cullmann, Oscar. *Baptism in the New Testament.* London: SCM, 1961.

Culpepper, R. Alan. "George Beasley-Murray." In *Baptist Theologians*, edited by Timothy George and David S. Dockery, 573–76. Nashville: Broadman, 1990.

Dagg, J. L. *Manual of Theology. Second Part. A Treatise on Church Order.* Harrisonburg: Gano Books, 1982.

Dargan, Edwin. *Ecclesiology: A Study of the Churches.* Louisville: Chas T. Dearing, 1897.

Davids, Peter. *The First Epistle of Peter.* NICNT. Grand Rapids: Eerdmans, 1990.

Davies, H. *Worship and Theology in England.* Vol. 5, *The Ecumenical Century 1900–1965.* Oxford, 1965.

Dawson, Christopher. *The Spirit of the Oxford Movement*. London: Sheed & Ward, 1934.
Delf, W. M. "Christian Baptism." *Baptist Times*, February 11, 1960.
Dilday, Russell. *The Doctrine of Biblical Authority*. Nashville: Convention, 1982.
Dockery, David, ed. *Southern Baptists and American Evangelicals: The Conversation Continues*. Nashville: Broadman, 1993.
Dockery, David, and Timothy George. "Preface." In *Theologians of the Baptist Tradition*, edited by David Dockery and Timothy George, xiii–xviii. Nashville: Broadman & Holman, 2001.
Dodd, C. H. *The Apostolic Preaching and Its Developments*. Chicago: Willett, Clarks & Company, 1937.
———. *The Epistle of Paul to the Romans*. London: Hodder and Stoughton, 1937.
———. *Johannine Epistles*. New York: Harper & Brothers, 1946.
———. *The Meaning of Paul for Today*. London: Swarthmore, 1930.
Draper, James. *Authority: The Critical Issue for Southern Baptists*. Old Tappan: Fleming H. Revell, 1984.
Dunkerley, Roderic, ed. *The Ministry and the Sacraments*. London: Student Christian Movement, 1937.
Dunn, J. D. G. "Baptised as Metaphor." In *Baptism, the New Testament and the Church: Historical and Contemporary Studies in Honour of R.E.O. White*, edited by Stanley Porter and Anthony Cross, 294–310. Sheffield: Sheffield Academic, 1999.
———. *Baptism in the Holy Spirit*. Philadelphia: Westminster, 1970.
———. *Romans*. Nashville: Thomas Nelson, 1988.
Ellis, Christopher. "Baptism and the Sacramental Freedom of God." In *Reflections on the Water: Understanding God and the World Through the Baptism of Believers*, edited by Paul Fiddes, 23–45. Macon: Smyth and Helwys, 1996.
———. *Understanding God and the World Through the Baptism of Believers*. Macon: Smyth and Helwys, 1996.
Elwell, Walter, and J. D. Weaver, eds. *Bible Interpreters of the 20th Century*. Grand Rapids: Baker, 1999.
Evans, Percy. *Sacraments in the New Testament*. London: Tyndale, 1946.
Fee, Gordon. *The First Epistle to the Corinthians*. Grand Rapids: Eerdmans, 1987.
Ferguson, Sinclair. *The Holy Spirit*. Downers Grove, IL: InterVarsity, 1996.
Fiddes, Paul. "Baptism and Creation." In *Reflections on the Water: Understanding God and the World Through the Baptism of Believers*, 47–63. Macon: Smyth and Helwys, 1966.
———. *Charismatic Renewal: A Baptist View*. London: Baptist Union, 1980.
———. "Daniel Turner and a Theology of the Universal Church." In *Pulpit and People: Studies In Eighteenth Century Life and Thought*, edited by John H. Y. Briggs, 112–27. Milton Keynes: Paternoster, 2009.
———. "Ex Opere Operato." In *Baptist Sacramentalism 2*, edited by Anthony Cross and Philip E. Thompson, 219–38. Milton Keynes: Paternoster, 2008.
———. *Participating in God: A Pastoral Doctrine of the Trinity*. London: Darton, Longman and Todd, 2005.
———. *Tracks and Traces: Baptist Identity in Church and Theology*. Eugene, OR: Wipf & Stock, 2003.
———, ed. *Reflections on the Water: Understanding God and the World Through the Baptism of Believers*. Macon: Smyth and Helwys, 1996.

Fitzmeyer, Joseph. *The Acts of the Apostle*. Anchor Bible. New York: Double Day Dell, 1998.
Flamming, James. "Could God Trust Human Hands?" In *Is the Bible a Human Book*, edited by Wayne E. Ward and Joseph F. Green, 10ff. Nashville: Broadman, 1970.
Flemington, W. F. *The New Testament Doctrine of Baptism*. London: SPCK, 1957.
Ford, S. W. "Christian Baptism." *Baptist Times*, November 5, 1959.
Fowler, Stanley. *More Than a Symbol: The British Baptist Recovery of Baptismal Sacramentalism*. Waynesboro: Paternoster, 2002.
France, R. T. *The Gospel of Mark*. Grand Rapids: Eerdmans, 2002.
———. *The Gospel of Matthew*. Grand Rapids: Eerdmans, 2007.
Gadsby, Will. "Gadsby's Catechsim." http://www.the-faith.org.uk/gadsby.html
Gaebelein, Frank E., ed. *Ephesians through Philemon*. Grand Rapids: Zondervan, 1981.
Garland, David E. *1 Corinthians*. Grand Rapids: Baker, 2003.
Garrett, James Leo, Jr. *Baptist Theology: A Four-Century Study*. Macon: Mercer University Press, 2009.
———. "Baptists Concerning Baptism: Review and Preview." *Southwestern Journal of Theology* (March 2001) 52–67.
———. *Systematic Theology*. Grand Rapids: Eerdmans, 1995.
Gee, Donald. *Wind and Flame: The Pentecostal Movement*. Nottingham: Assemblies of God Publishing, 1967.
George, Timothy. "Catholics and Evangelicals in the Trenches." *Christianity Today* 38 (1994) 16–17.
———. "Evangelicals and Catholics Together: A New Initiative." *Christianity Today* (1997) 34–35.
———. "Faith-Based Bathing." *Christianity Today* 47 (2003) 62.
———. "Foreword." In *Believer's Baptism: Sign of the New Covenant in Christ*, edited by Thomas Schreiner and Shawn Wright xv–xix. Nashville: B&H, 2006.
———. *Galatians*. New American Commentary. Nashville: Broadman & Holman, 1994.
———. "George Huntston Williams: A Historian for All Seasons." In *The Contentious Triangle*, edited by Rodney L. Peterson and Calvin Augustine Pater, 15–34. Kirksville: Thomas Jefferson University Press, 1999.
———. "Is Jesus a Baptist?" In *Southern Baptist Identity: An Evangelical Denomination Faces the Future*, edited by David Dockery, 89–105. Wheaton, IL: Crossway, 2009.
———. "Keeping Truth Alive as a Holy Calling." *Harvard Divinity Bulletin* 29 (2000) 4–6.
———. Personal email, January 7, 2016.
———. *Pilgrims on the Sawdust Trail: Evangelical Ecumenism and the Quest for Christian Identity*. Grand Rapids: Baker, 2004.
———. "The Priesthood of All Believers." In *The People of God: Essays on the Believers' Church*, edited by Paul Basden and David Dockery, 85–93. Nashville: Broadman, 1991.
———. "The Reformed Doctrine of Believers' Baptism." *Interpretation* 47 (1993) 242–54.
———. "The Sacramentality of the Church: An Evangelical Baptist Perspective." In *Baptist Sacramentalism*, edited by Anthony Cross and Philip Thompson, 21–35. Waynesboro: Paternoster, 2003.

———. "The Sacramentality of the Church: An Evangelical Baptist Perspective." *Pro Ecclesia* 12 (2003) 309–23.
———. "The Southern Baptists." *Baptism & Church: A Believer' Church Vision*, edited by Merle Strege. Grand Rapids: Sagamore, 1986.
———. *Theology of the Reformers*. Nashville: Broadman & Holman, 1988.
———. "What Baptists Can Learn from Calvin." *The Founders Journal* 78 (2009) 19–22.
———. "What I'd Like to Tell the Pope About the Church." *Christianity Today* 42 (1998) 41–44.
George, Timothy, and David S. Dockery, eds. *Baptists Theologians*. Nashville: Broadman, 1990.
George, Timothy, and Denise George, eds. *Baptist Confessions, Covenants, and Catechisms*. Nashville: Broadman & Holman, 1996.
Gill, John. *A Body of Practical Divinity*. Grand Rapids: Baker, 1978.
Gilley, Sheridan. *Newman and His Age*. London: Darton, Longman and Todd, 1990.
Gilley, Sheridan, and Brian Stanley, eds. *The Cambridge History of Christianity* Vol. 8. Cambridge: Cambridge University Press, 2006.
Gillies, Donald. *Unity in the Dark*. London: Banner of Truth, 1964.
Gilmore, Alec. *Baptism and Christian Unity*. Valley Forge: Judson, 1966.
———. *The Pattern of the Church; A Baptist View*. London: Lutterworth, 1963.
———, ed. *Christian Baptism*. Chicago: Judson, 1959.
Gloer, W. Hulitt, ed. *Eschatology and the New Testament: Essays in Honor of George Raymond Beasley-Murray*. Peabody, MA: Hendrickson, 1988.
Goodliff, Andy. "Book Review: Recovering the Evangelical Sacrament by Anthony R. Cross." AndyGoodliff, June 26, 2013. http://andygoodliff.typepad.com/my_weblog/2013/06/book-review-recovering-the-evangelical-sacrament-by-anthony-r-cross-pickwick-2013.html.
———. "British Baptist Theologians No. 4: Nigel G. Wright." AndyGoodliff, May 8, 2006. http://andygoodliff.typepad.com/my_weblog/2006/05/british_baptist_3.html.
———. "British Baptist Theologians No. 6: Anthony R. Cross." AndyGoodliff, May 22, 2006. http://andygoodliff.typepad.com/my_weblog/2006/05/british_baptist_2.html.
Gorday, Peter, ed. *New Testament IX, Ancient Christian Commentary on Scripture*. Chicago: Fitzroy Dearborn, 2000.
Graves, J. R. *The Relation of Baptism to Salvation*. Memphis: Graves, 1881.
Gros, Jeffrey, Eamon McManus, and Ann Riggs, *Introduction to Ecumenism*. Mahwah: Paulist, 1998.
Gros, Jeffrey, Harding Meyer, and William Rusch, eds. *Growth in Agreement II*. Geneva: WCC, 2000.
Grudem, Wayne. *Systematic Theology*. Grand Rapids: Zondervan, 2000.
Gunstone, John. *Signs and Wonders: The Wimber Phenomenon*. London: Daybreak, 1989.
Gunton, Colin. *The Actuality of Atonement: A Study of Metaphor, Rationality, and the Christian Tradition*. Grand Rapids: Eerdmans, 1989.
———. *A Brief Theology of Revelation*. Edinburgh: T. & T. Clark, 1995.
———. *The Christian Faith: An Introduction to Christian Doctrine*. Malden, MA: Blackwell, 2002.

———. *The Triune Creator: A Historical and Systematic Study*. Grand Rapids: Eerdmans, 1998.

Guzie, Tad. *The Book of Sacramental Basics*. New York: Paulist, 1981.

Hagner, Donald. "The Bible: God's Gift to the Church of the Twenty-First Century." *Currents in Theology and Mission* 35 (2008) 19–31.

Hall, Chad. "When Orphans Became Heirs: J. R. Graves and the Landmark Baptist." *Baptist History and Heritage* 37 (2002) 112–27.

Hall, Robert. *The Works of Robert Hall, A. M. With a Brief Memoir of His Life by Dr. Gregory; and Observations on His Character as a Preacher by John Foster*. Vol. 2. London: Olinthus Gregory, 1841.

Hardy, Edward R., ed. *Christology of the Later Fathers*. Louisville: Westminster John Knox, 1954.

Harmon, Steven. *Ecumenism Means You, Too: Ordinary Christians and the Quest for Christian Unity*. Eugene, OR: Cascade, 2010.

———. Personal email, July 22, 2010.

———. *Towards Baptist Catholicity: Essays on Tradition and the Baptist Vision*. Eugene, OR: Wipf & Stock, 2006.

Harnack, Adolf von. *History of Dogma*. Translated by Neil Buchanan. New York: Dover, 1961.

Harrison, Frank Mott. *John Bunyan: A Story of His Life*. London: Banner of Truth Trust, 1964.

Hartman, L. *Into the Name of the Lord Jesus: In Baptism in the Early Church*. Edinburgh: T. & T. Clark 1997.

Haymes, Brian. *A Question of Identity: Reflections on Baptist Principles and Practice*. Leeds: Yorkshire Baptist Association, 1986.

———. *Understanding God and the World Through the Baptism of Believers*. Macon, GA: Smyth and Helwys, 1996.

Haymes, Brian, Ruth Gouldbourne, and Anthony Cross. *On Being the Church: Revisioning Baptist Identity*. Bletchley: Paternoster, 2008.

Henry, Carl F. *God, Revelation, and Authority*. Waco: Word Books, 1976.

Hobbs, Herschel. *Fundamentals of Our Faith*. Nashville: Broadman, 1960.

———. "People of the Book." In *Baptist Why and Why Not?*, edited by Timothy George and Richard Land, 15ff. Nashville: Broadman and Holman, 1997.

Hodge, Charles. *Systematic Theology*. Vol. 3. Grand Rapids: Eerdmans.

Hodgson, Leonard, ed. *Convictions*. London: Student Christian Movement, 1934.

Hughey, J. D., Jr. "The New Trend in Baptism." *Baptist Times*, February 18, 1959.

Hull, William. "Baptism in the New Testament: A Hermeneutical Critique." *Review and Expositor* 65 (1968) 3–12.

Humphreys, Fisher. *Thinking About God: An Introduction to Christian Theology*. New Orleans: Insight, 1994.

———. *The Way We Were: How Southern Baptist Theology Has Changed and What It Means to Us All*. Macon, GA: Smyth and Helwys, 2002.

Humphreys, Fisher, and Philip Wise. *Fundamentalism*. Macon, GA: Smyth and Helwys, 2004.

"Interdenominational Spirit." Beeson Divinity School, Samford University. https://www.beesondivinity.com/articles/interdenominational-spirit.

Jaeger, L. S. Letter to *The Baptist Times*, September 24, 1959.

Jensen, Peter. *The Revelation of God*. Downers Grove, IL: InterVarsity, 2002.

John, S. B. "Christian Baptism." *Baptist Times*, February 25, 1960.
Justin Martyr. "First Apology 61." In *Early Christian Baptism and the Catechumenate: Italy, North Africa, and Egypt*, edited by Thomas Finn, 38–39. Collegeville, MN: Liturgical, 1992.
Kay, William K. *Pentecostals In Britain*. Waynesboro: Paternoster, 2000.
Keach, Benjamin. "Keach's Catechisms." In *Baptist Confessions, Covenants, and Catechisms*, edited by Timothy George and Denise George, 241–55. Nashville: B&H, 1996.
Kiffin, William. *A Sober Discourse of Right to Church Communion*. London: Larkin, 1681.
Kinghorn, Joseph. *Baptism, a Term of Communion at the Lord's Supper*. Norwich: Bacon, Kinnerbrook, and Co, 1816.
Kinnamon, Michael. "Assessing the Ecumenical Movement." In vol. 3 of *A History of the Ecumenical Movement*, edited by John Briggs, Mercy Oduyoye, and George Tsetsis, 51–81. Geneva: WCC, 2004.
Knight, George W., III. *The Pastoral Epistles*. Grand Rapids: Eerdmans, 1992.
Kostenberger, Andreas. *John*. Grand Rapids: Baker, 2004.
Kruse, Colin. *Paul's Letter to the Romans*. Grand Rapids: Eerdmans, 2012.
Lalleman, Pieter. Personal email, July 10, 2015.
Lane, William. *The Gospel of Mark*. Grand Rapids: Eerdmans, 1974.
Latourette, Kenneth Scott. "Ecumenical Bearings of the Missionary Movement and the International Missionary Council." In *A History of the Ecumenical Movement 1517–1948*, edited by Ruth Rouse and Stephen Neill, 353–73. Philadelphia: Westminster, 1967.
Lewis, John. *Revelation, Inspiration, Scripture*. Nashville: Broadman, 1985.
Lindsell, Harold. *The Battle for the Bible*. Grand Rapids: Zondervan, 1976.
———. *The Bible in the Balance*. Grand Rapids: Zondervan, 1979.
Livingstone, E. A., ed. *Oxford Concise Dictionary of the Christian Church*. Oxford: Oxford University Press, 2000.
Lloyd-Jones, D. M. *Romans*. Grand Rapids: Zondervan, 1973.
The London Confession (1644). In *Baptist Confessions, Covenants, and Catechisms*, edited by Timothy George and Denise George, 46. Nashville: Broadman & Holman, 1996.
Lord, F. Townley. *Baptist World Fellowship*. London: Carey Kinsgate, 1955.
Lumpkin, William. *Baptist Confessions of Faith*. Valley Forge, PA: Judson, 1969.
Luther, Martin. *The Large Catechism*. Philadelphia: Fortress, 1959.
MacArthur, John. *1 Corinthians*. Chicago: Moody, 1984.
———. *Acts 1–12*. Chicago: Moody, 1994.
———. *Ephesians*. Chicago: Moody, 1986.
———. *Titus*. Chicago: Moody, 1996.
Mare, Harold. "1 Corinthians." In *Romans through Galatians*, edited by Frank Gaebelein, 173–297. The Expositor's Bible Commentary. Grand Rapids: Zondervan, 1976.
Marsden, George. *Reforming Fundamentalism: Fuller Seminary and the New Evangelicalism*. Grand Rapids: Eerdmans, 1987.
Matthews, I. G. "The Point of View of the Baptists." In *The Ministry and the Sacraments*, edited by Roderic Dunkerley, 223–29. London: Student Christian Movement, 1937.
Matthews, Kenneth. *Genesis 1–11:26*. Nashville: B&H, 1996.

McNeill, John T. "The Ecumenical Idea and Efforts to Realise It, 1517–1618." In *A History of the Ecumenical Movement 1517–1948*, edited by Ruth Rouse and Stephen Neill, 27–69. Philadelphia: Westminster, 1967.

McSwain, Larry L. "Swinging Pendulums: Reform, Resistance, and Institutional Change." In *Southern Baptists Observed*, edited by Nancy Tatom Ammerman, 256–57. Knoxville: University of Tennessee Press, 1993.

Melick, Richard R., Jr. *Philippians, Colossians, Philemon*. Nashville: B&H, 1991.

Middleton, Paul. *The God of Love and Human Dignity: Festschrift for George Newlands*. London: T. & T. Clark, 2007.

Miller, Matt. "SBC Severs Ties with BWA as Theological Concerns Remain." *Baptist Press*, June 15, 2004. http://www.bpnews.net/bpnews.asp?id=18475.

Moo, Douglas. *The Epistle to the Romans*. Grand Rapids, Eerdmans, 1996.

Moody, Dale. *Baptism: Foundation for Christian Unity*. Philadelphia: Westminster, 1967.

———. "Baptism in the New Testament." *Review and Expositor* 60 (1963) 232–34.

———. "Baptism in Recent Research." *Review and Expositor* 65 (1968) 13–22.

———. "The Nature of the Church." In *What Is the Church?*, edited by Duke McCall, 15–27. Nashville: Broadman, 1958.

———. "The Shaping of Southern Baptist Polity." *Baptist History and Heritage*, July 1, 1979.

———. *The Word of Truth: A Summary of Christian Doctrine Based on Biblical Revelation*. Grand Rapids: Eerdmans, 1981.

Morris, Leon. *The Gospel According to Matthew*. Grand Rapids: Eerdmans, 1992.

———. *Spirit of the Living God*. London: InterVarsity, 1969.

Moule, C. F. D. *The Holy Spirit*. Grand Rapids: Eerdmans, 1978.

Mullins, E. Y. *Baptist Beliefs*. Valley Forge, PA: Judson, 1962.

Murch, James. *Cooperation Without Compromise*. Grand Rapids: Eerdmans, 1956.

Neal, George. "The Recovery of Baptism." *Baptist Times*, April 24, 2008.

Neighbour, R. E. "The Moral Significance of Baptism." *Review and Expositor* 8 (1911) 420–30.

Nettles, Thomas. "A Baptist Response." In *Understanding Four Views on Baptism*, edited by John Armstrong, 145–48. Grand Rapids: Zondervan, 2007.

———. "Baptist View." In *Understanding Four Views on Baptism*, edited by John Armstrong, 25–41. Grand Rapids: Zondervan, 2007.

———. *The Baptists: Key People in Forming a Baptist Identity*. Vol. 3. Scotland: Christian Focus, 2007.

———. *James Petigru Boyce: A Southern Baptist Statesman*. Phillipsburg: P&R, 2009.

———. Personal email, January 31, 2015.

———. "Salvation and Ministry Testimony." Sermon Audio, October 26, 2013. http://www.sermonaudio.com/sermoninfo.asp?m=t&s=1026132146503.

New Hampshire Confession of Faith. http://biblehub.com/library/schaff/the_creeds_of_the_evangelical_protestant_churches/the_new_hampshire_baptist_confession.htm.

Newlands, George. *Theology of the Love of God*. Atlanta: John Knox, 1980.

Newman, John. *J. H. Newman's Parochial and Plain Sermons*. Vol. 3. London: Rivingtons, 1877.

Nicholls, Mike. *Lights to the World: A History of Spurgeon's College 1856–1992*. Harpenden: Nuprint, 1984.

Ollard, S. L. *A Short History of the Oxford Movement*. London: Faith Press, 1963.
Owen, John. *A Discourse Concerning the Holy Spirit*. The Works of John Owen 3. Edinburgh: Banner of Truth, 1965.
———. *The Holy Spirit: His Gifts and Power*. Evansville: Sovereign Grace, 1960.
Pawson, David. *Jesus Baptises in One Holy Spirit*. London: Hodder & Stoughton, 1997.
———. *The Normal Christian Birth: How to Give New Believers a Proper Start in Life*. London: Hodder and Stoughton, 1989.
Payne, Ernest A. *The Baptist Union: A Short History*. London: The Baptist Union of Great Britain and Ireland, 1982.
Pelikan, Jaroslav. *The Christian Tradition*. Chicago: Chicago University Press, 1984.
Pendleton, J. M. *Distinctive Principles of Baptists*. Philadelphia: American Baptist Publication Society, 1882.
Pierard, Richard V., ed. *Baptists Together in Christ 1905–2005*. Falls Church: Baptist World Alliance, 2005.
Pinnock, Clark. *Biblical Revelation: The Foundation of Christian Theology*. Chicago: The Moody Bible Institute, 1971.
———. *A Defense of Biblical Infallibility*. Phillipsburg: Presbyterian and Reformed, 1967.
———. *Flame of Love: A Theology of the Holy Spirit*. Downers Grove, IL: InterVarsity, 1996.
———. *A New Reformation*. Tigerville: Jewel, 1968.
———. *The Scripture Principle*. San Francisco: Harper & Row, 1984.
Piper, John. "Response to Grudem on Baptism and Church Membership." Desiring God, August 9, 2007. https://www.desiringgod.org/articles/response-to-grudem-on-baptism-and-church-membership.
Polhill, John. *Acts*. The New American Commentary. Nashville: Broadman, 1992.
Porter, Stanley, and Anthony Cross, eds. *Baptism, the New Testament and the Church: Historical and Contemporary Studies in Honour of R.E.O. White*. Sheffield: Sheffield Academic, 1999.
———, eds. *Dimensions of Baptism: Biblical and Theological Studies*. New York: Sheffield Academic, 2002.
Pratt, Richard. "A Reformed Response." In *Understanding Four Views on Baptism*, edited by John Armstrong, 42–46. Grand Rapids: Zondervan, 2007.
Pusey, Edward Bouverie. *Tract Sixty-Seven: Scriptural Views of Holy Baptism in The Oxford Movement*. Edited by Eugene R. Fairweather. New York: Oxford University Press, 1964.
Quarles, Charles. "Ordinance or Sacrament: Is the Baptist View of the Ordinances Truly Biblical?" *Journal for Baptist Theology and Ministry* 1 (2003) 47–57.
Randall, Ian. "Part of a Movement: Nigel Wright and Baptist Life." *Challenging to Change*, edited by Pieter J. Lalleman, 143–62. London: Spurgeon's College, 2009.
———. *A School of the Prophets: 150 Years of Spurgeon's College*. London: Spurgeon's College, 2005.
Rausch, Thomas. *Catholics and Evangelicals: Do They Share a Common Future?* Downers Grove, IL: InterVarsity, 2000.
Read, L. A. "The Ordinances." *The Fraternal* 67 (1948) 8–10.
Robeck, Cecil M., Jr., and Amos Yong, eds. *The Cambridge Companion to Pentecostalism*. Cambridge: Cambridge University Press, 2014.
Robert-Thomson, E. *Baptists and Disciples of Christ*. London: Carey Kingsgate, 1960.

Robinson, H. Wheeler. *Baptist Principles*. London: Carey Kingsgate, 1960.
———. *The Christian Experience of the Holy Spirit*. London: Nisbet & Co., 1947.
———. "The Five Points of a Baptist's Faith." *Baptist Quarterly* 11 (1942) 4–14.
———. *The Life and Faith of the Baptists*. London: Kingsgate, 1946.
———. "The Place of Baptism in Baptist Churches Today." *Baptist Quarterly* 1 (1922) 209–18.
Rouse, Ruth, and Stephen Neill, eds. *A History of the Ecumenical Movement 1517–1948*. Philadelphia: Westminster, 1967.
Rowell, Geoffrey. *The Vision Glorious: Themes and Personalities of the Catholic Revival in Anglicanism*. Oxford: Oxford University Press, 1983.
"The SBJT Forum: The Lord's Supper." *Southern Baptist Journal of Theology* 6 (Fall 2002).
"The SBJT Forum Interview: How Did You Come to Teach at Southern Seminary and What Are Your Impressions of the Decade You Spent on the Faculty There?" *Southern Baptist Journal of Theology* 13 (2009) 100–113.
Schlatter, Adolf. *The Church in the New Testament Period*. Translated by Paul Levertoff. London: SPCK, 1961.
———. *The Theology of the Apostles: The Development of New Testament Theology*, Translated by Andreas Kostenberger. Grand Rapids: Baker, 1998.
Schnackenburg, Rudolf. *Baptism in the Thought of St. Paul*. New York: Herder and Herder, 1964.
———. *The Gospel According to St. John*. New York: Herder and Herder, 1968.
———. *Present and Future: Modern Aspects of New Testament Theology*. Notre Dame: University of Notre Dame Press, 1966.
Schreiner, Thomas. *1, 2 Peter, Jude*. The New American Commentary. Nashville: Broadman, 2003.
———. "Baptism in the Epistles: An Initiation Rite for Believers." In *Believer's Baptism: Signs of the New Covenant in Christ*, edited by Thomas Schreiner and Shawn Wright, 67–96. Nashville: B&H, 2006.
———. Faculty Profile. The Southern Baptist Theological Seminary. http://www.sbts.edu/academics/faculty/thomas-r-schreiner/.
———. *Galatians*. Zondervan Exegetical Commentary on the New Testament. Grand Rapids: Zondervan, 2010.
———. *Interpreting the Pauline Epistles*. Grand Rapids: Baker, 2011.
———. *New Testament Theology: Magnifying God in Christ*. Grand Rapids: Baker, 2008.
———. *Paul: Apostle of God's Glory in Christ*. Downers Grove, IL: Intervarsity, 2001.
———. Personal email, November 22, 2014.
———. *Romans*. Baker Exegetical Commentary on the New Testament. Grand Rapids: Baker, 1998.
———. "The Theology of Paul the Apostle." *Trinity Journal* 20 (1999) 95–100.
Schreiner, Thomas, and Shawn Wright, eds. *Believer's Baptism: Sign of the New Covenant in Christ*. Nashville: B&H, 2006.
Shepherd, Peter. *The Making of a Modern Denomination: John Howard Shakespeare and the English Baptists 1898–1924*. Waynesboro: Paternoster, 2001.
Shurden, Walter. "The Problem of Authority in the Southern Baptist Convention." *Review and Expositor* 75 (1978) 219–34.
Sibbes, Richard. "A Description of Christ." In vol. 1 of *The Complete Works of Richard Sibbes*, edited by Alexander B. Grosart, 1–32. Edinburgh: Banner of Truth, 1973.

Slater, David, ed. *A Perspective on Baptist Identity*. Kingsbridge: Mainstream, 1987.
Smail, Tom. "In Spirit and in Truth: Reflections on Charismatic Worship." In *Charismatic Renewal: The Search for a Theology*, edited by Tom Smail, Andrew Walker, and Nigel Wright, 95–103. London: SPCK, 1993.
Smail, Tom, Andrew Walker, and Nigel Wright, eds. *Charismatic Renewal: The Search for a Theology*. London: SPCK, 1993.
———. *The Love of Power or the Power of Love: A Careful Assessment of the Problems Within the Charismatic and Word-of-Faith Movements*. Minneapolis: Bethany House, 1994.
Smith, William. *A Critical Investigation of the Ecclesiological Thought of WO Carver*. ThD Dissertation, The Southern Baptist Theological Seminary, 1962.
Smyth, John. *The Short Confession of Faith*. In *Baptist Confessions of Faith*, by William Lumpkin. Valley Forge: Judson, 1969.
Sparkes, Douglas. "The Revd Dr. George Raymond Beasley-Murray." *Baptist Times*, March 23, 2000.
Spivey, James. "Benajah Harvey Carroll." In *Theologians of the Baptist Tradition*, edited by Timothy George and David Dockery, 163–80. Nashville: B&H, 2001.
Spurgeon, Charles. "Baptism—A Burial." In vol. 27 of *The Metropolitan Tabernacle Pulpit*, 624–25. London: Banner of Truth, 1971.
———. "Baptism Essential to Obedience." In vol. 39 of *The Metropolitan Tabernacle Pulpit*, 617–28. Pasadena: Pilgrim, 1969.
———. "Baptismal Regeneration." In vol. 10 of *The Metropolitan Tabernacle Pulpit*, 313–28. Pasadena: Pilgrim, 1969.
———. *The Metropolitan Tabernacle Pulpit, 1865*. Pasadena: Pilgrim, 1970.
———. *The Metropolitan Tabernacle Pulpit, 1866*. Pasadena: Pilgrim, 1970.
———. *Sermons of the Rev. C. H. Spurgeon*. Vol. 8. New York: Sheldon, 1871.
———. *Spurgeon on Baptism*. Worthing: Henry E. Walter Ltd.
"Staff—John E. Colwell." Spurgeon's College staff bio. http://www.spurgeons.ac.uk/about/staff/other-academic-staff/john-colwell.
St. Basil the Great. *On the Holy Spirit*. Crestwood: St. Vladimir's Seminary, 1980.
Stott, John. *Basic Christianity*. Downers Grove, IL: InterVarsity, 1971.
———. *The Cross of Christ*. Downers Grove, IL: InterVarsity, 2006.
———. *God's Words*. Downers Grove, IL: InterVarsity, 1981.
———. *The Message of Acts*. Downers Grove, IL: InterVarsity, 1998.
———. *The Message of Ephesians*. Downers Grove, IL: InterVarsity, 1986.
———. *Romans*. Downers Grove, IL: InterVarsity, 1994.
"Summons to Witness to Christ in Today's World: Part I, The Conversation in Review." 1988. http://www.pro.urbe.it/dia-int/b-rc/doc/e_b-rc_report1988_01.html#PartI.
Sutton, Jerry. *The Baptist Reformation: The Conservative Resurgence in the Southern Baptist Convention*. Nashville: Broadman & Holman, 2000.
Synan, Vinson. *The Holiness-Pentecostal Tradition: Charismatic Movements in the Twentieth Century*. Grand Rapids: Eerdmans, 1997.
Tatom Ammerman, Nancy. *Baptist Battles: Social Change and Religious Conflict in the Southern Baptist Convention*. New Brunswick: Rutgers University Press, 1990.
———, ed. *Southern Baptists Observed: Multiple Perspectives on a Changing Denomination*. Knoxville: University of Tennessee Press, 1993.

Taylor, Justin. "An Interview with Tom Schreiner on Baptism." The Gospel Coalition, January 14, 2007. http://www.thegospelcoalition.org/blogs/justintaylor/2007/01/14/interview-with-tom-schreiner-on/.

———. "Interview with Tom Schreiner on NT Theology." The Gospel Coalition, August 1, 2008. http://www.thegospelcoalition.org/blogs/justintaylor/2008/08/01/interview-with-tom-schreiner-on-nt/.

Taylor, Mark. *1 Corinthians*. Nashville: B&H, 2014.

Thielman, Frank. *Ephesians*. Grand Rapids: Baker Academic, 2010.

Thiselton, Anthony. *The First Epistle to the Corinthians*. Grand Rapids: Eerdmans, 2000.

Thompson, David. "Ecumenism." In vol. 9 of *The Cambridge History of Christianity*, edited by Hugh McLeod, 50–70. Cambridge: Cambridge University Press, 2006.

Thurian, Max, ed. *Churches Respond to BEM*. Vol. 1. Faith and Order Paper 129. Geneva: WCC, 1986.

Tillich, Paul. *The Protestant Era*. Chicago: University of Chicago Press, 1948.

Towner, Philip. *The Letters to Timothy and Titus*. Grand Rapids: Eerdmans, 2006.

Trigg, Jonathan. *Baptism in the Theology of Martin Luther*. Boston: Brill Academic, 2001.

Tull, James. *Shapers of Baptist Thought*. Macon: Mercer University Press, 1984.

Turner, Frank. *John Henry Newman: The Challenge to Evangelical Religion*. New Haven: Yale University Press, 2002.

Underwood, A. C. "Baptist." In *The Ministry and the Sacraments*, edited by Roderic Dunkerley, 223–29. London: Student Christian Movement, 1937.

Visser't Hooft, Willem. *The Genesis and Formation of the World Council of Churches*. Geneva: WCC, 1982.

———. "The Genesis of the World Council of Churches." In *A History of the Ecumenical Movement 1517–1948*, edited by Ruth Rouse and Stephen Neill, 697–724. Philadelphia: Westminster, 1967.

Walker, Michael. *Baptists at the Table: The Theology of the Lord's Supper Amongst English Baptists in the Nineteenth Century*. Oxford: Tyndale, 1992.

Walton, Robert. *The Gathered Community*. London: Carey, 1946.

Ward, Wayne, and Joseph Green, eds. *Is the Bible a Human Book*. Nashville: Broadman, 1970.

Ware, Bruce. *Father, Son, & Holy Spirit: Relationships, Roles, and Relevance*. Wheaton, IL: Crossway, 2005.

Webster, John, Kathryn Tanner, and Iain Torrance, eds. *The Oxford Handbook of Systematic Theology*. Oxford: Oxford University Press, 2007.

West, Morris. *To Be a Pilgrim: A Memoir of Ernest A. Payne*. Guildford: Lutterworth, 1983.

White, B. R. "The Frontiers of Fellowship Between English Baptists 1609–1660." *Foundations* 11 (1968) 244–56.

———. "Open and Closed Membership Among English and Welsh Baptist." *Baptist Quarterly* 24 (1972) 330–34.

White, R. E. O. *The Biblical Doctrine of Initiation*. London: Hodder and Stoughton, 1960.

Williams, N. P. *Ideas of the Fall and Original Sin*. London: Longmans, 1929.

Wood, A. Skevington. "Ephesians." In *Ephesians through Philemon*, edited by Tremper Longman III and David E. Garland, 19–174. Grand Rapids: Zondervan, 2005.

World Council of Churches. *Baptism, Eucharist and Ministry*. Faith and Order Paper 111. Geneva: WCC, 1982.

World Council of Churches, Commission on Faith and Order. *One Lord One Baptism*. London: SCM, 1960.

Wright, David. *What Has Infant Baptist Done to Baptism?: An Enquiry at the End of Christendom*. Waynesboro: Paternoster, 2005.

Wright, Nigel. *Baptist Churches: An Introduction*. Didcot: Baptist Union of Great Britain, 2009.

———. *Believers' Baptism?* Oxon: Baptist Union of Great Britain, 2009.

———. *Children in the Church*. Didcot: Baptist Union of Great Britain, 2009.

———. *The Church*. London: Scripture Union, 1984.

———. *Church Membership*. Didcot: Baptist Union of Great Britain, 2009.

———. *Disavowing Constantine: Mission, Church, and the Social Order in the Theologies of John Howard Yoder and Jurgen Moltmann*. Carlisle: Paternoster, 2000.

———. *Free Church, Free State: The Positive Baptist Vision*. Eugene, OR: Wipf and Stock, 2005.

———. *God on the Inside: The Holy Spirit in Holy Scripture*. Oxford: The Bible Reading Fellowship, 2006.

———. *The Lord's Supper*. Didcot: Baptist Union of Great Britain, 2009.

———. *New Baptists, New Agenda*. Waynesboro: Paternoster, 2002.

———. Personal email, June 20, 2015.

———. "A Pilgrimage in Renewal." In *Charismatic Renewal: The Search for a Theology*, by Tom Smail, Andrew Walker, and Nigel Wright, 22–32. Longon: SPCK, 1993.

———. *The Radical Kingdom*. Eastbourne: Kingsway, 1986.

———. "The Theology and Methodology of 'Signs and Wonders.'" In *Charismatic Renewal: The Search for a Theology*, by Tom Smail, Andrew Walker, and Nigel Wright, 71–85. Longon: SPCK, 1993.

———. *Why Be a Baptist?* Oxon: Baptist Union of Great Britain, 2009.

Zaspel, Fred. "Thomas J. Nettles Retires from SBTS." Books at a Glance, May 19, 2014. http://booksataglance.com/author-interviews/thomas-j-nettles-retires-from-sbts.